Expressive Arts for Social Work and Social Change

Expressive Arts for Social Work and Social Change

Tuula Heinonen, Deana Halonen,
and Elizabeth Krahn

OXFORD
UNIVERSITY PRESS

OXFORD
UNIVERSITY PRESS

Oxford University Press is a department of the University of Oxford. It furthers
the University's objective of excellence in research, scholarship, and education
by publishing worldwide. Oxford is a registered trade mark of Oxford University
Press in the UK and certain other countries.

Published in the United States of America by Oxford University Press
198 Madison Avenue, New York, NY 10016, United States of America.

© Oxford University Press 2019

Library of Congress Cataloging-in-Publication Data
Names: Heinonen, Tuula, 1952– author. | Halonen, Deana, author. |
Krahn, Elizabeth, author.
Title: Expressive arts for social work and social change /
Tuula Heinonen, Deana Halonen, and Elizabeth Krahn.
Description: New York, NY : Oxford University Press, [2019] |
Includes bibliographical references and index.
Identifiers: LCCN 2018015256 (print) | LCCN 2018016002 (ebook) |
ISBN 9780190912413 (updf) | ISBN 9780190912420 (epub) | ISBN 9780190912406 (pbk. : alk. paper)
Subjects: LCSH: Social service—Practice. | Arts—Therapeutic use.
Classification: LCC HV10.5 (ebook) | LCC HV10.5 .H395 2019 (print) | DDC 361.3/2—dc23
LC record available at https://lccn.loc.gov/2018015256

CONTENTS

PREFACE

This book arose from our various arts-based teaching, inquiry, writing, and creative experiences over a decade or more. After many years of discussion about our ideas on social work and the arts and in our respective projects, we thought it was time to write a book about such methods. There were few books available on integration of the arts in social work at the time. We wanted primarily to write about the arts as complementary methods in social work practice but also include content on the arts in inquiry and in social work education.

This book draws not only from expressive arts methods that have been more often used in practice and inquiry but also from others that are newer or less developed in social work. At the time of writing we were unable to find other books that combine social work with creative, arts-based methods for practice, although some that describe expressive arts therapies as group or individual therapy approaches (visual art, movement and dance, music, and others) are available. These are written from the perspective of professionals registered and/or licenced in these fields. In contrast, this book begins from a social work orientation and adds to it expressive arts–based methods as complementary resources for social workers who have been prepared through training, experience, and/or study while adhering to social work codes of ethics and principles for practice. Some social workers have chosen to complete programs of study in expressive arts–based fields such as art therapy, music therapy, movement and dance therapy, or others, to widen their scope of practice.

As practitioners, researchers, and scholars ourselves, we wrote this book because there is an increased interest in applying creative arts methods in social work. We think that there is need for a book that connects social work with a range of expressive arts–based methods and uses in different practice settings and client populations. Responding to people's needs often requires more than verbal communication, and creative arts offer rich possibilities for other formats. A holistic view of human beings that draws upon the expressive arts and the creative potential we all have within us is fundamental to this book as are methods that help people to express their feelings and ideas. So, too, is a vision of creative arts as a powerful means to address social injustice and catalyze social change, paving the way for individual and collective transformation for our clients and for ourselves.

ACKNOWLEDGMENTS

We are grateful to David Follmer at Lyceum and to Oxford in New York (Andrew Dominello, Dana Bliss and others contracted by Oxford on this project) for their help in getting this book ready for publication. We also thank our anonymous reviewers for their suggestions and comments.

Tuula Heinonen: I am thankful to this book's coauthors, Deana Halonen and Elizabeth Krahn. We developed the ideas for the book and spent many hours working as we wrote, reviewed, and revised the chapters. I also thank coauthors Tracey Lavoie and Sarah Roche, who coauthored individual chapters with me. I am also grateful to Jessica Canard whose interview material was useful in one of the Chapter 3 and to Don Stevens for his contribution. Finally, the Faculty of Social Work at the University of Manitoba granted me a research leave so I could spend time working on this book, and for that I am grateful. For Jordan, Derek, and Christopher: I wish you all the best in life and success in overcoming challenges that you meet along the way.

Deana Halonen: I am deeply indebted to Tuula Heinonen, who initiated the discussions about this exciting endeavor, as well as for her generosity with this opportunity to coauthor this book with Elizabeth Krahn and me. Her extensive knowledge and experience as an author, along with her never-ending belief in the value of this work, her creative facilitation of many deep explorations of key ideas and concepts, and her ongoing encouragement to bring it to completion, have been absolutely invaluable. I also say *kitchi-meegwetch* (huge thank-you) to my spiritual sisters, Margaret Tamara Dicks, coauthor of *Music, Singing, and Drumming*; Dr. Carolyn Kenny, who generously shared her wisdom, teachings, creative energy for discovery, and Indigenous perspective on the power of healing within music and the arts; and *Dewe-igen* the drum; *Dewe-igan* for her insightful analysis, wisdom, and humor. Dr. Kenny's commitment to the process of decolonization within the profession of music therapy and using music and the arts in the revitalization of traditional wisdom and societies are a part of her treasured legacy.

Elizabeth Krahn: I would like to express my gratitude to Tuula Heinonen and Deana Halonen for the invitation to join them as a coauthor in this creative endeavor. It has been a privilege to not only write about the art of narrative and story in relation to personal and collective healing and transformation, a passion of mine, but also to engage in the collaborative and productive process of envisioning, writing, and completing an anthology of expressive art forms that enrich and enhance the effectiveness of social work practice and research. I would also like to give special recognition to Laura Simms and David Baxter, each storytellers in their own right, who contributed to the storytelling and poetry content of this book. A special acknowledgment goes to my children and grandchildren, who add so much richness and inspiration to my life.

ABOUT THE AUTHORS

Tuula Heinonen is Professor in the Faculty of Social Work, University of Manitoba, where she has been employed for 24 years. Her scholarly interests are in arts-informed qualitative inquiry, social work and health, newcomer settlement and transitions, and international social development, aging, and gender. She is also an art therapist who is interested in the integration of drawing, painting, and collage in social work practice, inquiry, and education, and for individual well-being.

Deana Halonen is a Metis/Anishinaabe-kweg from the Grassy Narrows area, and more currently Kenora, in the northwest area of Treaty Three territory (Northwestern Ontario). She is an Instructor in the Faculty of Social Work, University of Manitoba, working for the past 10 years as Coordinator of the Distance Delivery Social Work Program, and teaching both online and blended learning courses using educational technology. She is a collaborative, experiential teacher and learner who takes every opportunity available to integrate the expressive arts into social work practice, inquiry, and education.

Elizabeth Krahn is a social work counselor in her eighth year of private practice, having previously worked for a number of years as a mental health social worker with adults of all ages and stages of life. She has also spent the last 10 years engaged in ethnographic and oral history research and the restorying of collective trauma and its lifespan and intergenerational effects, particularly in relation to attachment insecurities. As counselor, researcher, and presenter, she integrates story and metaphor, visual art-making, and/or photographs to enrich the process.

ABOUT THE CONTRIBUTORS

Margaret Tamara Dicks is a member of the Peguis First Nation on Treaty One territory in Manitoba, Canada. Her training consists of degrees in music therapy, social work, and Indigenous studies. She currently works as a mental health therapist in First Nation communities and is enrolled in the PhD program in Native studies at the University of Manitoba. Her research interests include the role music plays in the process of decolonization, specifically in the lives of women. Learning and participation in both traditional and contemporary music genres allow her to integrate music into her personal life.

Tracey Lavoie is an Instructor at the University of Victoria, School of Social Work, and PhD candidate at McGill University, School of Social Work. Having both experienced and witnessed the great power and potential of contemplative, creative, and arts-informed practices and pedagogies, she continues to weave them into her practice, teaching, and research. Her doctoral research is a phenomenological study that explores social work educators' lived experience of the intersection of mindfulness and antioppressive practice in their pedagogical philosophy and practices.

Sarah Roche is an elementary dance and music educator within Winnipeg School Division. She has worked as a professional contemporary dancer and artist educator for 10 years prior to becoming a full-time teacher after receiving an education degree from Queen's University in 2014. She has had the opportunity to train with a variety of experts within the field of dance, dance therapy, expressive arts, and dance education. Sarah has provided training and movement experiences for children and adults within the public school system, hospitals, senior care homes, and at the University of Manitoba in the Faculties of Social Work and Education.

NOTES ON SOURCES

David Baxter for extracts from his poem, "One More Time," from his book of poetry entitled *Emerging*, published by PetalPress: www.palford.com and printed in Salmon Arm, British Columbia. Copyright by David Baxter, 2011. Used in Chapter 6.

Laura Simms for her adaptation of a traditional fairytale, "The Giant Who Had No Heart," which inspired a new mythical tale, written by Elizabeth Krahn, entitled "The Kingdom That Lost Its Heart" and found in Chapter 6 of this book. Simms's fairytale is published in her book entitled *Becoming the World*, by Laura Simms Productions. Copyright by Laura Simms, 2009.

Expressive Arts for Social Work and Social Change

1

Why Expressive Arts for Social Work and Social Change?

TUULA HEINONEN, DEANA HALONEN,
AND ELIZABETH KRAHN

In social work, the arts can offer unique perspectives, approaches, and tools to meaningfully and effectively engage people through creative expression. At the individual and group levels, expressive arts are not new and can be found in the repertoires of social work practitioners in many fields of practice. In 1968, Ruth Middleman, writing about nonverbal approaches in social work with groups, asks social workers to draw on creative arts to encourage imagination and meaning in their work. Middleman saw the pervasive power of the arts as a vehicle for change. She noted that expressive arts, when used in social work, can promote communication either directly or indirectly and resolve problems or issues. They have been integrated in social work as complementary or alternative forms of expression, therapy, and healing that are aimed at individual and group change (Huss, 2013). Social workers who work with children have used creative forms of play (Carroll, 2002), drawing, and music because this teaches them about children's experiences and ideas (Huss, Kaufman, & Sibony, 2014; Lefevre, 2004).

Transformation at community and societal levels has also been an area of interest in social work, whether it is part of macro-level practice, social research, or both. Individual and group engagement may be connected with or lead to a higher level of change, as in social action projects that integrate expressive arts (Levine & Levine, 2011; Sinding & Barnes, 2015). Expressive arts applications in social work are increasingly gaining ground in the human service professions, including social work (e.g., Conrad & Sinner, 2015; Sinding & Barnes, 2015; Wilson, 2008; Zingaro, 2009).

Creative arts approaches are used by many human service professions, such as nursing, education, psychology, medicine, and occupational therapy, as complementary methods. Those who view themselves more specifically as professional expressive arts practitioners may have their own distinct professional fields, such as art, music, dance, and movement therapies, in which each is separately organized with a unique professional education, identity, a practice code of ethics, principles, and professional association. However, social workers use expressive arts, including visual arts, music, photography, drama, storytelling, movement and dance, and more, as complementary approaches that they combine with social work practice methods. Doing so makes sense for social workers who have learned how to draw on the expressive arts in their practices. Social workers, and other professionals who make use of expressive arts, see the potential in creative arts for healing, growth, learning, and expression. Some creative arts are newer to social work (e.g., movement and dance), and little has been written about them in relation to social work practice or inquiry. It is useful, however, to consider how such approaches could be utilized in combination with social work approaches and methods for specific populations.

This book begins with some key concepts and perspectives that reflect the orientation from which we write about the integration of social work and expressive arts-based approaches. These elements are listed next and are threaded through the chapters that follow. They offer a lens for the areas of expressive arts described in the individual chapters and the examples given in them.

Six individual chapters about expressive arts methods are included: (1) visual methods, including drawing, painting, and collage; (2) photography and video; (3) movement and dance; (4) storytelling, poetry, narrative, and writing; (5) songs and drumming; and (6) theater and drama. These chapters represent a selected group of methods in expressive arts for social work, but others, such as fiber arts, sculpture, and more, could be added. Further, each form of expressive arts may be combined, for example: drawing or photography with stories; music with movement and dance; or singing and drumming with storytelling. Some combinations may be well suited for specific situations or groups of people.

PURPOSE AND AIMS OF THE BOOK

This book is useful for practitioners interested in learning about the potential for the creative arts in social work and ways in which they are and could be applied in practice. Researchers interested in how expressive arts can add innovative methods and activities, greater depth, and new viewpoints to their research process and topics of inquiry will also find uses for the book. Educators who seek creative ways to enhance learning experiences of their students may also find the book helpful. Examples and illustrations in each chapter describe how creative methods have been used. The examples include a wide range of settings and populations that will provide insights for readers. The topics in the book might be also of interest to human service professionals outside of social work. However, throughout the book, we refer primarily to practices, principles, and concepts from social work.

ORGANIZATION OF THE BOOK

The book's chapters include content on the nature of the expressive arts, examples of applications, and, in some, interview material from those we spoke to about their use of such approaches in their work. At the end of each expressive arts chapter, reflection questions and resources that include additional literature references, video links, and websites are provided. The information about arts-based methods will enable readers to determine how their own social work and inquiry practices might be extended and enhanced through integration of creative arts approaches. Each chapter, although connected by common threads from expressive arts, is unique. Some are coauthored with one of the book's authors, whereas other chapters are written by one of the book's coauthors.

Chapter 2 provides the orientation that underlies our writing of this book on expressive arts in social work, and it includes concepts from green social work; the significance of place and the environment; Indigenous perspectives, principles, and practices; social justice and social action; cultural safety and respect; and the need for creative expression for people's well-being. The elements of the framework have been developed by the book's authors and are loosely woven into the book's chapters.

Chapter 3 describes visual arts approaches that have been used by social workers in many fields and settings such as mental health, family-centered practice, child and youth work, disaster intervention, and more. Drawing, painting, and collage have been particularly useful to practitioners in helping people explore their feelings when words are insufficient or difficult to use.

Chapter 4 on the use of photography and video is less established in social work, with the exception of photographic images for documentation or therapeutic use by social workers with families and children or other groups. Video, as a relatively new medium, is now seen in a number of community and youth projects as well as in education and social action. This medium sometimes overlaps with storytelling and narrative where video-making is aimed at capturing stories of people, events, or actions. Photography, useful in qualitative research, involves the participation of those who are the subjects of social research as active participants.

Chapter 5 discusses the field of movement and dance and its potential uses in social work, showing how physical movement in a wide range of forms and applications can be helpful for people. Although not evident in social work literature, movement and dance are beneficial for many client groups, including children and youth, older persons in long-term care residences, cancer survivors, disabled persons, and women who have survived abuse.

The art of storytelling, poetry, narrative, and writing as a way of engaging with *oneself* and the *other,* and restorying individual and/or collective lives is discussed in Chapter 6 in relation to social work and social change. The transformative power inherent in the *telling* and *hearing* of an individual or collective story, whether it be the history of a life lived, a poetic reflection, or a mythic tale, can have profound personal and social implications. Several narrative styles and mediums are discussed in the chapter in relation to a wide range of clients and populations to offer a platform for marginalized voices to be heard; to inspire creative and reflexive social work education and practice; and to contribute to more powerful qualitative research that better informs policy and practice. In the case of digital storytelling, stories can be made public and disseminated locally and internationally, thanks to the accessibility of social media.

Chapter 7 is about drumming and music, methods that are not new but are not well known in social work practice. In Indigenous communities, drumming and forms of singing are important cultural traditions that connect people to the universe and life itself. An interview with an Indigenous music therapist gives a unique shape to this chapter. Many kinds of music from classical to hip-hop can be integrated in social work. Music can evoke deep feeling affecting people's emotions and behavior.

In Chapter 8, theater and drama are discussed. These approaches have been included in social work as role plays, enactments of the effects of social injustice on groups of people, and/or accounts of people's lives that we can learn from. The power of performance for those who act and for their audiences can generate strong feelings for actors and for audiences who witness the power of others' feelings, resulting in connection and individual and social transformation for both groups.

Finally, in Chapter 9, we summarize the key ideas, contributions, lessons, and challenges in integrating and implementing expressive arts into social work. We draw from the threads that hold the book's chapters together and on the framework outlined in Chapter 2. Finally, we make recommendations for the future of expressive arts in social work practice, inquiry, and education.

REFERENCES

Carroll, J. (2002). Play therapy: The children's views. *Child and Family Social Work, 7,* 177–187.

Conrad, D., & Sinner, A. (Eds.). (2015). *Creating together: Participatory, community-based, and collaborative arts practices and scholarship across Canada.* Waterloo, ON: Wilfrid Laurier University Press.

Huss, E. (2013). *What we see and what we say: Using images in research, therapy, empowerment, and social change.* New York, NY: Routledge.

Huss, E., Kaufman, R., & Sibony, A. (2014). Children's drawings and social change: Food insecurity and hunger among Israeli Bedouin children. *British Journal of Social Work, 44*, 1857–1878. doi: 10.1093/bjsw/bc034.

Lefevre, M. (2004). Playing with sound: The therapeutic use of music in direct work with children. *Child and Family Social Work, 9*, 333–345.

Levine, E., & Levine, S. (2011). *Art in action: Expressive arts therapy and social change.* London, UK: Jessica Kingsley.

Middleman, R. (1968). *The non-verbal method in working with groups.* New York, NY: Association Press.

Sinding, C., & Barnes, H. (Eds.). (2015). *Social work artfully: Beyond borders and boundaries.* Waterloo, ON: Wilfrid Laurier University Press.

Wilson, S. (2008). *Research is ceremony: Indigenous research methods.* Black Point, NS: Fernwood Press.

Zingaro, L. (2009). *Speaking out: Storytelling for social change.* Walnut Creek, CA: Left Coast Press.

2

A Social Work Orientation for Transformation Using Expressive Arts

TUULA HEINONEN, DEANA HALONEN,
AND ELIZABETH KRAHN

Individual and social change and transformation are important goals at the core of social work practice and inquiry. Social workers aim to use a range of methods and approaches to address these goals for the benefit of people with whom they work. In inquiry and education, where knowledge is generated and shared, individual and social transformation among students, researchers, and community groups is also highlighted (e.g., Rutherford, Walsh, & Rook, 2011). The development of a social work orientation for individual and social transformation using expressive arts in social work is viewed by us as comprising the following elements: the environment—including green social work and the significance of place; Indigenous perspectives, principles, and practices; social justice and social action; cultural safety; and creative expression as a compelling human need for people's well-being. These concepts and ideas shape our orientation and are loosely woven through many of the chapters on expressive arts in this book.

THE ENVIRONMENT: GREEN SOCIAL WORK AND THE CONCEPT OF PLACE

John Coates and Mel Gray (2011) note that, although the environmental movement has been evident for nearly four decades, social work has been slow in responding to its issues. They point to an edited work by Hoff and McNutt, published in 1994, that offered strategies for social work involvement in environmental issues. However, the impact on the social work profession was limited. McKinnon (2013) questioned whether social workers (in Australia) viewed the environment as a private concern for individuals or as an issue for the social work profession. She cited the Australian code of ethics for social workers, indicating recently integrated concerns for the environment and human interaction with it, but suggesting that social workers may have limited opportunity to take these up given frontline practice responsibilities and demands, as well as uncertainty on how to proceed. She concluded that for the 20 social workers who participated in her study, most "had not found a way to successfully incorporate their environmental understanding and concerns into their professional practice" (p. 167). McKinnon found that shifting the concern for environmental issues from an individual to professional social work practice level remained a challenge.

Green social work and environmental justice have become important issues in social work both at local and global levels (Alston, 2015; Dominelli, 2014; Drolet, Wu, Taylor, & Dennehy, 2015; Norton, 2011), not only because it is important that social work includes the broad picture of current ecological issues, climate change, and the health of our earth, but because environmental problems tend to affect those who are poor and least able to adapt to these events and processes. Zapf (2009) states that social work scholars have conceptualized the environment as composed primarily of social elements, with little attention paid to physical and other kinds of environments. He also noted that social work had been outside of the discourses on ecology and the environment and, as a result, has not engaged in the issues that other social and physical sciences were writing about. Hawkins (2010), an American social work scholar, urged social workers to act in order to teach students and others and to curb the damage to human and animal habitats caused by intense and unbridled pursuit of economic progress. She writes about the urgency of including environmental justice as part of the human rights agenda and people's collective rights all over the world. Hawkins also argues for a more rapid and focused response to stop resource depletion. She states:

> Social work, as the helping profession that traditionally focused on linkages across systems, must actively join this movement [environmental justice] if we are to stay relevant in the contemporary global 21st century. Our professional mission of advocating for and acting toward social and economic justice must be expanded to include environmental justice. (p. 6)

Gray and Coates (2013) introduced a framework for ecospiritual social work, setting out its principles and underpinning ideas reflecting a holistic view, similar to an Indigenous worldview. Ecospirituality embraces as its primary principles: "[A]ll is one, interdependence, diversity, inclusivity, sacredness of the

Earth, and personal responsibility for the well-being of all" (p. 362). Its aim is to establish a "deep connection and concern for the well-being of the Earth and its sustainability for future generations" (p. 262). At the same time, it seeks alternatives to destructive economic practices that harm the earth and its inhabitants and looks beyond individuality in order to do so.

Currently, the rise of green social work and its concerns with ecology and the environment has turned the attention of scholars toward use of a structural analysis in examining the social, economic, and political forces that cause harm to the earth and its inhabitants (see Dominelli, 2014). Social workers who seek environmental justice believe that it is in our interest to work with like-minded colleagues from a range of disciplines, to bring to light the issues and mobilize allies who can together seek strategies, methods, and tools to alleviate, slow down, and end harmful practices that hurt our earth's environment.

As Gray and Coates (2015) state, "[A] broad encompassing theoretical framework that incorporates an understanding of environmental issues and their impact" is needed because the interdependence of humans and all forms of life require it (p. 6). Social work can join forces with other groups to work toward social transformation, both locally and globally. There is much room for social workers to engage in addressing environmental protection and justice, not only in local efforts, such as reducing fuel consumption, growing community gardens, innovating for recycling programs, but also by participating in efforts at broader levels with international and national organizations aiming for social change on issues of the environment.

The Concept of Place

Related to the physical environment is *place*, which Zapf (2009) refers to as a geographical site or space that excludes online sites or communities of people with common goals and interests. Rather, "a dynamic sense of context, of behaviour . . . is situated in places. Proximity, common ground, and shared aspirations contribute to neighbourhoods where physical features may be seen as assets and resources" (p. 78). However, as Zapf notes, the idea of place in social work is relatively new and requires further development. Place attachment and place identity concepts help in understanding how neighborhoods have meaning for people who live in them (Devine-Wright, 2013). People may be attached to several places at the same time and identify with them all in different ways. They are often able to change their attachment to neighborhoods or places by seeking new livelihoods or moving to new neighborhoods. The environment, land, and way of life are an important part of the concept of place, particularly for rural people and those whose lives and livelihoods depend on the land (see Scoones, 2015).

For many North American Indigenous people, place is especially important (Zapf, 2009). In a book about activist projects (Whitmore, Wilson, & Calhoun, 2011), Docherty (2011) describes, in a chapter highlighting the Storytellers' Foundation, the practice of living in relationship, and captures the concept of place in her reference to people who are "land-based citizens" (p. 127). She defines them as those people who are "deeply connected to place. Relationships that have been woven for one hundred years and relationships that have been woven for 10,000 years shape their families" (p. 127). This long history, and collective memory, of a specific geographical area as sustaining and familiar shapes the lives of those who live in proximity to one another and whose history, culture, and social ties profoundly connect to land, home, and physical space that root them to a place.

For many people, the places to which they have been deeply connected no longer exist as they once were and may evoke feelings of deep grief and loss. For Indigenous populations worldwide, this relates to the fallout of colonization and/or encroachment of corporate interests that have all but destroyed their natural habitats. In the case of refugees who have survived political persecution, genocide, or war, their attachment is to a place where their ancestors have lived for many generations and to which they can no longer return. North American settlers, after generations or a lifetime of being grounded in a place of strong community roots and family networks, have also experienced the fracturing of these land-based communities by a dominant corporate economic climate that not only damages their environment but requires geographic movement of family and community members seeking gainful employment. In *Another Country*, Mary Pipher (1999) discusses the plight of aging individuals who face living out their lives isolated in their homes or in long-term care facilities—and their children and grandchildren who are sometimes thousands of miles away. She likens this older population to those who are from "another country," because they have a different cultural mindset and no longer fit into the current norm. Moreover, the rise of mental health issues, poverty, homelessness, and violence within the context of local and global trends highlights large segments of the population who often struggle *to find* place and belonging in a fragmented world—who have literally been displaced or have perhaps never had the opportunity to experience a sense of attachment to place.

Social workers who work directly with these populations can integrate expressive arts approaches to engage with client stories and process the loss of place, of homeland, of previously long-standing cultural community that is now dispersed. Opportunities to share stories and express the emotional themes inherent in these experiences of displacement and loss (including institutional care or incarceration) can be very powerful, whether orally with others who deeply want to listen, through art-making, photography, or video; storytelling, poetry, or writing; music, dance, or drama—in one-on-one, group, or community contexts. Chapter 6 provides examples of how storytelling, poetry and writing, and other narrative approaches in social work practice and research can be used with a variety of populations to support individual, group, and community transformation and structural change. Although places of the past may never be restored, and what happened in the past cannot be changed, the art of relationship and community, which is supported by the sharing of stories, often in combination with other expressive art forms (as described in Chapters 4 to 8), can empower community building and a new, more sustainable construction of place. For a moving documentary on restorative justice grounded in the growing reconciliation and friendship between an Indigenous group who had lost their ancestral land and sacred places, and settlers who had farmed the land (and shared an attachment to it) for many decades, please follow the following link: https://www.reserve107thefilm.com/

INDIGENOUS PERSPECTIVES, PRINCIPLES, AND PRACTICES

Indigenous worldviews and values align with many of the ideas from environmental and green social work and challenge more conventional social work therapeutic approaches and practices in that they demand attention to the social structures that shape the lives of those with whom social workers engage (Gray & Coates, 2015). Gray and Coates suggest that social work is now more aware of the effects of environmental damage and climate change that, in addition to growing social inequality in most parts of the world, affect Indigenous people, those living in conditions of poverty, and those where conflict and war cleave and destroy communities.

Social action initiated by groups of people who struggle to uphold environmental values are presented by the media when demonstrations and events showing opposition to corporate economic projects threaten the environment. One example is seen in recent efforts to stop the building of pipelines across large areas of land across North America (see Council of Canadians website at http://canadians.org/pipelines). They believe that the environment needs to be protected and maintained for future generations to enjoy and that when there is the potential for pollution and destruction, economic gain should not drive decisions. When environmental harm poses risks to humans, animals, air, water, and land that sustain us all, there is a need to pay close attention to decisions being made.

Indigenous peoples draw on spiritual and cultural beliefs and practices to maintain well-being, through drumming and singing (Goudreau, Weber-Pillwax, Cote-Meek, Madill, & Wilson, 2008; Kenny, 2006) and healing rituals such as smudging and use of sweat lodge, the medicine wheel, and sharing circles

(Hart, 2002; Sinclair, Hart & Bruyere, 2009). These approaches are framed by values that prioritize protection and appreciation of the natural world as well as care, concern, and respect for nature and all living beings in relationship with one another. Chapter 7 describes expressive arts approaches based on songs and drumming in an Indigenous worldview and cultural context. This chapter discusses the role of the drum and drumming for Indigenous people and how the growing acceptance of the healing power of music, drumming, and singing among therapists, mental health professionals, and social workers situates traditional Indigenous approaches to health and well-being on the leading edge of therapeutic healing. It provides examples of how these forms of expression connect people to the land and the environment, and encourage the development of consciousness about these matters and a deep respect for Indigenous knowledges and traditional ways of helping and healing.

SOCIAL JUSTICE AND SOCIAL ACTION

Social Justice

In the history of social work, social injustice has been a concern that the profession sought to address. Seeking social justice was a part of the settlement movement in the early days of social work, and it belongs in a profession that works for individual and collective change and transformation to address issues of poverty, inequality, human rights, and oppression. Social justice is a core principle in social work and is contained in the code of ethics for social workers, not only in Canada, but in many other countries. As Lundy writes, "Social justice and equality need to be seen as integrally linked to the need for economic security and access to better social services and programs" (2011, p. 30). Lundy also notes that issues such as the environment, human rights, and armed conflict strengthen social work's resolve for social justice. Unfortunately, these aims are not easily pursued in the day-to-day world of social work practice, given the demands at the front line that focus social work energy and time in the delivery of social services. Nevertheless, there are examples of social work practitioners, researchers, and scholars, sometimes in conjunction with community groups or organizations, whose commitment to social justice has led to social action, and to social change and transformation.

Social Action

The methods used in social action aim to raise people's consciousness, produce critical questions, and draw attention to issues that concern groups of people. Social action refers not only to a range of methods that bring to attention views and ideas about social justice to make them known locally, nationally, and/or internationally but also generates action that leads to collaboration for better social policies, laws, programs, new initiatives, and supportive resources. Social action initiatives do not aim to hurt people or other living things through violence, but they can be loud, brash, or strident. There are many examples of social action involving community groups and social workers in events and activities for social change.

In Canada, the Calgary Raging Grannies (Montgomery, 2011), with their engaging songs and costumes, draw public attention to many issues of social concern, such as the need to protect the environment or the closure of needed social programs. As one member explained, being part of—belonging—to something with others who share common values and ideas offers its own rewards. With the Grannies, humor and the element of surprise can add to their effectiveness. An example from the United States is the International Fiber Collective (Weida & Marsh, 2011), which combines art and activism. In its Gas Station Project, this group has produced wrappings out of yarn, fiber, and other materials to wrap an abandoned gas station in order to raise awareness about society's dependence on fossil fuels and the damaging results to the environment. The finished product is striking, and those who stop to view it more closely are exposed to the purpose of the work and why it was made (see https://www.youtube.com/watch?v=neOqItgVoTY). Weida and Marsh (2011) refer to this social action approach as public art and digital documentation as it uses both methods to disseminate its message. (For more information on the organization, see https://ifcprojects.com). Other examples of social action are described throughout the chapters of this book.

CULTURAL SAFETY

The concept of cultural safety was developed in New Zealand by nursing professionals seeking to improve health care for Maori Indigenous people (Williams, 1999). Cultural safety can be viewed as the farthest point on a continuum where cultural awareness is on the opposite side and cultural competence is at the midpoint (Brascoupé & Waters, 2009). Social workers are encouraged to *start where the client is*, which means attempting to understand the significance of culture to individuals and groups of people and how it shapes their lives (Heinonen & Spearman, 2010). It is not possible for social workers to learn about all cultures or even expect that they can generalize that a person from one particular cultural background will have the same beliefs and practices as another and, therefore, will think and behave in similar ways. It is possible to be aware of cultural difference, but to become competent in working with people across our own cultures and those of others is rarely achieved.

Cultural safety as a concept is imprecise and difficult to define. Rather, it might be easier to understand what is culturally unsafe (e.g., lack of respect, minimizing needs and interests, and control over decisions that affect another person). Some refer to cultural safety as representing a shift from cultural aware-ness and cultural competence where "cultural safety represents a more radical, politicized understanding of cultural consideration, effectively rejecting the more limited culturally competent approach for one based not on knowledge but on power" (Brascoupé & Waters, 2009, p. 10). In this conceptualization, power in the relationship between professionals and those to whom they pro-vide service needs to be attended to in order to build safety. For example, for Indigenous peoples who have experienced oppression, colonization, residential schools, and other harmful acts and processes, power in the relationship is an issue that needs attention. This view can be applied to working with social work and with expressive arts and is explained further in Chapter 7 in relation to Indigenous singing and drumming.

Although different histories, circumstances, and needs may characterize the realities of people from other cultural backgrounds, it would be helpful to consider promoting culturally safe practices. For example, refugees who have experienced war, conflict, and other trauma will need to be treated with care and understanding. Of course, others who perceive themselves as powerless or controlled by others who exercise power over them may feel unsafe (e.g., people who are homeless, struggle with mental health issues or addictions). They have likely experienced marginalization in their lives and could benefit from treatment that includes greater sensitivity and understanding of the need for safety, whether due to ethnocultural or other background.

Despite the many differences between people based on cultural back-ground, what has been demonstrated throughout history is the potential for individuals of all cultures to be both victims and perpetrators of horrific trau-matic acts enacted between one another as well as within their own cultural groups. In light of personal experience as well as the growing research and lit-erature on the intergenerational transmission of collective trauma, Armand Volkas, a drama therapist based in the United States, facilitates Healing the Wounds of History (HWH) workshops internationally to address the impact that such trauma has on the personal and collective psyche (see http://www.healingthewoundsofhistory.org/)

Given its transformative potential—its ability to humanize both the *victim* and the *enemy* and, in that way, find common ground and empathy with one another despite historical abuses—Volkas facilitates HWH workshops with service providers; grassroots community-building groups; and groups of participants from two cultures with a common legacy of conflict and historical trauma, such as descendants of Nazi perpetrators and descendants of Jewish

Holocaust survivors, Palestinians and Israelis, Armenians and Turks, to name a few. He states:

> By working with the specific participants who are representatives of their cultures I seek to make a therapeutic intervention in the collective or societal trauma. In this way my work is related philosophically to Psychodrama's founder Jacob Moreno's idea that "A truly therapeutic procedure cannot have less an objective than the whole of mankind" (Moreno, 1953). HWH, which takes a psychological approach to conflict, provides a map to help polarized groups traverse the emotional terrain to reconciliation. In this sense the approach is a form of social activism. (Volkas, 2009, p. 147)

As social workers (or representatives of any other professional discipline), expressive artforms such as psychodrama can also support us in deconstructing our own cultural location and its historical legacies, which may be unconsciously influencing our relationships with others.

CREATIVE EXPRESSION AS A COMPELLING HUMAN NEED

Social work scholars (e.g., Conrad & Sinner, 2015; Sinding & Barnes, 2015) have described a range of expressive arts methods that can be useful in social work practice and research. These methods add to social work repertoires, benefiting those they work with and contributing innovation to the profession. For many practitioners, time constraints, lack of experience, little support from supervisors or managers, and/or agency mandates may limit social workers' application of art, music, story, writing, or other expressive arts approaches in their work. Over the last decade, an increasing number of journal articles and books (e.g., Conrad & Sinner, 2015; Leavy, 2015; McLean & Kelly, 2011; Sinding & Barnes, 2015) have appeared; and workshops, courses, and conferences have engaged social workers' interest in expressive arts methods.

We view the concepts and principles discussed in this chapter as perspectives and views that shape our thinking about social work and expressive arts. These are loosely woven through chapters where there are clear connections. In all chapters we address individual and social change and transformation. The elements that construct our orientation to expressive arts approaches, when integrated into social work and other helping professions, also inform readers about our values and views. Diverse examples are referred to in the chapters that follow. Literature from cognate disciplines of social work, such as education, psychology, sociology, and Indigenous studies, are also referred to when they resonate with the purposes, aims, and uses of the expressive arts as described in this book (e.g., Levine & Levine, 2011; McGregor, 2012). These ideas offer a means by which to orient the book.

REFERENCES

Alston, M. (2015). Social work, climate change and global cooperation. *International Social Work, 58*(3), 355–363. doi:10.1177/0020872814556824

Brascoupé, S., & Waters, C. (2009). Cultural safety: Exploring the applicability of the concept of cultural safety to Aboriginal health and community wellness. *Journal of Aboriginal Health, 5*(2), 6–41.

Coates, J., & Gray, M. (2011). The environment and social work: An overview and introduction. *International Journal of Social Welfare, 21,* 230–238.

Conrad, C., & Sinner, A. (Eds.). (2015). *Creating together: Participatory, community - based and collaborative arts practices and scholarship across Canada.* Waterloo, ON: Wilfrid Laurier University Press.

Devine-Wright, P. (2013). Think global, act local? The relevance of place attachments and place identities in a climate changed world. *Global Environmental Change, 23,* 61–69.

Docherty, A. (2011). Storytellers' Foundation: Learning for change. In E. Whitmore, M. Wilson, & A. Calhoun (Eds.), *Activism that works* (pp. 124–132). Halifax, NS: Fernwood.

Dominelli, L. (2014). Promoting environmental justice through green social work practice: A key challenge for practitioners and educators. *International Social Work, 57*(4), 338–345.

Drolet, J., Wu, H., Taylor, M., & Dennehy, A. (2015). Social work and sustainable social development: Teaching and learning strategies for "green social work" curriculum. *Social Work Education, 34*(4), 528–543.

Goudreau, G., Weber-Pillwax, C., Cote-Meek, S., Madill, H., & Wilson, S. (2008). Hand drumming: Health-promoting experiences of Aboriginal women from a northern Ontario urban community. *Journal of Aboriginal Health, 4*(1), 72–83.

Gray, M., & Coates, J. (2013). Changing values and valuing change: Toward an ecospiritual perspective in social work. *International Social Work, 56*(3), 356–368. doi:10.1177/0020872812474009

Gray, M., & Coates, J. (2015). Changing gears: Shifting to an environmental perspective in social work education. *Social Work Education: The International Journal, 5,* 502–512. doi:101.1080/02615479.2015.1065807

Hart, M. (2002). *Seeking mino-pimatisiwin: An Aboriginal approach to helping.* Halifax, NS: Fernwood.

Hawkins, C. (2010). Sustainability, human rights, and environmental justice: Critical connections for contemporary social work. *Critical Social Work, 11*(10). Available at http://www1.uwindsor.ca/criticalsocialwork/the-nexus-of-sustainability-human-rights-and-environmental-justice-a-critical-connection-for-contemp

Heinonen, T., & Spearman, L. (2010). *Social work practice: Problem solving and beyond.* Toronto, ON: Nelson.

Hoff, M. D., & McNutt, J. G. (Eds). (1994). *The global environmental crisis: Implications for social welfare and social work.* Aldershot, UK: Ashgate Publishers.

Kenny, C. (2006). *Music and life in the field of play: An anthology.* Gilsum, NH: Barcelona.

Leavy, P. (2015). *Method meets art: Arts-based research practice.* New York, NY: Guilford Press.

Levine, E., & Levine, S. (2011). *Art in action: Expressive arts therapy and social change.* London, UK: Jessica Kingsley.

Lundy, C. (2011). *Social work, social justice, & human rights*. Toronto, ON: University of Toronto Press.

McGregor, C. (2012). Arts-informed pedagogy: Tools for social transformation. *International Journal of Lifelong Education, 31*(3), 309–324. doi:10.1080/02601370.2012.683612

McKinnon, J. (2013). The environment: A private concern or a professional practice issue for Australian social workers? *Australian Social Work, 66*(2), 156–170. doi:10.1080/0312407X.2013.782558

McLean, C., & Kelly, R. (Eds.). (2011). *Creative arts in research for community and cultural change*. Calgary, AB: Detselig Enterprises/Temeron Books.

Montgomery, S. (2011). Calgary Raging Grannies: Affective and effective. In E. Whitmore, M. Wilson, & A. Calhoun, *Activism that works* (pp. 64–79). Blackpoint, NS: Fernwood.

Moreno, J. L. (1953). *Who shall survive?* New York, NY: Beacon House.

Norton, C. (2011). Social work and the environment: An ecosocial approach. *International Journal of Social Welfare, 21*, 299–308.

Pipher, M. (1999). *Another country: Navigating the emotional terrain of our elders*. New York, NY: The Berkeley Publishing Group/Penguin Putnam.

Rutherford, G., Walsh, C., & Rook, J. (2011). Teaching and learning processes for social transformation: Engaging a kaleidoscope of learners. *Journal of Teaching in Social Work, 31*(5), 479–492. doi:10.1080/08841233.2011.614206

Scoones, I. (2015). *Sustainable livelihoods and rural development*. Blackpoint, NS: Fernwood.

Sinclair, R., Hart, M., & Bruyere, G. (2009). *Wichitowin: Aboriginal social work in Canada*. Black Point, NS: Fernwood.

Sinding, C., & Barnes, H. (Eds.). (2015). *Social work artfully: Beyond borders and boundaries*. Waterloo, ON: Wilfrid Laurier University Press.

Volkas, A. (2009). Healing the wounds of history: Drama therapy in collective trauma and intercultural conflict resolution. In D. Johnson & R. Emunah (Eds.), *Current approaches in drama therapy* (pp. 145–171). Springfield, IL: Charles C. Thomas.

Weida, C., & Marsh, J. (2011). Weaving provocations for social change: The International Fiber Collaborative. In C. McLean & R. Kelly (Eds.), *Creative arts in research for community and cultural change* (pp. 109–114). Calgary, AB: Detselig.

Whitmore, E., Wilson, M., & Calhoun, A. (Eds.). (2011). *Activism that works*. Black Point, NS: Fernwood.

Williams, R. (1999). Cultural safety—what does it mean for our work practice? *Australia and New Zealand Journal of Public Health, 23*(2), 213–214.

Zapf, M. (2009). *Social work and the environment: Understanding people and place*. Toronto, ON: Canadian Scholars' Press.

Visual Arts

Drawing, Painting, and Collage

TUULA HEINONEN

INTEGRATION OF VISUAL ARTS IN THE CONTEXT OF SOCIAL WORK

Visual arts offer a vast and rich treasure chest of media, methods, and applications for arts-based social work and social development. Art and expressive therapists know that drawing, painting, collage, mixed media, and combinations of these methods are available for their use. Social workers, too, can make use of these as complementary methods in their practice work with people in a wide range of practice settings. Materials to create visual art pieces are often easy to find and can include use of paint, inks, pencils, pens and pastels, and/or recycled papers and images. Applications can be introduced as part of assessment or intervention activities in work with clients. The process of art-making is usually more important than the product, or both may be equally important for some. Using visual art media for individual and social transformation can produce powerful expression, insights, and empowerment for people.

In visual arts work with individuals and groups, there is a wide and deep practice history. The pioneers of art therapy, such as Helen Landgarten (1987) and Edith Kramer (1971), were associated with psychiatry and psychology and practiced with patients in hospitals and in other health care settings. Art therapy has grown and changed over the years, and human service professions, such as nursing, education, and social work, have adopted the use of visual arts in their own professional practices, although not art therapy as art therapists apply it.

Social work professionals in many fields of practice may find in the visual arts a welcome complement for practice with individuals, families, groups, and communities, and have developed or adapted visual arts–based methods and tools to suit the needs of those with whom they work. Furthermore, some social workers with an interest in using art in their work with individuals or groups have added to their credentials by completing art therapy or expressive arts diplomas or degrees to broaden their repertoires and skills. Such education and/or experience in the art-making process is essential because it enables those practitioners with only a little art background to learn about materials, methods, exercises, and their applications. They can also try out art-making projects, methods, and exercises in order to experience for themselves the profound power of the visual arts to effect change.

When arts-based methods are effectively and appropriately applied in practice, they can promote healing and well-being, build community cohesion, and lead to transformation in individuals, groups, and communities (Coholic, Cote-Meek, & Recollet, 2012; Moxley, 2013; Phinney, Moody, & Small, 2013; Slayton, 2012). Some exercises can generate emotions or insights that are profound. It is necessary for a social worker to be prepared and to know how to respond to strong feelings and emotional pain. The effects on social work clients in their use of materials such as paint, pastels, pencils, or images may also generate discomfort or fear where such materials are associated with judgment and criticism (e.g., "you have no skill in art"). It would be inappropriate for a social worker to use visual arts in his or her work with clients without having knowledge of such methods themselves and of the reasons why clients might not accept the use of visual arts intervention. Making use of visual arts media and methods without sufficient knowledge, skill, and training to deal with the complex human problems that social workers experience in their practices can present risks and be harmful for clients (Damianakis, 2007). They may even be professionally irresponsible (Reamer, 2004).

Social workers using new or experimental methods have always needed to consider how they would protect their clients and provide sufficient information for clients so they can choose whether or not to consent when intervention involves an approach or methods that they do not agree with. However, it is also useful and desirable for professionals to innovate and to try new intervention methods that might result in better outcomes for their clients. As Hocoy (2006) notes, just as with the pioneers of art therapy, it is possible for professionals to complement their knowledge, build skills, and learn about integrating the arts to help people "through reading, workshops and local practitioners" (p. 134). Good supervision and consultation with experienced and knowledgeable practitioners is invaluable for social workers who wish to add new complementary methods such as drawing, painting, and collage work to their practices.

Currently, the visual arts (and other art forms) are used by social work practitioners and have been found effective in helping people whose issues and situations require, or respond best to, alternative methods of treatment. For example, drawing, painting, collage, and other creative methods have been helpful when used with groups of vulnerable children involved in the mental health and child protection systems in Ontario, Canada (Coholic, Oystrick, Posteraro, & Lougheed, 2016). The range of issues such children had and the difficult home environments they had experienced resulted in poor self-esteem and confidence. As Coholic, Oystrick, Posteraro, and Lougheed (2016) describe, a means to build the children's strengths and social skills was needed and arts-based activities (with a mindfulness approach) offered an alternative that suited the children's needs.

Ephrat Huss, an Israeli social worker and art therapist, has produced a book (2013) and authored and coauthored articles on social work practice and the use of visual arts in individual and group work with children and adults (e.g., Huss & Ben-Gurion, 2014; Huss, Elhozayel, & Marcus, 2012; Huss, Nuttman-Shwartz, & Altman, 2012; Huss, Sarid, & Cwikel, 2010). She has written about using visual arts methods to help children who experienced disaster, women affected by abuse, and women with refugee experiences. In fact, there are many people whose situations and issues could be addressed through participation in visual art-making, and social workers may find it beneficial to introduce these in their practices.

Huss and Ben-Gurion (2014) describe how differences in ways of seeing and speaking about artwork can occur due to varying professional backgrounds and training. For example, a visual artist would likely appreciate the art from an aesthetic orientation, looking at composition, color, and technique, whereas a social worker would likely want to know about the social and cultural aspects of the art and the meaning attributed to it by the person who created it. On the other hand, art therapists, particularly those trained in psychotherapy, might draw from psychological concepts and theories and use such a knowledge base when working with an artist and her or his artwork. Damianakis (2007) notes that it is beneficial for social work practitioners to understand the perspective and orientation of art professionals so that they can learn from them about how social work values and perspectives differ or intersect with those of artists. She states that it would then make it possible "to generate insights that in turn contribute to social work practices and knowledge bases" (p. 525). Social workers can better understand what the arts can contribute to their work and how they might be useful in various practice settings and situations. However, as Damianakis (2007) suggests, the social work profession's humanistic and creative elements have not led to a committed engagement with the arts in social work practice. In contrast, it seems that the drive to apply evidence-based practices and technical solutions to people's complex problems has overshadowed social work's creative potential. For example, US social work educator Patricia Walton notes that she sees much richness and range in applications of the arts in other human service professions. Social work "remains entirely fixed on talk and text" (2012, p. 725). She questions why this should be the case when social work requires creativity to work in complex and often-changing practice situations. Further, the need to foster emotional expression as part of work with clients should direct social workers to the potential power of the arts in practice.

Walton (2012), in her application of visual arts work (collage) with students in social work field placements, found that using visual expression as a starting point led to deeper awareness in which the students were able to "more wholly acknowledge their own feelings, responses and reactions, including doubt, ambivalence, disapproval and discomfort" (p. 736). Although referring primarily to creative writing, Damianakis (2007) stresses that art may "disrupt the worker's reliance on conventional routines and social norms and to facilitate surprise and innovation" (p. 530).

In social work practice where visual arts are used, there is often a greater focus on the process of art-making as a means of individual and collective expression, transformation, and empowerment, although the artwork produced may have significance as well. Clients who participate in visual art-making may experience dissemination of their artwork in small groups or in public settings as empowering. When issues that affect a group of people who experience stigma are presented in the form of an exhibition of artwork produced by the group, dialogue and greater understanding may result. This was the case in Hong Kong during "a systematic arts dialogue . . . among people living with mental illness and those from the general population" (Ho, Potash, Ho, Ho, & Chen, 2017, p. 479). A collaborative art-making activity generated opportunities for education, discovering common interests and goals and fostering public awareness about mental illness.

An example of visual arts use with a group of people living with cancer follows. It is based on a report produced by Don Stevens for his final art therapy diploma project in 2013. As a fine arts graduate, Don had past experience with making art and in facilitating groups of people who wanted to participate in making their own artwork to enhance their well-being.

Art Therapy in a Health Care Setting: Don Stevens, Halifax Art Therapist

Don Stevens is an art therapist from Nova Scotia who has agreed to have his graduate work highlighted as an example of visual arts with groups of people facing serious health challenges. He made use of group work in his practice because it fit with the needs of the clients and the purposes of his practice work. Group work using creative methods is not new. Ruth Middleman, an American social worker, wrote in 1968 about "the non-verbal method in working with groups" and describes the power of the imagination and creative process in group work as important to explore because it is a part of human life (Middleman, 1968).

As Don describes, "Two groups were comprised of people living with chronic pain while the other was made up of people living with cancer. The clients developed their own strategies for resilience by manipulating simple art materials and sharing their experiences in an open studio environment" (Stevens, 2013, p. ii). Both health and mental health care services have noted the significance of art for clients' recovery (Bates, Bleakley, & Goodman, 2014; Collie, Bottorff, & Long, 2006; Malchiodi, 2013; Secker, Loughran, Heydinrych, & Kent, 2011).

Don draws on Winnicott (1971) to explain the importance of a holding space for people who engage in therapeutic art-making in order to "feel free to express themselves through creative play" (Stevens, 2013, p. 4). For people living with pain and uncertain futures, it is important to offer such a space and to be open to individual and group needs and interests. In this space, everyone was accepted, and all art-making efforts were appreciated. Don was sensitive to the fact that "many had mobility issues in addition to chronic pain, fatigue and illness" (2013, p. 12). In the therapeutic setting, "[a] level of trust was established that all work was honoured, respected and free from judgment" (2013, p. 14). As Don explained, those who were living with cancer can feel a sense of belonging and caring for one another in the group as they were living with challenges that all could relate to, despite different views and backgrounds. The clients learned from one another and from the art process as they spent time together in the group sessions.

In Don Stevens's written work, he describes individual group members' situations and shows their artwork with titles given by the group members. The weekly art-making sessions held over a 10-month period were opportunities for the participants to explore their ideas, feelings, and experiences, addressing different themes and interests. Given the long term of the art therapy, Don heard poignant stories of the group members' lives with cancer. He also experienced the death of one member, which motivated him to create his own artwork in response. The practice of professionals making their own art to express and "contain" emotions that arise from their practice work with clients is not uncommon in art therapy (Fish, 2012). It can offer insights that enhance practice and offer a means to make sense of troubling situations. However, as Don notes, more research is needed on self-care for practitioners to learn about the uses and outcomes of art-making for them. In fact, many art therapists believe that is important for them to engage in art-making themselves because it is essential to their professional development and well-being. Brown (2008) asserts, "Administrators of the agencies where creative arts therapists work along with their credentialing bodies and national organizations should take note of this and create standards of practice that support this" (p. 207).

Don Stevens also worked with a group of people who lived with chronic pain. They used art-making, drawing from a range of media, to express their ideas and feelings. One of these is entitled the "self-box" in which clients can depict what they present to the outside world on the outside of the box and, on the inside of the box, their inner thoughts and feelings. The use of this exercise has been described by Frings-Keyes (1974, p. 14) as a self-help method to learn about oneself and to experience making a visual record with art materials. Those who practice using art with clients can themselves benefit from painting, drawing, or other methods of art-making (Frings-Keyes, 1974; Stevens, 2013, p. 53).

A discussion of the concept of "safe space" (Oster, Aström, Lindh, & Magnusson, 2009) is useful. As Don states, "I have found that some clients insist that they never really feel safe, so I don't feel comfortable in imposing that label on them. I suppose I would prefer for the description to arise more organically" (2013, p. 54). He infers that it is better that clients themselves explore what a safe space might mean for them, if anything. It is possible that some people do not feel a sense of safety due to their past experiences of trauma or some other factors. They might, however, be able to identify whether such a place could be imagined or constructed in some way.

Communities as Sites of Visual Arts Application

In community organizations, visual arts projects have helped to bring youth and other groups of people together to take part in art-making for social change on issues of concern, such as building stronger neighborhoods, promoting care of the environment, and confronting violence and racism. There are differences in purpose and approach in the use of the arts for individual and group therapy, on one hand, and, on the other hand, in collective projects where social justice is the main goal. Yet there are important connections between these that have been noted (e.g., Hocoy, 2007; Levine & Levine, 2011; Moxley & Washington, 2013). Estrella (2007) notes that a process of social change may start with individuals, groups, communities, or in a society. She states, "Individual efforts to become more culturally competent and tolerant, more socially and politically aware and active, taking more personal responsibility for one's behavior, or developing an inner contemplative/spiritual practice, are all potential forms of social action" (p. 47).

Seeds may be planted within an individual that can lead to transformative change within and beyond the individual. People might then take action on their own, for example, by writing or speaking out on an issue of importance to them, or they may form like-minded groups with a social agenda that they wish to pursue. In visual arts therapies, discourse has centered on individual or group work, less on community or social change. This is likely because the pioneers of these therapies, practicing and writing from the time of World War II, tended to be psychiatrists and psychologists whose work drew on micro-level theories of professional practice in these fields (Hogan, 2001). There is a paucity of theories in the art therapy profession that connect art therapy together with social action (Hocoy, 2007), although some art therapists (e.g., LeBaron, 2011) have noted the dual roles of "social activism and restorative work" that exist in the expressive arts (p. 10). The potential for an interdisciplinary approach in practice and education between art and social work has been discussed by Wehbi, McCormick, and Angelucci (2016), who state that social work needs to innovate and find other ways of providing services than traditional counseling interventions. They describe how engaging with the arts (socially engaged art [SEA]) can help social workers to meaningfully work for social justice goals alongside communities. Through developing a course that combined social work and art, Wehbi and her colleagues (2016) aimed to involve students in a process of critical questioning and creative exploration that would lead to collaborative exchange, community engagement, and enhanced creativity. Like them, we concur that arts-informed social work practice can offer new ways of working with people that can lead to rewarding and effective results.

With the increasing proliferation of online media technologies and applications for communication of a wide range of issues of concern to different groups in society, it is possible to disseminate images produced to many people all at once. For example, the use of community collage murals for discussions on ecology and green communities is depicted on a website at http://collagemuralproject.blogspot.ca/. The format is public and welcoming to those who approach it online or at the physical sites where collage and mural-making events took place in London and Cape Town, South Africa. The events began informally with youth and other people taking part in collage-making using old magazines to depict ideas about climate change, a topic of concern to those who participated in it. In London, the project proceeded from weekend collage sessions to a gallery exhibition. The creative potential to develop communities through collective art-making and the spread of such projects to other groups and parts of the world illustrates the power of the arts to communicate and catalyze people who aim for a just society. Chapter 4 describes in more detail some possibilities and examples of these.

Social work concepts and theories can contribute to social action or social transformation goals. For example, Bob Mullaly (2007) calls for social workers to see that people's troubles and situations are located and rooted in a social-structural context that is characterized by inequality, injustice, poverty, oppression, and marginalization.

Social worker David Moxley (2013) has written that among groups of people experiencing oppression, art-making contributes to survival of the group (through its effects on cohesion) and makes it an act of self-definition in the face of oppression and marginalization. Art-making may emerge within a group as its principal source of pleasure, interpretation of the world, and coping (p. 237).

In another publication, Moxley and Washington (2013) describe the impact of art-making on a group of African American women who wanted to overcome homelessness. The authors found that making art was important not only for expression of emotional and difficult experiences but also for the discovery of common themes and the development of group strength and cohesion, which led the women from a process of arts-based expression to community action.

Illustrations and examples from arts-based practice and research in social work both from the literature and in practitioner experience show the ways in which community settings have offered possibilities for the use of visual arts–based methods. What follows is an example, based on an interview with a young artist, of the way that visual arts have been used to enhance Indigenous and other young people's lives. Although the practitioner whose work is represented is not a social worker, she works in a community service organization and the work she does is comparable and relevant to community-based social work; thus, it could offer lessons and practice ideas for social workers.

EXAMPLE OF AN ART PROJECT FOR COMMUNITY SOCIAL CHANGE: JESSICA CANARD, COMMUNITY ARTIST

Former Canadian Lieutenant Governor Michaëlle Jean and her cochair, Jean Daniel Lafond, embarked on a mission to use the arts "to empower underserved youth to transform lives and revitalize communities in Canada" (see http://www.fmjf.ca/en/). Through their organization, the Michaëlle Jean Foundation (MJF), they focus on using the arts to promote dialogue, community mobilization, and social change, and many young persons have used creativity of the arts "to build new solutions to pressing issues affecting them. These young leaders are proving that the arts can change lives and give hope to communities hit by such challenges as violent extremism, the disproportionate incarceration of minority youth, delinquency, violence and suicide" (http://www.fmjf.ca/en/about-us/). One of the young people who received assistance and mentorship through the organization is Jessica Canard, who related how important art has been in her young life. She was accepted into Winnipeg's Graffiti Gallery Urban Canvas Program in 2009. Eight young Aboriginal artists were selected and financially supported to take part in a 48-week intensive art internship. As Jessica said, "It was the kind of mentorship I was looking for and it was really like I was living my dream already. They had professional artists who have been to schools in other countries to learn about art; [they shared] what they'd learned with us."

Jessica later participated in other initiatives where she combined visual art and social change activities. In 2011, new opportunities arose that she embraced:

I was a part of Graffiti Art Programming Aboriginal Youth Advisory Council (GAPAYAC), and in 2011 we hosted an event called Voicing Youth's Rights to the City. It invited youth from different schools, professors, government officials, and community members to participate. This is where I first met the 27th Governor General at the time, Michaëlle Jean. We talked about safety, city planning, and its effects on health, as well as how much access we as youth have in making decisions in our communities. The members of GAPAYAC created art pieces on our views of living in Winnipeg. I sold the art piece I made for the event to the Michaëlle Jean Foundation (MJF). The art piece is titled "Untitled 2011" and is a multimedia piece created on a door. Skateboards were jigsawed to look like a cityscape. The buildings looked like the ones you'd find in the Exchange [Stock Exchange District of Winnipeg]. Streets shoot out from the cityscape like sun's rays, with the bus numbers that I use most stencilled on the top. The Foundation partnered with the Canadian Museum for Human Rights (CMHR) to display my artwork at their head office.

I [have] continued making art and doing a lot of community-building work through the Graffiti Gallery. In 2013 I was asked to give a testimonial at the first Power of the Arts National Forum held at Carleton University, [where] I talked about how the arts impacted my life as well as the partnership between the MJF and the CMHR.

Jessica refers to herself as a visual artist and produces large paintings, for example, murals. She refers to her style as "bright, bold, and colourful." She explained that she is particularly interested in art as social commentary "for the people who are in the streets." Jessica views this kind of art as accessible and its purpose is to communicate ideas and opinions. She also sees street art as an alternative to the paid advertising of businesses with the resources to promote "their messages, products, and services." She adds, "Street art to me is a way of subverting the idea that you have to pay to share visually." She also believes that artists need more constructive channels to make art, such as through mural festivals.

Jessica described a project in Winnipeg in which she has been involved:

I work a lot in the North Point Douglas area [in the inner city of Winnipeg], and one of the public art projects I had the opportunity to work on is the community oven located in Michaëlle Jean Park. The community oven was an idea brought over from Vancouver, and the lead artist on the project was Leah Decter. It took the whole summer of 2012 for a team of eight of us to design, create, and install a tile mosaic around the whole oven. The community oven is an outdoor oven heated by fire that takes four hours to heat up. You can cook all day long in it. The community oven was a project initiated by the North Point Douglas Women's Centre NPDWC, and Graffiti Art Programming were the ones who added the creative elements of a tile mosaic. The NPDWC hosts community pizza nights, cultural bread night, and training nights for people who want to learn how to use the oven. These food making . . . events are for anyone in the community. . . . It's to celebrate the community and the people who make it up. . . . During these events, art projects are happening alongside the food making because why not make art and delicious food together?

Jessica refers to art as a means to "beautify and build stronger communities. . . . Art isn't just crafts and what you do in your free time . . . it's a serious tool for creating change. It's for the individual who makes art for their own personal growth, as a way to connect with others and the world around them."

Art can help to break down the alienation experienced by people who have been marginalized in society. The Graffiti Gallery, Jessica's employer, provides youth access to create art on their own terms. As Jessica says, "the organization also partners with many local agencies serving young people . . . to offer creative opportunities and events for them." She explained that, at a recent event, staff at the organization asked youth what kind of persons they wanted to be when they grew up: "For example, do you want to be a caring person or a helpful person?" Jessica said that this approach was very different from the pressure involved when they were asked what they wanted to *be* when they grew up. She described what occurred next:

> The youth then wrote about the kind of persons they wanted to be; they drew where they saw themselves in a few years; and they also did some drama activities where they dressed up as their future selves. Videos were taken of them as their future selves that were then turned into holograms and everything the youth created was displayed at the gallery. Over 100 youth [took part] and it left me with hope for the future. Here [were] all these people, younger than me . . . wanting to make the world a better place for the people around them.

For people who have experienced oppression, racism, exclusion, pain, and/or trauma, there can be great significance attached in presenting to others their works of art produced on the issues they have faced. A public exhibition of visual art by those who are troubled or who have been socially marginalized can represent a valorization of their identity, struggles, and efforts toward healing and growth. For example, in relation to a project with participants affected by war, art-making accompanied by an expressive writing activity was used (Stepakoff et al., 2011). In this project, the Iraqi survivors of torture and war that Stepakoff and associates (2011) wrote about gained the ability to cope with individual pain and trauma by sharing and being acknowledged by others who had lived through similar experiences. Through sharing their art with others, the participants enhanced "public awareness of the realities of suffering and resilience among Iraqis who have been forced to seek refuge in other lands" (p. 142). Such acts require trust in the expressive arts to promote healing, courage to take part in the process of art-making, and the desire to communicate through and about the art with a wider audience.

USE OF VISUAL ARTS METHODS IN RESEARCH

Recent books that describe arts-based research by social work scholars and those in other professional human service fields, such as education and psychology (e.g., Bryant, 2016; Butler-Kisber, 2010; Knowles & Cole, 2008; Leavy, 2015; McLean & Kelly, 2010; Sinding & Barnes, 2015), demonstrate the many ways in which visual and other expressive arts methods can be framed and applied and how such methods can offer new perspectives and insights in research. In social work, there is emerging interest in applying arts-based methods in qualitative research.

Visual arts are viewed as qualitative research, and in social work inquiry it often appears in the form of photovoice, in which research participants usually take photographs related to the research topic and later discuss them with other participants and the researcher. Both the photos and the narratives comprise data (e.g., Harley & Hunn, 2015; Lewinson, Robinson-Dooley, & Grant, 2012). (These are discussed in more detail in Chapter 4.)

Drawing and painting are not often seen in social work research projects, although they may be used as a means for generating ideas or included in a group process such as drama, storytelling, or reflection (e.g., McGillicuddy, Cross, Mitchell, Halifax, & Plummer, 2015; Paton, 2015). Collage as a method in qualitative research has been described by Butler-Kisber (2008, 2010) as an appealing art form in which elements such as images and text are positioned on a surface "as a way of expressing the said and unsaid, and allows for multiple avenues of interpretation and greater accessibility" (p. 268). The images, texts, and other materials on a collage surface comprise data which also requires interpretation from the person who created the work. The process of making a collage involves placing fragments together to express ideas and feelings. Sometimes through the process of reflecting or discussing the collage, previously unspoken ideas and insights arise that result in new understanding and knowledge about topics being discussed. Butler-Kisber (2010) notes greater interest in collage in research (and in teaching, supervision, practice, and art journaling), making it likely that collage will continue to be prominent in arts-based social research in the future. When collage is used for practice (exploration, expression, and/ or healing for individual or social change), the aim is therapeutic; when collage is used to explore or answer a question, it is usually conducted for research purposes (Chilton & Scotti, 2014).

Use of collage can be helpful to social work and other human service practitioners where it offers a means of exploring issues and difficult experiences as well as possible resolution. Helen Landgarten, in *Clinical Art Therapy* (1981), developed the magazine photo collage process for use by professionals in the field of mental health as a tool for assessment. Since that time, new ways of using collage by professionals have been developed mostly for practice in-tervention. The method has been shown to be useful in reminiscence to re-view memories or make sense of life with older adults living with dementia, where verbal communication can be augmented by collage-making (Woolhiser Stallings, 2010). Provision of precut images labeled according to a theme (e.g., workplaces, sports, etc.) is helpful because it offers choice in image selection that, for many experiencing dementia, may be limited in daily life. The selection of images should be done by the persons who are participating in the activity because each person has unique associations with different images, colors, and themes. Collage-making can also help in promoting interpersonal communica-tion (Woolhiser Stallings, 2010). Some assistance by a caregiver might be nec-essary when clients are challenged in manipulating magazine images or glue.

In response to a theme or question posed by a practitioner (group worker, therapist, community worker, or social worker), those who are being provided with services participate in a collage exercise. Materials, such as images and words cut from magazines or newspapers, glue and scissors, and time to com-plete the exercise are provided by the practitioner. An individual or group selects from a variety of compiled magazine or precut images and words, assembling and gluing them down on a piece of paper or other ground into a completed collage. The point is not to find an image that exactly fits with one's idea or ex-perience, but one that is a metaphor, symbol, or color that represents it. Most of us can imagine what these might be for ourselves. For example, poverty might be represented by an old gray shack, an empty bowl, or a person looking down at the ground. Social clinical practice differs from inquiry because both have different purposes. With graduate students, I have used such exercises to ex-plore with them the transitions they experienced in the academic setting or key points in their past year of studies. The students were also encouraged to combine collage-making with pastels, markers, or pencil crayons. This method

Figure 3.1 Rocks and sky. Collage courtesy of Tuula Heinonen.

was particularly useful when the student was interested in using the arts for exploring their study progress; however, not all students were.

Collage is also useful for professional development. The opportunity to focus on self-reflection and expression in relation to professional issues and emotions that arise in the course of a trying week can be helpful. I have found that collage-making offers an opportunity to create order, harmony, and reflection that reaches beyond work life and restores well-being and effectiveness. As shown in Figure 3.1), one of the collages that I produced recently after a particularly challenging and tiring week provides a sense of peace as I view it and think of the significance of the images, textures, and colors to me.

CONCLUDING THOUGHTS

Chambon (2009) states that there is a role for the arts in social work research. Social work "can benefit from encounters with practices of art to the extent that such practices can point to and question what is perceived as *natural* ways of relating in society—homelessness, precarious living conditions, unequal access to various forms of capital, appropriation of and exercising knowledge" (p. 600). In other words, the two divides of practitioners and clients are more clearly seen as related and interconnected in society.

Visual art methods offer important tools for practitioners and, increasingly, for researchers. Creativity is an available resource for human beings and can offer to social workers complementary methods that foster individual and social transformation for individuals and groups of people experiencing pain, suffering, loneliness, oppression, and social exclusion at different periods in life. This is not a new idea for those in human services, including social work, since the arts have been applied for a long time by professionals to foster education, expression, and well-being among clients, often without much documentation. Social workers, in working with people needing services to live with, recover, and transform from the effects of individual distress, family conflict, troubling issues common to specific groups, or problems that originate in a community, would find it helpful to integrate arts-based methods into their practice. Drawing, painting, and collaging can help people express what is difficult or unspeakable in a way that can represent a tentative idea that is being explored, a statement of need, an angry scream, or a forceful voice that seeks to be acknowledged and understood. All these can be beneficial to those who produce the art and those who view and respond to it.

QUESTIONS FOR REFLECTION

1. Have you used visual arts–based methods in your practice? If so, how has it shaped the way in which you work?
2. What barriers have you observed in social workers (or a different human service profession that you belong to) complementing their practice with visual arts methods?
3. In your own work with people, how do you think the visual arts can generate individual change?
4. How might visual arts methods promote or lead to social change?
5. What do you see as the benefits and pitfalls of using visual arts methods in qualitative research?

RESOURCES

Breast cancer survivors heal through art: https://www.youtube.com/watch?v= rXPw_g7MjFc

Michaëlle Jean Foundation, regarding social innovation: http://www.fmjf.ca/ en/programming/social-innovation/

The Painter of Jalouzi, a video about color in the slums of Haiti: https://www.youtube.com/watch?v=Eyr9NwyszNY and http://my.happify.com/hd/artist-bringing-joy-to-his-community/

Painting in twilight: An artist's escape from Alzheimer's: https://www.youtube.com/watch?v=I_Te-s6M4qc

REFERENCES

Bates, V., Bleakley, A., & Goodman, S. (Eds.) (2014). *Medicine, health and the arts: Approaches to the medical humanities.* Abingdon, Oxon: Routledge.

Brown, C. (2008). The importance of making art for the creative arts therapist: An artistic inquiry. *The Arts in Psychotherapy, 35*(3), 201–208.

Bryant, L. (2016). *Critical and creative research methodologies in social work.* Farnham, MA: Taylor and Francis.

Butler-Kisber, L. (2008). Collage as inquiry. In G. Knowles & A. Cole (Eds.), *Handbook of the arts in qualitative research* (pp. 265–276). Thousand Oaks, CA: Sage.

Butler-Kisber, L. (2010). *Qualitative inquiry: Thematic, narrative and arts-informed perspectives.* Thousand Oaks, CA: Sage.

Chambon, A. (2009). What can art do for social work? *Canadian Social Work Review, 26*(2), 217–223.

Chilton, G., & Scotti, V. (2014). Snipping, gluing, writing: The properties of collage as an arts-based research practice in art therapy. *Art Therapy Journal of the American Art Therapy Association, 31*(4), 163–171.

Coholic, D., Cote-Meek, S., & Recollet, D. (2012). Exploring the acceptability and perceived benefits of arts-based group methods for Aboriginal women living in an urban community within northeastern Ontario. *Canadian Social Work Review, 29*(2), 149–168.

Coholic, D., Oystrick, V., Posteraro, J., & Lougheed, S. (2016). Facilitating arts-based mindfulness group activities with vulnerable children: An example of nondeliberative social group work practice. *Social Work With Groups, 39*(2–3), 155–169.

Collie, K., Bottorff, J., & Long, B. (2006). A narrative view of art therapy and art making by women with breast cancer. *Journal of Health Psychology, 11*(5), 761–775.

Damianakis, T. (2007). Social work's dialogue with the arts: Epistemological and practice intersections. *Families in Society: The Journal of Contemporary Social Services, 88*(4), 525–533.

Estrella, K. (2007). Social activism within expressive arts "therapy": What's in a name? In F. Kaplan (Ed.), *Arts in action: Expressive arts therapy and social change* (pp. 42–52). London, UK: Jessica Kingsley.

Fish, B. (2012). Response art: The art of the art therapist. *Art Therapy: Journal of the American Art Therapy Association, 29*(3), 138–143. doi:10.1080/07421656.2012.701.594

Frings-Keyes, M. (1974). *The inward journey: Art as psychotherapy for you.* Millbrae, CA: Celestial Arts.

Harley, D., & Hunn, V. (2015). Utilization of photovoice to explore hope and spirituality among low-income African American adolescents. *Child and Adolescent Social Work Journal, 32*(1), 3–15.

Ho, R. T. H., Potash, J., Ho, A. H. Y., Ho, V. F. L., & Chen, E. (2017). Reducing mental illness stigma and fostering empathic citizenship: Community arts collaborative approach. *Social Work in Mental Health, 15*(4), 469–485. doi:10.1080/15332985.2016.1236767

Hocoy, D. (2006). Art therapy: Working in the borderlands. *Art Therapy: Journal of the American Art Therapy Association, 23*(3), 132–135. doi:10.1080/07421656.2006.10129621

Hocoy, D. (2007). Art therapy as a tool for social change. In F. Kaplan (Ed.), *Art therapy and social action: Treating the world's wounds* (pp. 21–39). London, UK: Jessica Kingsley.

Hogan, S. (2001). *Healing arts: The history of art therapy.* London, UK: Jessica Kingsley.

Huss, E. (2013). *What we see and what we say: Using images in research, therapy, empowerment, and social change.* New York, NY: Routledge.

Huss, E., & Ben Gurion, H. M. (2014). Toward an integrative theory for understanding art discourses. *Visual Arts Research, 40*(2), 44–56.

Huss, E., Elhozayel, E., & Marcus, E. (2012). Art in group work as an anchor for integrating the micro and macro levels of intervention with incest survivors. *Clinical Social Work Journal, 40,* 401–411.

Huss, E., Nuttman-Shwartz, O., & Altman, A. (2012). The role of collective symbols as enhancing resilience in children's art. *The Arts in Psychotherapy, 39,* 52–59.

Huss, E., Sarid, O., & Cwikel, J. (2010). Using art as a self-regulating tool in a war situation: A model for social workers. *Health & Social Work, 35*(3), 201–209.

Knowles, G., & Cole, A. (2008). *Handbook of the arts in qualitative research.* Thousand Oaks, CA: Sage.

Kramer, E. (1971). *Art as therapy with children.* New York, NY: Schocken Books.

Landgarten, H. (1981). *Clinical art therapy: A comprehensive guide.* New York, NY: Routledge.

Landgarten, H. (1987). *Family arts psychotherapy.* New York: Brunner/Mazel.

Leavy, P. (2015). *Method meets art: Arts-based research practice* (2nd ed.). New York, NY: The Guilford Press.

LeBaron, M. (2011). Foreword: Eureka! Discovering gold in a leaden world. In E. Levine & S. Levine (Eds.), *Art in action: Expressive arts therapy and social change* (pp. 9–18). London, UK: Jessica Kingsley.

Levine, E., & Levine, S. (Eds.). (2011). *Art in action: Expressive arts therapy and social change.* London, UK: Jessica Kingsley.

Lewinson, T., Robinson-Dooley, V., & Grant, K. (2012). Exploring "home" through residents' lenses: Assisted living facility residents identify homelike characteristics using photovoice. *Journal of Gerontological Social Work, 55*(8), 745–756. doi:10.1080/01634372.2012.684758

Malchiodi, C. (2013). *Handbook of art therapy* (2nd ed.). New York, NY: The Guilford Press.

McGillicuddy, P., Cross, N., Mitchell, G., Halifax, N. D., & Plummer, C. (2015). Making meaning of our experiences of bearing witness to suffering: Employing A/R/Tography to surface co-remembrance and (dwelling) place. In C. Sinding & H. Barnes (Eds.), *Social work artfully: Beyond borders and boundaries* (pp. 205–219). Waterloo, ON: Wilfrid Laurier University Press.

McLean, C., & Kelly, R. (Eds.) (2010). *Creative arts in interdisciplinary practice: Inquiries for hope and change.* Calgary, Alta.: Detselig Temeron Books.

Middleman, R. (1968). *The non-verbal method in working with groups*. New York, NY: Association Press.

Moxley, D. (2013). Incorporating art-making into the cultural practice of social work. *Journal of Ethnic & Cultural Diversity in Social Work, 22*(3–4), 235–255. doi:10.1080/15313204.2013.843136

Moxley, D., & Washington, O. (2013). Helping older African American homeless women get and stay out of homelessness: Reflections on lessons learned from long haul development action research. *Journal of Progressive Human Services, 24,* 140–164.

Mullaly, R. (2007). *The new structural social work*. Don Mills, ON: Oxford University Press.

Oster, I., Aström, S., Lindh, J., & Magnusson, E. (2009). Women with breast cancer and gendered limits and boundaries: Art therapy as a "safe space" for enacting alternative subject positions. *The Arts in Psychotherapy, 36,* 29–38.

Paton, C. (2015). Bringing relating to the forefront: Using the art of improvisation to perceive relational processes actively in social work. In C. Sinding & H. Barnes, H. (Eds.), *Social work artfully: Beyond borders and boundaries* (pp. 191–203). Waterloo, ON: Wilfrid Laurier University Press.

Phinney, A., Moody, E., & Small, J. (2013). The effect of a community-engaged arts program on older adults' well-being. *Canadian Journal on Aging, 33*(3), 336–345.

Reamer, F. (2004). Non-traditional and unorthodox interventions in social work: Ethical and legal implications. *Families in Society, 87*(2), 191–197.

Secker, J., Loughran, M., Heydinrych, K., & Kent, L. (2011). Promoting mental health and social inclusion through art: Evaluation of an arts and mental health project. *Arts & Health, 3*(1), 51–60.

Sinding, C., & Barnes, H. (Eds). (2015). *Social work artfully: Beyond borders and boundaries*. Waterloo, ON: Waterloo University Press.

Slayton, S. (2012). Building community as social action: An art therapy group with adolescent males. *The Arts in Psychotherapy, 39,* 179–185.

Stepakoff, S., Hussein, S., Al-Salahat, M., Musa, I., Asfoor, M., Al-Houdali, E., & Al-Hmouz, M. (2011). From private pain toward public speech: Poetry therapy with Iraqi survivors of torture and war. In E. Levine & S. Levine (Eds.), *Art in action* (pp. 128–144). London, UK: Jessica Kingsley.

Stevens, D. (2013). *Art therapy and resilience in a health care setting*. Final project for the diploma in advanced art therapy, Vancouver Art Therapy Institute, Vancouver, BC.

Walton, P. (2012). Beyond talk and text: An expressive visual arts method for social work education. *Social Work Education: The International Journal, 31*(6), 724–741, doi: 10.1080/02615479.2012.695934.

Wehbi, S., McCormick, K., & Angelucci, S. (2016). Socially engaged art and social work: Reflecting on an interdisciplinary course development journey. *Journal of Progressive Human Services, 27*(1), 49–64.

Winnicott, D. (1971). *Playing and reality*. New York, NY: Basic Books.

Woolhiser Stallings, J. (2010). Collage as a therapeutic modality for reminiscence in patients with dementia. *Art Therapy: Journal of the American Art Therapy Association, 27*(3), 136–140.

4

Photography and Video Methods

TRACEY LAVOIE AND TUULA HEINONEN

CONTEXT: PHOTOGRAPHY AND VIDEO IN SOCIAL WORK

Photography and video can be used as effective expressive arts methods for individual and collective change or transformation and in qualitative arts-based inquiry. In photography, the wide scope in methods and tools available to practitioners and researchers continues to expand, enabling many applications and combinations with other expressive arts methods useful in a range of practice fields and with diverse groups of people. The use of videos and their production (i.e., film-making) has also increased in social work and other human service fields. Videos have been useful as a means of expressing individual or collective histories and records of events and processes, as well as offering creative tools for exploring issues that are meaningful for producers of videos or for videographers who engage in research projects. In social work education, videos may be useful in recording enactments (role plays), in student assignments, and in distance education, to illustrate methods for working with people facing complex issues.

This chapter describes uses of both photography and video and provides explanations and examples of various projects. Greater attention is paid to photography due to its broader adoption and current usage in many human service professions, including social work. What is important to note in the history of photography and video in social work is how the focus on a primarily individual practice has shifted to uses that can catalyze people's strengths and capacities, and provoke individual and collective transformation. However, it is also necessary to identify and consider potential problems and challenges related to ethics involved in representing people in images, the ownership of images, and issues in image dissemination to audiences and the public in general (see, for example, Webhi & Taylor, 2013).

Photography

The term *photography* is derived from Greek words meaning "light" and "draw." Simple pin-hole cameras were described in the fifth century BC in Chinese texts, and these devices were used a century earlier to capture images using light focused on a subject or object on light-sensitive material. Making images using this type of simple still camera is quite easy (see https://www.photo.net/learn/create-a-digital-pinhole-camera/).

Once the still camera was further developed, photographers replaced many painters in creating more quickly produced and realistic portraits of people. A camera could also document events, places, and objects, providing a record of events across time and space. As cameras became cheaper and more easily available, multiple private and public uses arose. More recently, social scientists, such as anthropologists Bateson and Mead (1942), used photography in their field research. Other social scientists found that photography and the photographic image had much potential for human expression, capturing events and people that hold significance and meaning for both photographer and viewers. Professional photographers, working on their own or as employees in companies who own the images taken, took photographs of individuals and groups of people, sometimes without knowledge or permission from the subjects in the photos. Further, just like *facts*, images can be skewed for particular purposes and referred to as truth. The image can convey the power relations that exist between people at a particular time, place, and/or situation (Webhi & Taylor, 2013). Today, social media (as in videos of events) can be used for the purpose of civic engagement on the Internet (James et al., 2010).

Photographs may be seen as works of art that reflect compelling beauty, as seen in the portraits of Jusuf Karsh, who photographed famous people such as Audrey Hepburn, Winston Churchill, and Martin Luther King (see http://121clicks.com/inspirations/the-greatest-portraits-ever-taken-by-yousuf-karsh). Another area of photography that can show intensity of human suffering, with an emotional impact on viewers, is photojournalism, for example, in images of wars and disasters. The purpose of such images is that they are for news stories broadcast to the public by the media. The photos of individuals or groups of people may not involve the knowledge or permission of the subjects in their photos. Furthermore, even when news stories compel photographers to record events, decisions need to be made about what photos are appropriate to present to the public (see Martin Kratzer & Kratzer, 2003).

Photographic images can represent a valuable chronology or document of people's lives and of social history. As Kopytin (2004) highlights, photographs have the power to unite people and "'speak' much more eloquently and convincingly than words" (p. 49). Photographs provide windows of understanding because they can also "serve as vivid and concentrated fragments of external reality as well as the objectified representation of our inner worlds" (p. 49). Personal discoveries can be unveiled through the unfolding process of "cohesion and continuity to experience" (p. 49). Currently, photography, including video production, is readily available to many as a result of rapid dissemination of cameras of lower cost, enhanced quality, and availability, especially in smartphones, tablets, watches, and more.

Photographs can also be useful for social workers, educators, and researchers in fostering reflexivity, expressing feelings in relation to a professional issue, or considering implications of a decision they are struggling with. The photograph in Figure 4.1 was taken by one of the authors (Tuula) to aid in reflection on the meaning in a practice decision I faced. In the photo are reflected fronds

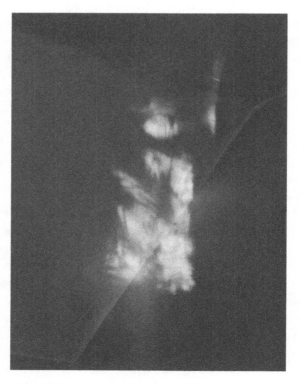

Figure 4.1 Plant fronds: Use of photo to foster reflexivity in social work practice. Photo courtesy of Tuula Heinonen.

of plants that sat on a table in my room. Before I took the photo, I recalled that the plant fronds moved gently in the breeze that entered from my window and the lighter reflection of the fronds mimicked their continuing movements. The reflection moved on the walls over the course of the day as the light in my room changed. I used the photo I took to meditate because it helped me to explore and reflect on my situation and prompted me to think about different perspectives and meanings in it. At that time, this photo was well suited for my purpose.

Photography in Social Work and Other Human Service Professions

The ease of taking photographs has enabled social work researchers and practitioners to apply photography and video-making and/or viewing in their work. Social work therapy and counseling practice make use of photographs as artifacts that can be a focus in the work of participants with their service providers. The people with whom the practitioners work may, for example, participate in taking photographs that represent to them a meaningful or emotive theme, such as strengths, aspirations, or life goals.

PhotoTherapy, an expressive arts approach, consists of techniques that use participants' own personal snapshots and family photos, along with the feelings, thoughts, memories, and information that they evoke, as catalysts for communication and healing (Weiser, 2004). The *Five Techniques of PhotoTherapy*, which are directly related to the various categories of relationship between the individual and the camera, are summarized as follows: (1) photos taken or created by the individual; (2) photos that have been taken of the individual by other people; (3) self-portraits; (4) family albums and other photo-biographical collections; and (5) "Photo-Projectives" (p. 25). Weiser (2004) thus holds that the meaning of a photo is created by the taking or planning of it; by its viewer[s] through viewing and witnessing it; and by inviting interest from another individual or therapist and, thus, has potential use in a therapeutic setting.

Forty years ago, family social workers used Polaroid photos and found them helpful in working with families in which infants experienced difficulties in growth and where home visits were carried out as part of the intervention (Woychik & Brickell, 1983). In addition to the photos documenting concrete physical changes in the developing child, the therapists discovered that, once confidentiality of the photos was ensured, the families enjoyed taking and keeping photos of themselves and family members and looked forward to subsequent visits in which photography was included, particularly when they saw their children's situation improve (Woychik & Brickell, 1983). (It is also possible that photos might have been used as evidence when neglect or abuse of children was suspected.)

Another use of photographs by social workers was described by Minton (1983), who worked in a neonatal intensive care unit where sick infants were cared for. Photographing an ill infant was done by a social worker as a means of connecting with the family during the infant's hospitalization. Minton refers to this act as a way to provide a concrete and often appreciated service to the parents so that a social worker could initiate a relationship with them during a difficult time. The photos provided affirmation of the child's existence to the parents and other family members and helped to elicit support. (However, being offered such photos to view may have been upsetting or inappropriate for some parents. Social workers first need to check to see if such a service is wanted at all.)

Journal articles written in 1975 by Nelson-Gee, and in 1976 and 1978 by Wolf, describe the use of *instant photography*. The use of the newly introduced Polaroid camera made it possible for clients to take photographs to express their feelings and ideas. The instant pictures could be cut up and pieces placed into drawings created by clients during sessions with their therapists. Although their orientation was in psychotherapy and analysis of the photograph or photograph-drawing, the techniques that were developed with Polaroid photography offered complementary new methods for therapists (Wolf, 1976, 1978). Nelson-Gee (1975), in therapy practice with children, noted that the Polaroid camera offered a meeting place where "the child and I could meet, a medium through which we could exchange perceptions and begin to establish communication," and she saw that the child would have an instant and concrete record in the photograph or, as she described, "a physical memory" (p. 159).

In another early work, Cosden and Reynolds (1982) wrote that photography did not constitute therapy, but "rather . . . an activity which can be 'therapeutic.'" Instead, these authors saw photography as providing additional material (photos taken by a client) for analysis in therapy (Wolf, 1978) or activities used to foster mastery and self-esteem through clients' successful completion of mounted photographs (Cosden & Reynolds, 1982).

THERAPEUTIC USE OF PHOTOS AND PHOTOTHERAPY WITH INDIVIDUALS, FAMILIES, AND GROUPS

In the realm of clinical social work and therapy, the scholarly literature suggests that photography holds great promise and potential for healing, growth, and transformation (DeCoster & Dickerson, 2014). Photography has been used in many clinical settings with individuals, families, and groups. Art therapists such as Judy Weiser (2004) and Alexander Kopytin (2004) have used photography in their practices to assist individuals in their healing journeys. As a visual art medium, photography is said to be accessible and enjoyable, inviting self-expression, creativity, and empowerment. As a mode of artistic expression, photography provides a structured way to share ideas and emotions. In their study that systematically identified, summarized, and rated previously tested clinical interventions that incorporate photos and/or photography in mental health practice, DeCoster and Dickerson (2014) highlighted the benefits of the therapeutic use of photography in clinical social work.

According to Alexander Kopytin (2004), further to its utility in therapeutic settings, photography instills feelings of safety, power, and control. He adds that, specifically, the physical density of a camera and photographs can foster feelings of safety and offer some distance from events, which is particularly important when negative events and difficult emotions are being explored. Furthermore, the social nature of photography unites people and stimulates visual thinking and communication. The sharing of stories often accompanies the sharing of photos, and the narratives that emerge can be vivid and complex and can pave the way for the expression of thoughts and feelings (Kopytin, 2004).

Through the use of photographic images, positive and negative memories and feelings are provoked and released, creating the conditions for resolution and healing (Kopytin, 2004). He explains that various sensory systems are stimulated, such as visual and tactile, thereby offering an affective and embodied experience. Photography actively engages individuals, groups, and/or families in the therapy process with the taking and sharing of images. Along with this more active stance in therapy and in the world, photography inspires "initiative and intentionality" (p. 51). The opportunity to recognize and understand change and growth at various levels, such as physical, environmental, and emotional, becomes possible through the exploration of individual photos, and exploring combinations of images taken from a variety of sources can also lead to the unearthing of connections and realization of new meanings. As such, the possibility for *self-reflection and reframing* highlighted by Kopytin (p. 51) appears vast. Further, expression through use of photography can help people to communicate indirectly and, for those with traumatic experiences in their background, offers some degree of protection for them to avoid directly speaking about their traumatizing stressful life events.

Illustrations and Applications

An example of the use of photography in the realm of social work practice and other human services and helping professions is hospice photography. Some photographers offer free portrait and documentary photography to hospice patients and their families. The photographs can help capture the essence of relationships, preserve memories, and chronicle this life transition. Hospice nurse Mary Landberg, who has photographed patients and their families, highlights the impact of such photos by stating, "Many people tell me their photographs are their most cherished objects and the images enable their love for each other to live beyond the last breath" (http://moments.nhpco.org/news-blogs/hospice-photography-%E2%80%93-preserving-moments-love-forever). More on hospice photography services can be found on various websites (see Resources section at the end of this chapter).

Dennett (2009) highlights the work of his late former partner, Jo Spence, a photographer and cancer activist from the United Kingdom who used photography as "a natural part of her preferred alternative and complementary cancer treatments" (p. 10). Initially for personal use in her breast cancer healing journey, Spence's "visual illness diaries" (p. 10) that emerged from her earlier passion for creating photo albums evolved into "critical campaign material" (p. 10) for women's and disability movements, for teaching purposes and publications, and for a touring photography exhibition called "The Picture of Health" (p. 10). Spence is regarded as being instrumental in the development of therapeutic photography in the United Kingdom. In linking her own personal issues to social justice causes, her photography practice has been said to "illustrate a commitment to the political potential of photography—a way to connect her own intimacies and traumas to a broader public discourse" (http://www.jospence.org/biography.html). More on Spence's life, work, and exhibits can be found via the following link: http://www.jospence.org/work_index.html.

New developments in technology for engagement with visual arts has made it possible for people who are blind or have limited vision to gain access to and participate in photography. For example, the rise of 3D printers provides a useful tool whereby, rather than an image reproduced in two dimensions on a sheet of paper, these printers enable the creation of three-dimensional sculptures. Thus, photos and other images are produced in three dimensions and felt with the hands so they can be *seen*. For many, it brings back memories in photographs, such as a family photo or activities in childhood, by making them accessible through tactile experience. See Tincho (n.d.) for additional details and stories of people who experienced images that could be felt through this technology, including a video on a recent project in action. For photos shared via social media, both Facebook and Twitter have introduced systems and functions that can *read* or describe photographs. With the use of artificial intelligence, specifically object recognition software, Facebook servers have the capacity to decode and describe images in audio format. Twitter users can manually add their own text descriptions to images (Baker, 2016).

In the realms of social work education and inquiry, Phillips and Bellinger (2011) demonstrated how photos can be used to teach about relationality and difference (p. 86). The authors analyzed photographic images from Diana Matar's exhibit *Leave to Remain*, which addresses the asylum-seeking process in the United Kingdom and "offers insightful conversations about the public discourses of asylum seeking and the effects of asylum seeking on individuals" (p. 87).

Phillips and Bellinger (2011) used "contemporary visual methodology" (p. 86) in their analysis of select photos (21 in total) and then shared portions of their conversation with each other about the process of the analysis against the backdrop of their commentary on the content and context of the images. Their analysis of the content and context of Matar's photos reveals that the photographer "is able to push our discussion of asylum seeking to the everyday, where the (surrounding) life is of primary interest" (p. 99). As such, the possibility for relationality and reflexivity emerges. Phillips and Bellinger shared that the photographs are useful in social work education in generating " 'a reflective self'. . . [by which] we are invited to pay close attention to the spaces where 'bodies and eyes meet' and to consider how we will ensure that in that space, both service users and social workers are humanized and can therefore be understood and encouraged to be active subjects" (p. 102). According to Sinding, Warren, and Paton (2012), "in offering such evocative alternate images, Matar's photos reconfigure contemporary social relations between citizens and 'others' " (p. 9). In teaching about relationality and difference, Phillips and Bellinger (2011) therefore demonstrate how the use of photography brings to life tenets of social justice and antioppressive practice (AOP) in social work education. Matar's *Leave to Remain* exhibit can be viewed via the following link: http://www.dianamatar.com/leave-to-remain. There is great power and potential for photography in social work classrooms and in field learning/practicum settings, such as fostering openness and awareness, connection to the environment and the larger social world, and encouraging dialogue, reflection, and tenets of collaborative and relational practice such as a *not-knowing* perspective (Anderson, 2005), as well as promoting affective and embodied learning experiences.

PHOTOGRAPHY FOR COMMUNITY INTERVENTION AND SOCIAL TRANSFORMATION: SOCIAL CHANGE

The collaborative photography project between Lindsay Katsitsakatste Delaronde, an Iroquois/Mohawk artist from Quebec, Canada, and a group of First Nations women is an example of photography aimed at consciousness-raising and social change. Entitled *Project Squaw*, it was exhibited as *In Defiance* in the fall of 2016 at a British Columbia, Canada, art gallery. The 3-year project used photographic images to resist the language and attitudes that oppress and marginalize Indigenous women. Delaronde photographed the 32 women, who ranged in age from 22 to 56 years, in a style and physical setting that was chosen by them (Madden, 2016). Coupled with defying and resisting the term *squaw*, the community of voices that emerged in the project rewrites the dominant discourse of trauma and tragedy that has been perpetuated from colonialism. Through the power of photography and the individual portraits, the narratives are transformed into alternate views of self and of strength, power, and resilience, reflecting truth and respect (Madden, 2016). (See also the University of Victoria Legacy Art Gallery's 2016 video, *In Conversation with Lindsay Delaronde & Sarah Hunt.*)

Although much of the literature echoes such claims as photographs having the potential to "speak louder than words" (Webhi & Taylor, 2013, p. 525); "'speak' much more eloquently and convincingly than words" (Kopytin, 2004, p. 49); and "be an emotionally powerful means of expressing human experiences" (DeCoster & Dickerson, 2014, p. 2), caution related to issues such as ethics, voice, and representation also exists with the use of photos. In keeping with codes of ethics and tenets of social justice practice, social work practitioners, educators, and researchers who use photography in their practice, teaching, and research should pay close attention to issues such as ownership of images, consent for the use of photos, and the risk of misrepresentation.

In their examples of international development workers' use of photography to document field work, Webhi and Taylor (2013) illuminate the links between photography and colonialism and imperialism, specifically how the use of photos in community and international development work can risk replicating and perpetuating pre-existing power imbalances in different areas of the world. Many important issues for consideration regarding the use of photographs in community and international development are highlighted, such as potential ethical dilemmas of representing the *other* and the risks of photographs conflating reality, making them a "tool to elicit reactions to a presumed truth" and, thereby, supporting and perpetuating colonial, neocolonial, and imperialist discourses and agendas (p. 526). What is proposed by Webhi and Taylor (2013) is a critical analysis of the purpose of the documentation, awareness of the use of images, and workers' roles in the reproduction of images so as not to advance a neocolonial agenda (p. 526). Along with awareness, the commitment to creating alternate discourses and anticolonial representations of North–South relations are suggested. Photography that builds on these ideals fits better with the social work aim of social transformation.

Photovoice Inquiry

Photovoice, a qualitative, community-based, participatory research approach, involves providing cameras to community participants so that they can visually represent (through photography) and communicate their lived experiences (Molloy, 2007; Ornelas et al., 2009; Woodgate, Zurba, & Tennent, 2017). The goals of photovoice include (a) the opportunity for participants to record and reflect their community's strengths and concerns; (b) the promotion of critical dialogue and knowledge about important community issues through group discussions and photographs; (c) the presentation of people's lived experiences through their own images and language; and (d) connecting communities to policymakers (Ornelas et al., 2009; Wang & Burris, 1997; Wang & Redwood-Jones, 2001).

Said to be developed by Wang and Burris (1997) and colleagues, and first used by village women in rural China to influence the policies and programs that impacted them (Photovoice Globally, n.d.; Wang & Redwood-Jones, 2001; Woodgate et al., 2017), photovoice is based on three major theoretical understandings: first, problem-posing education that is based on the work of Brazilian educator Paolo Freire (1970, 1973), feminist theory, and tenets of documentary photography (Bonnycastle & Bonnycastle, 2015; Wang & Redwood-Jones, 2001). The approach differs from the more traditional approach of documentary photography in that participants are active in the research process rather than "passive subjects of other people's intentions and images" (Wang & Burris, 1997, p. 371). Photovoice encompasses models and techniques such as photo-elicitation and digital storytelling, paving the way for participants, who often identify as marginalized and may not have access to photography equipment, to create their own visual images that capture their perspectives, illuminate their experiences, share their stories in their own voice, and promote social change and transformation (Photovoice Globally, n.d.).

Photovoice has been used as a tool to empower marginalized community members to collaborate, enhance their community, and build alliances (Bonnycastle & Bonnycastle, 2015). Peabody (2013) contends that photovoice is an "extremely promising tool" (p. 263) and has great utility in social justice and community development. With the participant photographer producing the images and influencing other aspects of the project in the role of coresearcher, Woodgate et al. (2017) contend that photovoice is a "tool for expression and empowerment in qualitative research" (p. 2).

Lee's (2009) MSW project, "Visualizing the Margins: The Experiences of Queer People of Colour," is one example of the use of photovoice in social work research. How "queer people of colour visualize, describe, and conceptualize their life experiences" (p. 48) and "resist interlocking systems of domination" (p. 2) was explored with the use of photovoice methods. Along with the participant-produced photos and narratives that illuminated their experiences and acts of resistance, a collaborative photo exhibit was also part of this project.

Coupled with use in and by communities, photovoice has also been incorporated into social work education settings to illuminate concepts and meanings (Phillips & Bellinger, 2011); as a tool for students to learn about, engage with, and experience research (Bonnycastle & Bonnycastle, 2015); and as a method to engage social work students in social justice (Peabody, 2013). In referencing both photovoice literature and the insights gained from studies connected to a research program with youth and their families over a 15-year period, Woodgate et al. (2017) highlight the many advantages, opportunities, and challenges (including ethical, relational, and procedural) in using photovoice in qualitative research. Cautions and ethical issues related to the use of photovoice, as discussed by Wang and Redwood-Jones (2001), include "the potential for invasion of privacy and how that may be prevented; issues in recruitment, representation, participation, and advocacy; and specific methodological techniques that should be used to minimize participants' risks and to maximize benefits" (p. 560). Many of these same cautions also apply to the production of videos and videography.

Video in Social Work

In contrast with photography, video has been utilized mostly in social work education, for example, in case study vignettes and experiences of practice situations and ideas and methods of intervention (e.g., Cartney, 2006; Rowan et al. 2015; Thomas & Marks, 2014). The need for such resources in social work is important since social work education often includes experiential learning using interactive media to simulate real-world situations for student learning. Social work inquiry has more recently involved video production. There are many videos produced about social issues that aim to raise awareness and understanding that can contribute new perspectives for social work. One can simply search online for topics on addictions, mental health, poverty, child welfare, climate change, and many more. (These can vary in quality and perspective, so it is best to select carefully.)

A Toronto-based social worker, Stephen "Buddha" Leafloor, who narrates a TEDxOttawa presentation (2011), *Social Work Through Hip Hop* (see https://www.youtube.com/watch?v=SzC8hb9Sr_w), describes how street dancing has helped him to connect better with youth than when working as a social worker in child protection agencies. He weaves his own story into his ideas about how learning hip-hop can lead to individual change and social transformation in Canada's Arctic and elsewhere. An American TEDxTalk video, entitled *Social Workers as Super-Heroes*, can also be found online (https://www.youtube.com/watch?v=A27QjpQ_Ieo). This TEDxTalk features a description, by Anna Scheyett (2015), of what social workers do and how they make contributions to US society.

Videos about social work projects for social change have been produced and mounted on Internet sites to help the public learn about the profession and social work practice. One such video explaining the need for change in social work education is the European video, *Mend the Gap—A Challenge for Social*

Work Education, by Lisa Blidnert (2015), which focuses on bridging gaps of understanding between social workers and those with whom they work.

A powerful video from the United States about poverty and child welfare on Indigenous reserves by Lakota Law is entitled *Social Service Workers Speak Out: Poverty Is Not Neglect*. This work brings to light shortcomings in practices and policies in relation to child protection services in reserve communities (see https://www.youtube.com/watch?v=QeGiF0zkIYo). Many more videos about social work, social work methods, and issues of social importance can be found on the World Wide Web by searching for keywords when making selections. The viewer, however, needs to realize that videos on the Internet may range widely in viewpoints, quality, and even accuracy.

There are now many ways for students to produce their own videos as part of their learning in social work, and these can generate powerful and creative learning opportunities (e.g., Thomas & Marks, 2014). Effective technologies are accessible and available through the capacities of easy-to-use, hand-held devices such as smartphones. Tetloff, Hitchcock, Battista, and Lowry (2014) describe students' involvement in video production for an assignment in a University of Alabama social policy course. The students were requested to focus on a "policy, law, or program; provide information about it; and argue for its importance in the United States. Collaboratively, students compile[d] videos, music, research, and interviews to craft interpretations of social policies" (p. 23). The point of the exercise was to help students to develop skills in critical thinking, assess the validity of material they encountered, and, finally, present their findings (Tetloff et al., 2014). Digital technology in this and other social work projects makes it possible for ideas to move beyond individual and small audiences to the public realm.

Thomas and Marks's (2014) exploratory study of the use of student-generated videos in a social work community practice course illuminates the power and potential of videos in social work education. Their MSW course, which focused on community practice and economic development theories, models, and strategies, required a visual presentation of the key components of the students' written papers. This experiential component was found to greatly enhance students' learning and understanding of community practice. Findings from the online surveys of the 37 participants indicated that participants valued the creative aspects of the video component and the new learning that emerged in the domains of praxis and technological skill development (Thomas & Marks, 2014).

VIDEOS FOR SOCIAL JUSTICE, HUMAN RIGHTS, AND SOCIAL TRANSFORMATION

An example of the use of video for the promotion of social justice, human rights, and social transformation is the hour-long video program *Compulsive*

Practice that was presented at the 2016 *Day With(out) Art* by the US community organization Visual AIDS. The "compulsive, daily, and habitual practices by nine artists and activists who live with their cameras as one way to manage, reflect upon, and change how they are deeply affected by HIV/AIDS" are highlighted (Carlomusto, Juhasz, & Ryan, 2016, para. 1, lines 2–3). Their video compilation includes a diversity of experiences, such as individual personal reflections and community-based activist demonstrations, and a range of older and more current video formats. The video practices of the featured artists and activists who are living with AIDS are said to "serve many purposes—cure, treatment, outlet, lament, documentation, communication—and have many tones—obsessive, driven, poetic, neurotic, celebratory" (Carlomusto et al., 2016, para. 2, lines 3–5). For more information, see visualaids.org/projects/detail/compulsive-practice.

Video in Social Work Inquiry

Videos in which research participants take part have become more prominent in social work. Videos in research (e.g., video ethnography) can very powerfully depict people and their circumstances, often bringing private events and experiences into a public forum. There are clearly implications regarding privacy and confidentiality which surface and that may not be understood until later when the videos are in process. Inquiry that involved migrant mothers living with their children in Italy posed just such a dilemma for researcher Hernandez-Albujar (2007), who realized that her plan to use ethnographic video recording in her study would reveal the identities of the migrant mothers, many of whom were undocumented. The researcher had to find some other way to hear the stories of the migrant women so that they would not be identified. Hernandez-Albujar wanted to use video because, she asserts, "it does more than just tell a story: It more closely reproduces the feelings, lived experiences and sensations of the participants" (p. 284). She was aware that a more vivid and textured result would be achieved if only still photos were used. In the end, the researcher arrived at a compromise, producing a video that used groupings of images (metaphors) to evoke feelings and experiences related by the study participants in interviews, but excluding their images. As is shown in this research, the use of video in inquiry does not need to be bound by conventional film formats or structures; creative solutions that capture stories and meaningful images that fit can succeed. Sara Pink (2001) states, in relation to video ethnography, "The visual technologies that ethnographers use, like the images they produce and view, will be invested with meanings, inspire responses and are likely to become a topic of conversation" (p. 35). There is no one way to achieve such a result. Digital video stories constituted data in Marlyn Bennett's (2016) doctoral research in Manitoba, Canada. Bennett was interested in documenting the stories of Indigenous youth, former foster children who had or were making a transition from foster care to emerging adulthood. Often youth were poorly prepared for this transition and experienced numerous roadblocks along the way. Through the use of digital video, youth who participated were able to tell their stories in their own ways, with technical help and support provided. Some videos made by the youth have been mounted onto public sites for viewing by others. Bennett's work effectively, and in a compelling way, describes how the young people learned and struggled in transitioning from foster care to emerging adulthood. The video stories could also be described as the youths' accounts of self-validation, affirmation, and/or survival. Their stories teach social workers and social service agencies about the effects of being in the care of child protection agencies and transitioning from them. Bennett's descriptions of the video accounts and the videos that are available for viewing point to the many needs in their young lives that have not been met and what would have helped.

Foster (2009) discussed the process and outcome of using video as a method of collecting and disseminating data in her *Sure Start* research study. She claimed that providing research participants the opportunity to "tell their stories through this medium is an ideal way to privilege their experiences and for the audience to gain insights into their lives" (p. 233). Foster also claimed that "participatory video is an effective method of gathering data" (p. 243). The use of video by research participants "encapsulated many of the findings that emerged through questionnaires and interviews and, whilst they were presented here amongst a variety of other forms of data, they received a particularly emotional response from the audience" (p. 243).

CONCLUDING THOUGHTS

Photographic technology has provided an abundance of equipment, methods, tools, and applications for social workers to draw from, combine, and generate by themselves. Such methods are gaining ground, especially in education and research areas. Use of photography in social work has a longer history, in work with children and families, women's groups, refugee newcomers, and youth facing difficulty. These are only some of the populations that can potentially benefit.

Videos by those who have been clients of social services and social workers provide accounts that can teach us from the perspective of the person who interacts with social service systems and their employees. Their stories contribute knowledge based on experience with service provision and serve to inform change in social welfare and agency policies and in social work practices, which can lead to individual and social change and transformation.

Many opportunities to make use of still and moving images exist for social work practitioners, educators, and scholars, and a vast array of methods and applications are available. The proliferation of books, articles, and websites about these methods and how they have been applied indicates an increased interest in the use of images in social work.

QUESTIONS FOR REFLECTION

1. When you think of your own work with individuals who have experienced some trouble in life, how do you think that reviewing family photos and talking about them could be of help?
2. What kind of exercise using photography could you imagine as being helpful for those for whom you provide services and what is your rationale for introducing it? What outcomes might result?
3. What are some ethical issues involved in making a video with adults who have experienced childhood abuse 20 or more years ago? What, if any, criteria would you use to exclude prospective participants, and why?
4. If you could make a video of the inspiring moments in your social work (or related) career, what would it contain? What could others learn from it?

RESOURCES

Photography

Photography use in hospice settings: https://www.slrlounge.com/lifes-end-documented-by-kindred-spirits-hospice-photography/ and http://www.hospiceportraits.com

PhotoTherapy, Therapeutic Photography, & Related Techniques: https://photo-therapy-centre.com/

Photovoice Canada: http://photovoice.ca/

Photovoice Hamilton, a project of the Community Centre for Media Arts: http://ccmahamilton.ca/portfolio/

Photovoice Worldwide: http://www.photovoiceworldwide.com

Some examples of photovoice projects in social work are available at http://inspireart.org/en/photovoice-in-montreal-photovoice-a-montreal/

Videos

The following link is for a short video that was developed with help from M. Bennett as part of her doctoral work (2016). It was made by a young Indigenous man who experienced challenges in transitioning from childhood experiences in foster care to, and emergence into, adulthood: https://assets. adobe.com/link/839d843d-170a-47d9-5c59-a3927e32c2ae?section=activity_ public. See https://socialworklicensemap.com/social-work-movies/ to see how Hollywood films have depicted social workers and social work practice, mostly in roles in which children and youth are provided services.

Additional details on three-dimensional printing technology, including a video on a recent project in action, can be found at http://www.boredpanda. com/touchable-memories-3d-printing-pirate3d/. Twitter users can manually add their own text descriptions to images (see http://www.bbc.com/news/ disability-35881779).

REFERENCES

Anderson, H. (2005). The myth of not-knowing. *Family Process, 44*(4), 497–504.

Baker, D. (2016). Identity 2016: Facebook lets blind people "see" its photos. *BBC News online*. Retrieved from http://www.bbc.com/news/disability-35881779.

Bateson, G., & Mead, M. (1942). *Balinese character: A photographic analysis (Vol. 2)*. New York, NY: New York Academy of Sciences.

Bennett, M. (2016). Digital storytelling with First Nations emerging adults in extensions of care and transitioning from care in Manitoba (PhD dissertation). Faculty of Social Work, University of Manitoba. Retrieved from http://mspace.lib.umanitoba.ca/ handle/1993/31252

Blidnert, L. (2015). *Mend the gap—A challenge for social work education* [Video]. Retrieved from https://www.youtube.com/watch?v=QExM_aA2Mus.

Bonnycastle, M. M., & Bonnycastle, C. R. (2015). Photographs generate knowledge: Reflections on experiential learning in/outside the social work classroom. *Journal of Teaching in Social Work, 35*(3), 233–250. doi:10.1080/08841233.2015.1027031

Carlomusto, J., Juhasz, A., & Ryan, H. (2016). Compulsive practice [Visual aids]. Retrieved from visualaids.org/projects/detail/compulsive-practice and https://vimeo. com/192798505

Cartney, P. (2006). Using video interviewing in the assessment of social work communication skills. *British Journal of Social Work, 36*, 827–844.

Cosden, C., & Reynolds, D. (1982). Photography as therapy. *The Arts in Psychotherapy, 9*, 19–23.

DeCoster, V., & Dickerson, J. (2014). The therapeutic use of photography in clinical social work: Evidence-based best practices. *Social Work in Mental Health, 12*(1), 1–19. doi:10.1-80/15332985.2013.81245

Dennett, T. (2009). Jo Spence's camera therapy: Personal therapeutic photography as a response to adversity. *European Journal of Psychotherapy & Counselling, 11*(1), 7–19.

Foster, V. (2009). Authentic representation? Using video as counter-hegemony in participatory research with poor working-class women. *International Journal of Multiple Research Approaches, 3*(3), 233–245.

Freire, P. (1970). *Pedagogy of the oppressed.* New York, NY: Seabury.

Freire, P. (1973). *Education for critical consciousness.* New York, NY: Continuum.

Hernandez-Albujar, Y. (2007). The symbolism of video: Exploring migrant mothers' experiences. In G. Stanczak (Ed.), *Visual research methods: Image, society and representation* (pp. 281–306). Thousand Oaks, CA: Sage.

James, C., Davis, K., Flores, A., Francis, J., Pettingill, L., Rundle, M., & Gardner, H. (2010). Young people, ethics and the new digital media. *Contemporary Readings in Law and Social Justice, 2*(2), 229–249.

Kopytin, A. (2004). Photography and art therapy: An easy partnership. *Inscape, 9*(2), 49–58. doi:10.1080/02647140408405677

Landberg, M. (n.d.). Hospice photography—Preserving moments of love forever. Retrieved from http://moments.nhpco.org/news-blogs/hospice-photography-%E2%80%93-preserving-moments-love-forever

Leafloor, Stephen (2011). *Social work through hip hop* [TEDxOttawa video]. Retrieved from https://www.youtube.com/watch?v=SzC8hb9Sr_w

Lee, W. J. E. (2009). Visualizing the margins: The experiences of queer people of color (master's thesis). McGill University, Montreal, QC.

Madden, A. (2016). In defiance: Indigenous women define themselves. *Focus Online.* Retrieved from http://focusonline.ca/node/1125.

Martin Kratzer, R., & Kratzer, B. (2003). How newspapers decided to run disturbing 9/11 photos. Media Studies of September 11. *Newspaper Research Journal, 24*(1), 34–47. doi:PDF/10.1177/073953290302400104

Matar, D. (n.d.). *Leave to Remain* [photo exhibit images]. Retrieved from http://www.dianamatar.com/leave-to-remain#0

Minton (1983). Uses of photographs in perinatal social work. *Health and Social Work, 8*(2), 123–125.

Molloy, J. K. (2007). Photovoice as a tool for social justice workers. *Journal of Progressive Human Services, 18*(2), 39–55. doi:10.1300/J059v18n02_04

Nelson-Gee, E. (1975). Learning to be: A look into the use of therapy with Polaroid photography as a means of recreating the development of perception and the ego. *Art Psychotherapy, 2,* 159–164.

Ornelas, I., Amell, J., Tran, A. N., Royster, M., Armstrong-Brown, J., & Eng, E. (2009). Understanding African American men's perceptions of racism, male gender socialization, and social capital through photovoice. *Qualitative Health Research, 19*(4), 552–565. doi:10.1177/1049732309332104

Peabody, C. G. (2013). Using photovoice as a tool to engage social work students in social justice. *Journal of Teaching in Social Work, 33*(3), 251–265. doi:10.1080/08841233.2013.795922

Phillips, C., & Bellinger, A. (2011). Feeling the cut: Exploring the use of photography in social work education. *Qualitative Social Work, 10*(1), 86–105. doi:10.1177/1473325010361999

Pink, S. (2001). *Doing visual ethnography.* London, UK: Sage.

Rowan, D., Järkestig-Berggren, U., Cambridge, I., McAuliffe, D., Fung, A., & Moore, M. (2015). The 6 continents project: A method for linking social work education classrooms for intercultural exchange through asynchronous video sharing. *International Social Work, 58*(4), 484–494.

Scheyett, A. (2015). *Social workers as super-heroes.* TEDxColumbiaSC [Video]. Retrieved from https://www.youtube.com/watch?v=A27QjpQ_Ieo

Sinding, C., Warren, R., & Paton, C. (2012). Social work and the arts: Images at the intersection. *Qualitative Social Work, 13*(2), 187–202. doi:10.1177/1473325012464384

Tetloff, M., Hitchcock, L., Battista, A., & Lowry, D. (2014). Multimodal composition and social justice: Videos as a tool of advocacy in social work pedagogy. *Journal of Technology in Human Services, 32*(1–2), 22–38. doi:10.1080/15228835.2013.857284

Thomas, K. A., & Marks, L. (2014). Action! Student-generated videos in social work education. *Journal of Technology in Human Services, 32*(4), 254–274. doi:10.1080/15228835.2014.922912

Tincho. (n.d.). Touchable memories: This company 3D-prints old photos to help the blind re-experience memories. Retrieved from https://www.boredpanda.com/touchable-memories-3d-printing-pirate3d/

University of Victoria Legacy Art Gallery (2016). *In conversation with Lindsay Delaronde & Sarah Hunt.* Retrieved from https://www.youtube.com/watch?v=BMLK1NunX-g

Wang, C., & Burris, M. (1997). Photovoice: Concept, methodology, and use for participatory needs assessment. *Health Education & Behavior, 24*, 369–387. doi:10.1177/109019819702400309

Wang, C., & Redwood-Jones, Y. A. (2001). Photovoice ethics: Perspectives from Flint Photovoice. *Health Education & Behavior, 28*, 560–572. doi:10.1177/109019810102800504

Webhi, S. & Taylor, D. (2013). Photographs speak louder than words: The language of international development images. *Community Development Journal, 48*(4), 525–539. doi:10.1093/cdj/bss050

Weiser, J. (2004). Phototherapy techniques in counseling and therapy—Using ordinary snapshots and photo-interactions to help clients heal their lives. *The Canadian Art Therapy Association Journal, 17*(2), 23–56.

Wolf, R. (1976). The Polaroid technique: Spontaneous dialogues from the unconscious. *Journal of Art Psycholotherapy, 3*, 197–214.

Wolf, R. (1978). The use of instant photography in creative expressive therapy: An integrative case study. *Art Psychotherapy, 5*, 81–91.

Woodgate, R. L., Zurba, M., & Tennent, P. (2017). Worth a thousand words? Advantages, challenges and opportunities in working with photovoice as a qualitative research method with youth and their families. *Forum: Qualitative Social Research [Sozialforschung], 18*(1), Art. 2.

Woychik, J. P., & Brickell, C. (1983). The instant camera as a therapy tool. *Social Work, 28*(4), 316–318.

Movement and Dance

SARAH ROCHE AND TUULA HEINONEN

BACKGROUND

A person who is engaging in movement uses space immediately around her or his body and in the environment. The "elements of space, time, force and shape" (Halprin, 2003, p. 111) characterize creative expression through movement. These elements can be observed by those who watch a dancer move across a room in different ways using parts of her body and the space around her and in the room.

Regarding the use of expressive movement and the body, Halprin (2003) writes that the physical, emotional, and mental levels work "experientially and metaphorically with our past and with the ways our life experiences live in us at unconscious as well as conscious levels," and we need to loosen ourselves "from these entanglements" to be able to "more fully and expressively present in the moment" (p. 105).

An interview with Sarah Roche, a contemporary dancer and educator, helps to shape the content of this chapter. Tuula has drawn upon Sarah's words and has positioned them with selected literature on movement and dance to deepen discussion on topics raised by Sarah. Sarah Roche's interest in movement and dance stems from early childhood when she first began dancing jazz and ballet and creative movement. Some of her elementary school teachers were influential in guiding her and inspiring her to teach children herself. Sarah also sang and acted in school but returned as a young woman to modern dance and ballet at The School of Contemporary Dancers in Winnipeg, Manitoba, and, later, in a university training program, the Senior Professional Program at the School of Contemporary Dancers affiliated with the University of Winnipeg, where she completed a 4-year degree. She apprenticed with the company Winnipeg's

Contemporary Dancers, and, while there, performed for six seasons before leaving to independently produce shows and perform commissioned works. While performing, she also worked as a teacher, especially in young children's dance. She has taught modern, jazz, ballet, and creative movement in dance studios to people in all age groups from toddlers to older adults. Sarah has also taught in urban and rural schools in Manitoba. Through organizations such as Learning through the Arts at the Toronto Conservatory of Music, The Integrated Arts, and Engaging Fusion, Sarah has helped teachers integrate curricular learning through dance and movement. This essentially meant using the creative process of dance with elementary school children to help deepen their learning in math, social studies, language arts, and other subjects. Sarah is interested in childhood development and finds helping children to learn through interactive movement and dance is rewarding. She has also brought her skills in these methods to local daycares and kindergartens. Sarah has recently finished an education degree from Queen's University in the area of Artist in Community and currently teaches music and dance in a Winnipeg elementary school.

MOVEMENT AND DANCE

Movement and dance have been a part of human life for as long as historical records have existed. Movement has always been necessary for basic survival in the search for food, safety, and human companionship. Living beings need to move. Dance to mark rituals and express emotions has been common over time and in the activities of all people (Kourkouta, Rarra, Mavroeidi, & Prodromidis, 2014). Dance might have occurred for the purpose of healing, spiritual expression, celebration, or communal entertainment, and for many this might have been a means of differentiating one group of persons from another as well as providing opportunities for cultural or spiritual expression and recreation.

The application of movement and dance as methods of helping and healing people, as in dance movement therapy or as complementary to more conventional talk therapies, is relatively new. In the United States, Isadora Duncan and, later, Martha Graham pioneered innovative approaches to dance that offered new ways to express experience and emotions through dance. Graham began a dance school in the 1920s that emphasized the capacity and power of the body to express mood, emotion, and social and psychological themes in contemporary dance (see https://www.youtube.com/watch?v=ieMO1Z0UhGQ for an example of dance that is based on Graham's method). Graham's work provided rich resource material for the development of dance therapy and was influential in its development (Paley, 1974; Root-Bernstein & Root-Bernstein, 2003).

Dance therapy was sometimes combined with psychotherapy, and other influences from the arts were also included (Paley, 1974). Marian Chase, considered the founder of dance movement therapy (Lohn, 1987), worked in hospital psychotherapy with groups of patients. She was a professional dancer, choreographer, and teacher of dance. Like dance movement therapists today, she saw the power of movement and dance, usually accompanied by music, as a vehicle for communicating through the body's expression. There are dance movement (sometimes written as dance/movement) therapy associations in many parts of the world. The American Dance Therapy Association (ADTA) states that dance movement centers on "movement behavior as it emerges in the therapeutic relationship. . . . Body movement, as the core component of dance, simultaneously provides the means of assessment and the mode of intervention for dance/movement therapy" (https://adta.org/faqs). Movement and dance can benefit a wide range of individuals and groups such as those who experience physical and mental health problems. The ADTA publishes the *American Journal of Dance Therapy* for its members. A recent journal issue celebrates the 50th anniversary of the Association, from 1966 to 2016 (Devereaux, Kleinman, Johnson, & Witzling, 2016).

In Canada, dance movement therapists are organized by the Dance Movement Therapy Association of Canada (DMTAC), whose mission is to continue development and training and promote the profession across the country. DMTAC refers to dance movement therapy as included in the family of creative arts therapies and states: "This innovative approach to psychotherapy aligns with current research into the brain and behaviour and the importance of movement for human development and mental health" and "Increasing an understanding of movement behaviour enables new insights into the connection of inner and outer realities" (http://dmtac.org). The DMTAC has compiled a list of key articles, books, and journals on movement and dance therapy on their website at http://dmtac.org. They define dance movement therapy in the following way: "Dance Movement Therapy is based on the premise that thoughts, feelings and the experience of self are expressed through the body and movement. It is a relational process that integrates the emotional, cognitive, physical and social aspects of self" (http://dmtac.org).

However, not all those who make use of movement and dance in their work with people have a psychotherapeutic orientation, especially those who use movement and dance methods as a complement to other forms of intervention (e.g., talk). Movement and dance do not need to be combined with psychotherapy but can be useful in developing confidence, self-esteem, and overall health.

Although dance does not involve the creation of visual arts or writing, the experience of movement remains in the mind of both participants and the observers and can have a profound and long-lasting emotional impact. If the dance evokes strong emotion or touches a chord in someone, its impact can be profound and long-lasting. Of course it is possible to reenact a dance or record a dance that can be kept on one's computer or other device and viewed over again.

Research (Murcia, Kreutz, Clift, & Bongard, 2010) has shown that dance can increase well-being at emotional, social, and other levels. Dance involves coordination of movement, rhythm, and music, which can affect individuals, groups, and communities who participate. As McNeill stated in 1995 (cited in Murcia et al., 2010, p. 150), "[K]eeping in time together has been a fundamental mechanism for strengthening social bonds between individuals and thus an effective way to create and sustain communities." Dance and movement also constitute methods of physical activity and exercise, which offer significant health benefits. These activities are based on beliefs "that body and mind are inseparable. Body and mind interact so that a change in movement affects total functioning" (Kourkouta et al., 2014, p. 230).

Movement and dance are available to everyone, no matter what their level of physical ability might be. In relation to dance, Sharon Took-Zozaya explains, "I've come to understand that not all disabilities can be seen with the untrained eye, that each individual has unique experiences of life and physical embodiment, and that in some way, we all have special needs or limitations" (2011, pp. 81–82). She also notes that there is a "transformational potential" in dance (p. 82). Took-Zozaya (2011) cites from her work with a group of people, some with profound limitations, her efforts to encourage them in expression yet respect each person's autonomy. She described using a mirroring exercise and a scarf to connect with a disabled woman who was unable to speak and who had been unable to engage in movement activities with others in the group. Took-Zozaya started by using scarves, draping one gently over the woman's head to see what she would do. From this small gesture, a type of game started where both repeated arm movements with and without the scarf, raising their arms upward. As Took-Zozaya states, the two of them were in a kind of dance together (p. 87). Movement can be simple and small, but its significance extends beyond a series of repeated physical actions. From this example, it is evident that interpersonal connection and creative expression were occurring (p. 87). Creative expression through movement can promote people's health throughout the life cycle. It is also possible to accommodate chronic health conditions, disability, and limited mobility by adapting movement and dance activities to individual needs and abilities (Lyons, 2010).

In the social work profession, few have written about expressive movement and dance applications in practice. Exceptions include works by Moe (2014), Huss and Haimovich (2011), and Mazza (2006). Dance and movement applications have tended to involve those who practice dance, yoga, or other physical movement and integrate these into their work with clients. These methods hold much potential for social work, for example, when dance movement therapists collaborate with social workers or when social workers adapt movement or dance exercises to complement their practice with people. There are many groups of people who could benefit from the expression and healing properties that movement and dance allow. Other forms of creative expression can also be combined with movement or dance (Cancienne & Snowber, 2003; Mazza, 2006). Mazza (2006) describes a method in which choreography and poetry are combined as a means of expressing grief. In his RES method, he introduces a poem, song lyrics, or other writing to his client or student and asks for a response. The person acts this out. In other activities, Mazza introduced a collaborative poem exercise to a group of dance students who then prepared a choreographed dance based on the poem (2006, p. 149). He adds, "The promise of integrating dance/movement with poetry therapy speaks to the inter-relationship of mind, body, and spirit. The poetic occurs when *story* and dance merge into a defining expression that affirms our humanity" (Mazza, 2006, p. 150). The author cautions those who wish to make use of such methods in their practice to reflect on whether the methods align with the purpose for application and that these techniques have not been well tested.

Potential of Movement and Dance and Applications

Research on the benefits of movement and dance at a young age shows, and Sarah agrees, that children develop culturally, socially, and physically through movement and their cognitive development is enhanced by learning to move (Davies, 2003). Movement also constitutes exercise that contributes to good health in children (Kourkouta et al., 2014) and people at all stages of life (e.g., Guzmán-Garcia, Hughes, James, & Rochester, 2013; Oliver & Hearn, 2008; Ritter & Low, 1996). Opportunities for self-expression and discovery offered through movement and dance can also promote children's imaginations and intellectual ability (Pica, 2009). According to Oliver and Hearn (2008), "When children create dances, they participate in decision-making and learn cooperation. They learn how to observe and develop into informed creators, participants and spectators" (p. 6). Children who are able to engage in creative expression through movement or dance also gain in self-esteem and confidence, especially when they are supported and encouraged to express themselves (Pica, 2009).

Inner-city communities where children's lives may be affected by poverty, transitions due to migration, or instability at home can offer programs that include expressive movement and dance that enrich children's learning and social life. Sarah Roche explains, "I've always been really interested in the idea that we're not just learning movement, not learning a set of shapes or patterns. Dance is teaching us about much more than that. Dance is allowing children [and other persons] to develop confidence and self-expression." Through dance, she adds, "there is an opportunity for much greater depth of learning: learning about what it means to be a human being, how to interact with other people, and how to become sensitive to your own body." Sarah refers to this as "emotional education," and it involves the therapeutic elements of dance and the idea of experiential dance. Creative expression through dance or movement thus offers opportunities for children to acknowledge their feelings and express them through movement when they feel safe. Jackson (2015) states that movement and dance connect people together, promoting bonding and belonging. The point, as Sarah also notes, is that dance is not viewed only as a performance but is an experience of bodily expression. In other words, the process of movement and dance is far more important than realizing an outcome.

Sarah Roche has furthered her interest in dance as an expressive art through workshop participation (e.g., at the Tamalpa Institute in San Francisco and DMT workshop with Dr. Suzi Tortora), where authentic movement and storytelling through dance were the focus (see Tortora, 2006). A key concept that Sarah gained from her work in dance and experience at the Tamalpa Institute is the idea of life-art metaphors. She explained that in the studio she learned that dance actually acts as a metaphor for how she could live every day. Through such means as contact improvisation, she realized that the skills needed to communicate through dance and the body were the same skills needed to interact with individuals outside of the dance room. Contact improvisation will be discussed further later in the chapter.

Daria Halprin (2003), renowned dancer Anna Halprin's daughter, states, "[W]hatever resides in our body—despair, confusion, fear, anger, joy—will come up when we express ourselves in movement. When made conscious, and when entered into as a mindful expression, movement becomes a vehicle for insight and change" (p. 18). By moving (or dancing), it is possible to express one's emotions and moods and to alter these through a process of physical movement. In her rich and detailed book containing descriptions of concepts and methods, she affirms the need for a person to "become aware of, express, and organize her life experiences, to make both symbolic and actual changes which lead to growth" (2003, p. 123). Movement and dance can help to bring to the surface emotions that the body expresses. Rage, fear, joy, hope, and other emotions can be released through body movements, and, in doing so, they are made available to the person expressing them and to those who observe them (see Leseho & McMaster, 2011). Through movement, the body enables an individual or group process aimed at growth and healing. (To view a video of Anna Halprin, age 95, dancing with Daria Halprin, see https://www.youtube.com/watch?v=GdpvC0-fi64).

An experience of healing and transformation that clearly demonstrates bodily expression through movement is described by South Asian dancer Lata Pada (2010), who lost her husband and children in the 1985 Air India bombing. Lata Pada was tormented by her emotions and instinctively turned to dance in order to express her feelings. As she states, "While my world as wife and mother had been cruelly wrenched from me, I came to understand that my identity as a dancer had survived" (Pada, 2010, p. 154). Pada immersed herself in the physical movement of dance, finding sources of support from other family members and friends. Her Hindu religion also helped her to cope with her emotional pain. Nine years later, Pada began to produce *Revealed by Fire*, a personal narrative presented through dance, sounds, images, and music about her experience of loss. Fire was a metaphor in this production, a frightening force as well as a strength she drew from, stating, "And in the moment of greatest pain, she, like Sita, saw that at the heart of the fire was its strength and its weakness, and so she embraced it and found that it embraced her" (Pada, 2010, p. 161). Through performance, Pada poignantly expresses the pain she experienced, using dance and movement combined with other creative media, to tell the story of what happened to her family, and how she lived and was transformed. A YouTube video of part of the performance, *Excerpts from Revealed by Fire*, can be viewed at https://www.youtube.com/watch?v=_nkEWZvx7cw.

Just as a process of healing and transformation can be realized in an individual through movement and dance and other expressive art forms, dance and movement can also offer benefits beyond an individual level, for groups of people in different circumstances and settings.

Sarah Roche's work as a dancer, dance teacher, and expressive dance and movement facilitator, can be summarized as bringing dance and movement to people, a contribution that can open up the possibilities of physical expression and the enjoyment of moving one's own body, even if the ability to move is limited. As Sarah states, when we are stressed and tense, we cannot feel or express our feelings easily to others because we are too tight to feel anything. We are blocked. Our bodies tighten to not feel pain, but then the body is too tight to feel pleasant sensations. The physical blocking may also be linked to an emotional or mental block. Such tightness and blocking can be experienced as an impediment to creative activity. However, Halprin (2003) explains in relation to such blocks, "[A]ctively giving over to the conscious expression of an impasse leads to a breakthrough. We go into it creatively; we sing the impasse, dance the impasse, or paint it. Blocks are not 'bad'; in fact they provide important thematic material for exploration" (p. 126). As Sarah states, "[W]hen you're working in contact improvisation or doing any kind of dance with another person, your body needs to be open to physically listen to the needs of the other person. If a body is tense, it cannot listen nor can it react freely. In the same way, when one is emotionally tense and upset, one is often not able to listen freely and openly to another person's perspective or feelings. Sometimes opening a physical block can then open emotional and mental blocks, too."

CONTACT IMPROVISATION

Contact improvisation involves interaction and response in movement or dance that involves a duet of improvisation. Houston (2009) describes contact improvisation in the following way: "Heads skim the ground, buttons rub against noses, legs wrap around arms and backs mould into torsos" (p. 101). Contact can be "subtle, powerfully physical, gentle or risky" (Houston, 2009, p. 101). Because there is no pre-planning of movements in the dance, there can be an element of risk involved. Like daily conversation that is unplanned, each person needs to read the other, give and take appropriately, so that the improvisation, the dance conversation, works for both. There are professional contact improvisation companies, but it has also been a form for those who are not trained in dance. According to Houston (2009), it has also been used by disabled dancers. However, it is less well accepted by persons for whom touching and receiving touch are issues. Letting go and being open to the touch from another person may be difficult for some.

Mirroring, a method of viewing another's actions or responding to his or her expressions, can help participants in a dance movement relationship to observe, be open, and to feel empathy. It takes place when "two people make similar body movements that are coordinated or slightly echoed in time" (McGarry & Russo, 2011, p. 178). There are technical descriptions related to mirroring and how it works through sensory input in the brain (see Rizolatti & Craighero, 2004); however, our interest here is in how it can be helpful in movement dance intervention.

Mirroring in dance movement activities often involves music, which brings with it the potential for coordination of rhythm and tempo in a multisensory experience (McGarry & Russo, 2011). Mirroring activities can also be used by therapists with groups and individuals (e.g., Wittig & Davis, 2012). Kinesthetic empathy, the ability on a bodily level to feel and understand what another is feeling through techniques of mirroring and attunement, is a core concept of DMT theory and practice and considered to be one of DMT's major contributions to psychotherapy (Fischman, 2009). In therapy with couples, communication and relationship insights and greater empathy and connectedness can be enhanced through mirroring one another's actions and expressions. There may be other adaptations for this exercise because it is highly interpersonal and can build empathy or even accentuate conflict. Participant trust in the practitioner is a prerequisite. In social work, complementary use of dance movement intervention requires specialized skills in order to understand the ways that dance movement can contribute to helping people and how to work effectively with this creative method as a complement in social work practice.

A Beginning: Walk-Dance to Music

A warm-up exercise that Sarah has employed, especially when people are nervous about participating in movement and dance, is to ease them into moving through an individual walk-dance, which is done to music of upbeat tempos and rhythms. She learned this technique from Daria Halprin at the Tamalpa Institute and has found it effective with groups. The activity starts with everyone simply walking to music that is being played. After some time, participants are given instructions to try new ways of walking (e.g., backwards, sideways, stopping, and changing directions with changes in rhythms and tempos). The participants are asked to find a walk-dance partner without speaking and to then experiment in attempting a walk-dance duet. Walking partners can team up with another group of two to create a walking quartet. This is a simple activity that helps ease people into moving and communicating through their bodies. Sarah's experience has been that people enjoy the walk-dance and begin to develop bonds with other participants.

Being mindful of body sensations, emotional reactions, and thoughts can form a part of the activities so that participants can reflect on personal feelings, leadership, decisions made in the selection of partners, and the kinds of actions and movements they include. In social work, for example, such activities can be helpful with groups where trust and belonging are important. It is important that these observations are made without judgment but are brought up for the sake of personal growth and awareness. Taking a stance of being curious, as opposed to judgmental or overly analytical, is an important part of the approach.

In Figure 5.1 Roche, Halonen and Heinonen show through movement and facial expression feelings of empowerment, freedom and fear.

Dance Performance Created by Children at a Community Center

While working at a community center with a group of children aged 6 to 11, Sarah was asked to help create a celebration for the anniversary of a special community leader who had died. She asked the eight children in the group what they liked most to do at the center. The children thought of a number of activities and then Sarah asked them what they were most thankful for about the center and how they would feel if the center ceased to exist. Sarah then asked the children to create some movements based on what they had said. The children were asked to create a shape with their bodies that reflected how they would feel if the center did not exist. They created several more shapes

Figure 5.1 Movement and dance with Sara Roche (*top*), Deana Halonen (*middle*), and Tuula Heinonen (*bottom*). Photo used with permission of all subjects.

and these were then arranged into a dance that reflected the loneliness and sadness at the loss of their center. The next stage was about their feelings about being there and what they did while there. Their expressions were happy and joyful ones and also demonstrated how they played together when they were at the center. The children were connected together in this group initiative. The fact that the children created the dance themselves based on their own feelings and ideas was important to them and to others with strong connections to the center. Feedback from Sarah's work with children has been positive and has shown her that many children who are not active in classes become energized by creative expression. Not only did the dance creation and song have an impact on the children, but they also touched the staff and community members who formed the audience.

ENGAGING SCHOOL CURRICULUM THROUGH MOVEMENT

Expressing emotions can be difficult, especially if one is asking a child to relay personal emotions. But using literature to explore emotions, gain empathy, and express feelings is a helpful tool to allow children to express a range of emotions. Sarah related how children in an inner-city school who were reading a book about slavery in their class were given an opportunity to express their ideas and feelings through movement. She worked with the class by dividing up the book's content on slavery into four sessions: (1) hiding; (2) what it means to be oppressed; (3) escape; and finally, (4) freedom. In each class session, Sarah helped the class to work with the four concepts to understand the emotions associated with each and to show how their bodies could express these states. The children also described what each person's bodily expression looked like to them (e.g., low to the ground, heavy, hanging, and more). Noticing what emotions look like helps children with their emotional education, helping them to relate to other children and adults.

The children then created a movement with their bodies to connect with what they had experienced about feeling sad or scared, feeling oppressed, escaping, and on what freedom felt like. The children expressed freedom by opening their arms to show joy, connecting with one another, and feeling closer to the sky.

The benefits for children to safely express their feelings are considerable. Using movement offers another way of exploring and learning about themselves and the world around them. As Sarah notes, some children feel alone or excluded at school for a variety of reasons, and activities that engage such children creatively can help them feel more connection to one another. Such activities can also aid in building empathy for others and for working together on common goals. Often children who experience bullying or teasing at school can benefit when ground rules are developed and creative activities are skilfully facilitated.

As in other creative expression methods, the practitioner's skill and knowledge is critical because feeling and expressing strong emotions might threaten the safety of some children. However, as Sarah remarked, movement and dance truly enable the learning of empathy for others because it is possible to try out somebody else's movement and to see what it feels like for oneself in comparison with another person. Sarah asserts that often teachers are surprised at the transformation that occurs in these children. Some of the children she has worked with in movement and dance sessions remember the impact it had on them many years later.

Expression of Movement and Voice With a Group of Women

Sarah also worked with adult women who struggled with disordered eating. When she started to work with them, she began by checking in and asking the women to show an action that represented how they felt that day. When the women were more comfortable, the walk-dance was introduced because this was a good way for them to get to know each other. Several women in the group reflected during check-in before the walk-dance that they felt "nervous and interested," "tired," "apprehensive," and "frustrated," but, after the walk-dance exercise, the women said they felt "at peace," "awake," "playful," "energized," "excited," and "relaxed." Although there was some anxiety felt by the women later, perhaps in anticipation of further risking through bodily expression, the women were able to explore their feelings in ways that interested and engaged them. Later, the women were invited to try out the movements of other women in the group while repeating their *check-in word* three times. This is another example of trying on another person's feeling or movement.

MOVEMENT AND DANCE WITH OLDER PERSONS

Sarah described her application of movement and dance to music in a residence for older persons in which the aim was social connection and promotion of wellness through group activity. Most of the participants were in wheelchairs or had other mobility challenges that were accommodated by sitting in chairs. The participants began each 40-minute session with a *name dance* where each performed an action to associate with their names and other participants repeated it back to them. Following this warm-up, Sarah helped the group to create a circle dance with music. From one group session to the next, the group members performed the actions with associated names or developed new ones. There was excitement and anticipation about this activity each week. Sarah created a playlist of music to include songs that reflected the participants' age cohorts, for example songs of Bing Crosby and others popular in the past. Many would join in by singing along and moving together from where they sat in the chairs or wheelchairs. As Sarah remarked, it was possible to kick their legs even while seated.

It is useful to make adaptations with movement and dance expression when needed so that those with physical limitations can participate and take a turn leading the dance. Including persons in creative ways that might not have seemed possible is important and adds to feelings of belonging. As Sarah said, "You can even move a nose, an arm, a hand, or one leg" (e.g., in the case of some stroke survivors with paralysis), and it does not matter how much movement there is as long as there is participation and inclusion. Even if people have knees or hips that limit activity, it is possible to adapt movement to enable participation in an activity.

For Sarah, and likely others who work with movement and dance, it can be gratifying to work with a range of age groups and populations. For example, seeing a parent–child relationship develop through movement together is meaningful. As Sarah has observed, a lot of learning occurs through expression of movement because one's body contains individual stories, not only muscles, bones, veins, and blood. She adds that the body also contains one's fears and emotions and explains that movement and dance are physical activities that increase endorphins and help people to feel better and happier.

Challenges of Participating in Movement and Dance

Not everyone has found dance or movement easy or even pleasurable. Some may associate these with unpleasant experiences and fears and feel uncomfortable or uncertain about participating. For example, when working with the group of women who experienced disordered eating, a discussion of their feelings and concerns about movement and dance participation was necessary before even beginning to move. Dance carries a lot of connotations for people, and it is best to have a conversation about them.

Sarah asked the women about their experiences in movement as observers and participants so that all the things that they saw as dance could be discussed, including skills, preconceptions, and concerns. She asked the women to reflect on their feelings about dance or movement. For most, body image was an issue that generated apprehension. It is useful, she states, to bring into the open and acknowledge these concerns and difficulties in dancing and moving. Sarah states that people may have associations of sexiness or other connotations with dance and feel uncomfortable about them. Sarah relates this to a general societal discomfort due to the fact that we do not tune in to our bodies often. Acknowledging this with clients is important because often feelings and ideas need to be worked out. It is not possible to force people to move because individual pacing needs to be considered.

Noting that one is moving, even in small ways, and then exploring and taking risks once it feels safe to do so is helpful. Exploration, even in small ways, opens up ideas for further movement. Starting with a discussion about safety and with graduated movement can help those who are reluctant to move or dance. It is possible to explore first what gently moving the fingers feels like and, later, graduate to more vigorous movements. Tuning in to an individual or a group is the best way to determine people's level of comfort with movement and dance activities.

Sarah says that she tries to normalize movement, asserting, "We all move," and movement is for all people. "When we breathe, we move." She also connects movement to music and rhythm, and to the idea that the experience of movement or dance can be only for oneself, not for others. For many, performance in front of an audience means dancing for somebody else or putting on a show. But dance can be experiential and not performative. This can happen by starting simply. For example, drawing circles with different body parts at different speeds, first with eyes closed and then open, helps people to become more comfortable. This simple step gave her disordered eating group participants a chance to express themselves by moving individually and to acknowledge that everyone produced a different, but correct, result. A safe space was also fostered from this small exercise in which the women claimed, "Wow, we all just moved and we all did it fine."

Music, cautions Sarah, can overpower one's internal sensation of movement and will influence immediately how one wants to move the body. Although that may be desirable and helpful, it is important to be conscious of its effects. Some associations might exist with certain pieces of music or certain songs, which could get in the way of enjoyment. It may be necessary to select alternative pieces.

Some people may have little awareness of what they are expressing through their body. "By doing body work through movement and dance and having [an opportunity] to experiment with different ways of moving, one can become more aware of their patterns," explains Sarah. For example, tension or tightness can be changed into more flowing and free movements and different sensations. Sarah states that it can be useful for participants to ask themselves how they interpret the music and how they would like to move to it. For many, music with a beat or rhythm tends to motivate them to move by tapping the feet, moving the head, or getting up and dancing. Such experiences when incorporated into daily life can promote well-being.

SAFETY AND MINDFULNESS

As suggested earlier, in any intervention with clients, safety needs to be built before they are able to take risks. Sarah stresses that she always approaches people in the room mindfully and without judgment, affirming that there is no right or wrong way of moving. However, Sarah asks that participants notice how they feel in the moment and note the choices they make in their movements because this awareness can contribute to sensitivity and mindfulness that deepen the benefits of creative expression.

Mindfulness is not a new concept and can be traced to Eastern approaches to philosophy and spirituality, such as Buddhism (Barton, 2011). Within mindfulness approaches, the practice of meditation and methods that enhance mind–body awareness have been used for healing purposes (Rappaport, 2014). The practices related to mindfulness have been introduced to the profession of social work, where its use can promote health and well-being among persons experiencing mental health problems and physical illnesses such as cancer (Carlson, 2012). Rappaport and Kalmanowitz (2014) refer to the professional use of mindfulness in professional practice as "simple, yet powerful transformative practices" (p. 13), and they caution against its application in the absence of good training. Mindfulness has become integrated into social work and other professions in health, mental health (including psychotherapy), arts therapies, such as drama, dance and movement, visual art, poetry, and more (Rappaport, 2014), and it is found in many health care and community-based practice settings. In movement and dance it can be helpful for focusing and developing one's awareness in order to express emotion and ideas. Sarah views the body as "another language," which can be a vehicle for expression through movement rather than words. For some people, expression through movement may be easier than using words to communicate.

Gender, Age, and Culture

Gender, as a key organizing feature in any society, group, and community, shapes the way people express themselves and participate in activities either as individuals or in groups. Action and expression may reflect gendered experiences and preferences. In some situations or populations, mixed-gender groups may not be a good idea (e.g., women who have experienced abuse by males).

Differences among potential participants may be related to gender, culture, age, socioeconomic status, or other features related to unique background or experience. For example, among older persons, the greater number of male war veterans might have different needs and interests than women who might have been caregivers for most of their lives. It is important to tune in to what an individual or a group wants in relation to movement and dance, and the music that accompanies such activities. When dance is associated with one partner over the course of a lifetime, it may be difficult to dance alone or with others to the same kind of music danced to in the past. Individuals do not always respond in the same way to music, and social workers need to be prepared to consider first how to anticipate and prepare for unique responses in individuals and groups. For older persons, many years of experiences provide memories that can be a source for triggered reactions; some might be adverse or difficult and others might be joyful.

Practitioner Knowledge and Skill

In any movement or dance activities, it is necessary for the social worker providing services to be confident and comfortable in what he or she is offering. Not only may participants sense a practitioner's lack of knowledge, but providing a service without adequate training and preparation is unethical and may even be harmful. Ethical practice is governed by professional codes of conduct (e.g., Canadian Social Work Code of Ethics) that are clear on taking on practice work for which one has insufficient experience and knowledge (CASW, 2005). On p. 8 of the CASW Code of Ethics document (2005), a section on competence in professional practice notes that clients have the right to expect competency from the social workers providing services to them and that social workers should seek to advance their knowledge and skills, adding innovation and increased proficiency to their practice (see https://casw-acts.ca/en/what-social-work/casw-code-ethics/code-ethics). Social workers could work in collaboration with those experienced in using dance as a therapeutic method if they wish to add dance and movement to their practices.

Sarah Roche mentioned that the practitioner without knowledge about movement and dance methods will not have the experience or knowledge to guide participants, plan appropriate activities, make adaptations to activities, or evaluate the activities effectively. Participants in dance and movement activities need to have access to a skilled practitioner who knows how to integrate, select, adapt, or develop activities suited to the needs of clients. Some clients may have had difficult past experiences that can affect their willingness or ability to participate. Accommodation and adaptation or other approaches may be more helpful. Movement and dance are not simply recreational exercises but are a purposeful part of a therapeutic program that may also include verbal methods.

Some individuals may be fearful of how they will be perceived by others or of how they will perform. Sarah suggests that since everyone knows how to walk (or ambulate in some way), it is good to start with walking and mirroring activities. Later, more complex movement, dances, or vigorous activities can be taught, as appropriate. Social work practice that includes complementary methods such as movement and dance can offer to social workers new ways of working with clients who seek healing, growth, and expression.

Group practice methods can help clients benefit from group support, encouragement, and collective expression through movement and dance (see Wittig & Davis, 2012). Through regular sessions of expressive movement, participants' experiences could lead to personal transformation; the group might experience it together as relationships with one another and with the group as a whole develop. Group work, a well-established mode of social work practice, has been shown to be effective across many client populations and settings (Sullivan, Mitchell, Goodman, Lang, & Mesbur, 2003). When expressive arts, such as movement and dance, are integrated in group intervention, an interpersonal process is introduced that can create deeper experiences for participants. Social workers who work in creative ways on their own or in collaboration with dance therapists or others with expressive arts backgrounds can offer a wider range of options to help clients express themselves, gain insights, heal from illness or traumatizing experiences, and, potentially, experience transformation.

Cultural background may shape the practice of dance for people, and diverse forms of dance are known around the world. Cultural background or a strong adherence to certain cultural beliefs may play a role in the way movement or dance is understood and experienced (Pada, 2010; Waterfall, 2011; Wilcox, 2011). One example is in Indigenous cultures. Waterfall, a Métis woman Sun Dancer of Anishnabe/Ojibway and European backgrounds, writes that her practice of the Sun Dance connects her to her culture, her traditions, and the Creator, and, according to her, "the Sun Dance as a spiritual practice" (2011, p. 124). She also notes the significance of Indigenous people's connection to the environment, particularly the land and a specific place, to nature, to ancestors, and to spirituality, stating that the knowledge in these realms "[has] accrued through time, passed down through our oral and written histories, such as our pictorial drawings, legends, stories, proverbs, songs, ceremonies and dances" (p. 125). Waterfall (2011) refers to the use of the circle in the Sun Dance, explaining that it reflects the idea that all of us "are connected and related" (p. 127). She also states that balance and harmony are important for the future of the earth and all living things. Waterfall (2011) states that the Sun Dance "has created a context for the healing and empowerment of many Anishnabec People" (p. 131), and it is important due to the harm caused by colonization and related effects of grief and loss. The Sun Dance allows the expression of many emotions and also affirms the connectedness of all people to the environment.

On a broader scale are movement and dance initiatives that address social injustice and seek social transformation. Little writing is available on the use of movement and dance for social change, although dance has been used to raise awareness about social issues. In public places, dance and sometimes other expressive arts methods are used to draw the attention of large audiences of people. Many are then posted on social media to further disseminate the event.

One example of this phenomenon is the *flash mob*, a performance that looks spontaneous (but usually is planned in advance). Some years ago, a flash mob focused public attention on the need for resistance in the face of the enactment of Bill C-45, affecting Indigenous rights in Canada. The flash mob events were held in a number of cities as part of the Idle No More movement. For example, the Indian Round Dance Flash Mob took place in Toronto and other Canadian cities (some were held in the United States as well). These events not only drew on cultural traditions, symbols, and art forms but also were effective in educating the public about issues that concerned Indigenous people and others in North America (see http://culturalorganizing.org/idle-no-more-and-the-round-dance-flash-mob/). The Kino-nda-niimi Collective (2014) compiled stories from these events, including the collective flash mob performances of round dances in a number of public malls in Canadian cities.

Dance that is meant to confront social injustice can be seen in genres that come from those who view themselves as oppressed or marginalized; for example, hip-hop dance emerged from poor African American neighborhoods. Hip-hop (including breakdancing) represents a powerful and effective expression of emotion and strong assertive way of reacting to the performer's perceptions on his or her reality (Kent, 2014), giving the youth who participate a sense of belonging and identity. These were "often racially divided areas where non-white youths had little opportunity to entertain themselves in lavish night clubs or even had the money to do this" (Kent, 2014). Kent describes how, in a South African community, breakdancing was uniquely adapted to the interests of this group of youth. He also describes dancing as protest: "By 'breaking the law', and using public property to dance on, in and around, the street becomes a symbol of the freedom that the dancers have over their bodies and their lives, even though there may be other constraints on them as individuals and groups" (p. 174). As Kent notes, the act of dancing (usually with portable music) represents a "way of breaking away from convention and constructing a place for themselves outside of social conventions" (p. 174). For the Black youth who take part, "it is the young and the marginalised who hold power, not the other way around. The road becomes a play and a means to reconstruct the 'coloured' body" (p. 174). The potential of hip-hop and breakdancing for youth is also noted in several other chapters of this book (see Chapters 4 and 8) in relation to theater and video, in which dancer and social worker Stephen Leafloor describes how he found hip-hop helped him and those he worked with as a social worker (see Blueprint for Life website at http://www.blueprintforlife.ca/about/founder/).

Dance that communicates social injustice through cultural expression, "choreographic agency," which can be combined with theater, for example, as in the performance of *Dying While Black and Brown*, produced by Zaccho Dance Theater (see Prickett, 2016). The performance explores possibilities of social mobilization beyond the performance to address the issue of imprisonment and the death penalty and their effects on Black men in the United States. The choreography includes dancers who take on characters and perform around a frame that resembles a house that is also a jail cell, in and around which the dancers move (Prickett, 2016). The dancers then take the topics of the performance to the audience and invite them to engage in discussion. (See a review of Zaccho Dance Theater's performance at http://www.bostonmagazine.com/news/blog/2015/03/09/dying-while-black-and-brown/.) These examples of movement and dance performance communicate to audiences and attempt to demonstrate realities and situations that are unjust. Their aim is to challenge people and to change their understanding of issues that oppress groups of people. In so doing, dance, often combined with music and theater, can address and highlight social injustices and work for social change through expressive arts.

Combining Movement and Dance With Other Forms of Creative Expression

While movement and dance may fit together well with music of all kinds, there is also room to engage other creative expression with these. For example, some 19th-century artists, such as Wassily Kandinsky, heard music being played in the colors they used on their canvas. Movement and dance can be combined with painting or collage artwork to explore emotions that arise in relation to one or the other activity in more depth. Sarah believes that such combinations of expressive arts can provide therapeutic benefits and insights for participants. For example, painting while moving one's arms in large shapes or responding to images or stories with movements can be good ways to warm up for movement and dance activities. Or in reverse order, a dance experience can be an excellent inspiration for poetry or a visual art representation.

INTEGRATION OF MOVEMENT AND DANCE INTO SOCIAL WORK

Movement and dance exercises are a complement for social workers who draw from them appropriately and safely for their clients. Ideally, consultation with an experienced movement and dance expert would be best prior to planning such activities with clients. Social workers who have experience in movement and dance themselves are in a better position to integrate such activities in their client interventions. Sarah Roche refers to her own work as using movement and dance in healing ways that may be therapeutic, but she does not call herself a therapist because she is not a certified DMT. She also states that social workers can learn about other forms of movement that are health promoting such as tai chi, yoga, or qi gong. These could be integrated into a social worker's practice when appropriate. Sarah adds that knowing how certain movements and dances feel for oneself helps social workers to imagine what their clients might feel, and it suggests to them how they can purposefully and effectively plan activities with specific goals and anticipated outcomes in mind. Knowing one's own fears, hesitations, and limitations is valuable for all social work practitioners before they work with clients.

Hannah Beach, a social worker who uses dance with children in Ottawa, engages children to create dances (see websites at https://hannahbeach.ca/ and http://dandeliondancecompany.ca/) using their own choreography and including children with different abilities. She has also produced a number of videos that are on the Dandelion Dance Company's website. Through creative choreography, children and young people explore their own identities, viewpoints, and values, and they develop important and transferable physical and creative skills that can be further developed as they grow up.

Social workers with movement dance therapy training can be found using movement and dance with persons in mental health and other fields of practice. In an article by Trainin Blank (2009), one such practitioner discusses his work in a hospital as creating dances with "everyday movements put into sequences" (p. 4 online at http://www.socialworker.com/feature-articles/practice/Based_

on_Mind-Body_Connection%2C_Dance_Therapy_Offers_Physical%2C_Psychic_Benefits/). The purpose of the movements is to help participants to express their feelings and, in doing so, search for metaphors about their lives that might enhance insight. Movement and dance, just like the visual arts, music, and theater, can help those who do not easily verbalize their feelings or thoughts. Expressive art methods thus can offer alternatives to spoken words.

Jackson (2014) encourages social workers to embrace the expressive arts in their work with clients because they can offer benefits that go beyond talk. She refers to people living with dementia who often have cognitive difficulty that affects memory. She points out that creative expression has sometimes been used in the form of arts and crafts or a programmed leisure-time activity. Although such methods can be enjoyable, their potential may be greater for individuals when they are used therapeutically without a focus on completing a product, such as a painting or craft item. Participation in movement and dance can enhance the quality of life for people who have dementia. Even though people may not be able to remember daily life skills such as making a salad, their memories will work much better when exposed to music or visual art-making. Different parts of the brain are brought into action and results may be remarkable. Dementia may be accompanied by feelings of loss and powerless-ness, but being able to dance a waltz or sing all the words to a favorite song can be both empowering and meaningful for the person and often for his or her family as well. However, few large studies have been conducted that demon-strate the benefits of creative and expressive arts in health care settings, so they tend to remain more marginal in health care.

Opportunities to experiment with movement and dance might also be useful for social workers for their own self-care or for professional development activ-ities to build insight and reflection on their practice. Reflection on the activity can also spur further creative development and ideas for work with clients. It can also help social workers to understand the limits of movement and dance activities for themselves and for their practice work.

CONCLUDING THOUGHTS

Sarah asserts that the body teaches one to be adaptable. It is constantly moving and changing and never stays the same, even as one breathes. A person can learn to tune in to one's own body and be attentive to minute changes such as when inhaling and exhaling; breathing is constant movement. All people can feel it as change and adapt. "Human bodies are meant to move," she adds, "and our movement communicates ideas whether we are aware of it or not."

In this chapter, we have drawn from the experience of Sarah Roche, a dancer and teacher who has witnessed the power of movement for children and adults and the meaning it holds for those who participate and learn about themselves and others in the process. We have also made connections to literature, video, and website sources that deepen understanding of movement and dance methods in working with people and their situations. From these materials, it is apparent that social work has a rich ally in movement and dance methods in many practice settings and client situations. There is much room to explore and collaborate in this area of the expressive arts because writing from the perspective of social work or by social work scholars and professionals is sparse. Several new articles, however, were found on practice interventions that have used movement or dance with older adults (Rodio & Holmes, 2017), and in persons in recovery from substance misuse (Roy & Manley, 2017).

QUESTIONS FOR REFLECTION AND SUGGESTED ACTIVITIES

1. How do movement and dance add to social work in your field of practice and with persons you work with? What are some ethical concerns that you can think of?
2. Write out a plan for a group where movement or dance is implemented for a professional development day in your workplace. The purpose of the day would be to raise awareness of dance movement methods and to invite participants to try out some exercises that you design or adapt from those you have learned about.
3. How might you combine movement or dance with some other expressive art methods, such as visual arts, poetry, or theater in your field of work and with those to whom you provide services?

RESOURCES

For a description of dance therapy and its application by Rena Kornblum, a registered dance therapist based in an American university's social work department, see https://www.youtube.com/watch?v=j3YgZiWieNk

For a description and videos on resources about movement and dance with children and on the Dandelion Dance Company in Ottawa, run by Hanna Beach, see the following websites at http://dandeliondancecompany.ca/ and http://dandeliondancecompany.ca/

For information on the Canadian Social Work Code of Ethics and Principles of Practice, see the website at https://casw-acts.ca/en/what-social-work/casw-code-ethics/code-ethics

The video, Sun Dance Ceremony, that took place in Pipestone, Minnesota, is available online for viewing at http://www.bing.com/videos/search?q=Sun+da

nces&FORM=VIRE3#view=detail&mid=E063758A97BAEFC02B32E063758A97BAEFC02B32

This video was produced by Meeches Video Production in Manitoba and describes the context and history of the Sun Dance and its purpose today.

REFERENCES

Barton, L. (2011). Movement and mindfulness: A formative evaluation of a dance/movement and yoga therapy program with participants experiencing severe mental illness. *American Journal of Dance Therapy, 33*, 157–181.

Cancienne, M., & Snowber, C. (2003). Writing rhythm: Movement as method. *Qualitative Inquiry, 9*, 237–253.

Carlson, L. (2012). Mindfulness-based interventions for physical conditions: A narrative review evaluating levels of evidence. *International Scholarly Research Notices (ISRN) Psychiatry*, Article ID 651583, 1–21. doi:10.5402/2012/651583.

Davies, M. (2003). *Movement and dance in early childhood*. London, UK: Sage.

Devereaux, C., Kleinman, S., Johnson, G., & Witzling, K. (2016). American Dance Therapy Association historical timeline: 1966–2016. *American Journal of Dance Therapy, 38*(2), 437–454.

Fischman, D. (2009). Therapeutic relationships and kinesthetic empathy. In S. Chaiklin & H. Wengrower (Eds.), *The art and science of Dance/Movement Therapy: Life is dance* (pp. 33–54). New York, NY: Routledge.

Guzmán-Garcia, A., Hughes, J., James, I., & Rochester, L. (2013). Dancing as a psychosocial intervention in care homes: A systematic review of the literature. *International Journal of Geriatric Psychiatry, 28*(9), 914–924.

Halprin, D. (2003). *The expressive body in life, art, and therapy : Working with movement, metaphor, and meaning*. London, UK: Jessica Kingsley.

Houston, S. (2009). The touch "taboo" and the art of contact: An exploration of Contact Improvisation for prisoners. *Research in Dance Education, 10*(2), 97–113.

Huss, E., & Haimovich, S. (2011). "The hips don't lie": Dancing around gendered, ethnic, and national identity in Israel. *Body, Movement and Dance in Psychotherapy, 6*(1), 3–16.

Jackson, K. (2014). Expressive therapies for people with Alzheimers and related dementias. *Social Work Today, 14*(1), 10–13. http://www.socialworktoday.com/archive/012014p10.shtml

Jackson, K. (2015). Beyond talk—Creative arts therapies in social work. *Social Work Today, 15*(3), 22–25.

Kent, L. (2014). Breaking Grahamstown; Breakin' the dance. Exploring the role of break dancing in the construction of a break dancer's identity. *The Journal of Hip Hop Studies, 1*(2), 168–184.

Kino-nda-niimi Collective. (Eds.). (2014). *The winter we danced: Voices from the past, the future and the Idle No More Movement*. Winnipeg, MB: ARP Books.

Kourkouta, L., Rarra, A., Mavroeidi, A., & Prodromidis, K. (2014). The contribution of dance on children's health. *Progress in Health Sciences, 4*(1), 229–232.

Leseho, J., & McMaster, S. (Eds.). (2011). *Dancing on the earth: Women's stories of healing through dance*. Forres, Scotland: Findhorn Press.

Lohn, A. (1987). Reflections about Marian Chase: An interview with Catherine Pasternak and Marion Gibbons. *American Journal of Dance Therapy, 10,* 11–26.

Lyons, D. (Ed.). (2010). *Creative studies for the caring professions.* Dublin, Ireland: Gill & Macmillan.

Mazza, N. (2006). Voices in flight: Integrating movement/dance with poetry therapy. *Journal of Poetry Therapy: The Interdisciplinary Journal of Practice, Theory, Research and Education, 19*(3), 147–150.

McGarry, L., & Russo, F. (2011). Mirroring in dance/movement therapy: Potential mechanisms behind empathy enhancement. *The Arts in Psychotherapy, 38*(3), 178–184. doi:10.1016/j.aip.2011.04.005.

McNeill, W. (1995). *Keeping together in time: Dance and drill in human history.* Cambridge, MA: Harvard University Press.

Moe, A. (2014). Healing through movement: The benefits of belly dance for gendered victimization. *Affilia, 29*(3), 326–339.

Murcia, C. Q., Kreutz, G., Clift, S., & Bongard, S. (2010). Shall we dance? An exploration of the perceived benefits of dancing on well-being. *Arts & Health: An International Journal for Research, Policy and Practice, 2*(2), 149–163. doi:10.1080/17533010903488582.

Oliver, W., & Hearn, C. (2008). Dance is for all ages. *Journal of Physical Education, Recreation & Dance, 79*(4), 6–8; 56.

Pada, L. (2010). Revealed by fire: A story of grief, dance and transformation. In C. McLean & R. Kelly (Eds.), *Creative arts in interdisciplinary practice: Inquiries for hope and change* (pp. 151–165). Calgary, AB: Detselig.

Paley, A. M. (1974). Dance therapy: An overview. *American Journal of Psychoanalysis, 34*(1), 81–83.

Pica, R. (2009, July). Can movement promote creativity? *Young Children, 64*(4), 60–61.

Prickett, S. (2016). Constrained bodies: Dance, social justice and choreographic agency. *Dance Research Journal, 48*(3), 45–57. doi:10.1017/S0149767716000309.

Rappaport, L. (Ed.). (2014). *Mindfulness and the arts therapies: Theory and practice.* London, UK: Jessica Kingsley.

Rappaport, L., & Kalmanowitz, D. (2014). Mindfulness, psychotherapy and the arts therapies. In L. Rappaport (Ed.), *Mindfulness and the arts therapies: Theory and practice* (pp. 24–36). London, UK: Jessica Kingsley.

Ritter, M., & Low, K. (1996). Effects of dance/movement therapy: A meta-analysis. *The Arts in Psychotherapy, 23*(3), 249–260.

Rizolatti, G., & Craighero, L. (2004). The mirror-neuron system. *Annual Review of Neuroscience, 27,* 169–192. doi:10.1080/01609513.2015.1066580.

Rodio, A., & Homes, A. (2017). Lessons learned from ballroom dancing with older adults. *Social Work With Groups, 40*(1–2), 69–76.

Root-Bernstein, M., & Root-Bernstein, R. (2003). Martha Graham, dance and the polymathic imagination: A case for multiple intelligences or universal thinking tools? *Journal of Dance Education, 3*(1), 16–27. doi:10.1080/15290824.2003.10387225.

Roy, A., & Manley, J. (2017). Recovery and movement: Allegory and "journey" as a means of exploring recovery from substance misuse, *Journal of Social Work Practice, 31*(2), 191–204. doi:10.1080/02650533.2017.1305336.

Sullivan, N., Mitchell, L., Goodman, D., Lang, N., & Mesbur, E. S. (2003). *Social work with groups: Social justice through personal, community, and societal change.* Binghamton, NY: Haworth Press.

Took-Zozaya, S. (2011). Dancing with (dis) abilities. In J. Leseho & S. McMaster (Eds.), *Dancing on the earth: Women's stories of healing through dance* (pp. 81–93). Forres, Scotland: Findhorn Press.

Tortora, S. (2006). *The dancing dialogue: Using the communicative power of movement with young children.* Baltimore, MD: Paul H. Brookes.

Trainin Blank, B. (2009). Based on mind-body connection, dance therapy offers physical, psychic benefits. *The New Social Worker.* Retrieved from http://www.socialworker. com/feature-articles/practice/Based_on_Mind-Body_Connection%2C_Dance_ Therapy_Offers_Physical%2C_Psychic_Benefits/

Waterfall, B. (2011). Sun Dancing as service to Mother Earth and all of creation. In J. Leseho & S. McMaster (Eds.), *Dancing on the earth: Women's stories of healing through dance* (pp. 123–136). Forres, Scotland: Findhorn Press.

Wilcox, H. (2011). Movement in spaces of liminality: Chinese dance and immigrant identities. *Ethnic and Racial Studies, 34*(2), 314–332. doi:10.1080/01419870.2010.528439.

Wittig, J., & Davis, J. (2012). Circles outside the circle: Expanding the group frame through dance/movement therapy and art therapy. *The Arts in Psychotherapy, 39,* 168–172.

6

Storytelling, Poetry, Writing, and the Art of Metaphor

ELIZABETH KRAHN

CONTEXT: STORY, MEANING-MAKING, AND SOCIAL WORK PRACTICE

Humans have been making meaning of and storying their lives for millennia, producing oral traditions, myths, and legends about past worlds which have served to create and preserve diverse cultural identities around the globe. Over the course of time and the evolution of civilizations, new contexts and experiences have created new meanings, narratives, and forms of expression; and new meanings, narratives, and expression have, in turn, stimulated new contexts and experiences—all of which have spoken of the interplay between harmony and strife.

It is not surprising, then, that for many cultural groups, the words for *story* and *history* are synonymous. Storytelling is one way that premodern peoples all over the planet transmitted collective memory, drawing wisdom from their collective pasts and guiding future generations, an oral tradition still valued and practiced to varying degrees by many Indigenous groups today. Traditional storytelling has the potential to unite and anchor a group of individuals in a collective sense of meaning, identity, and belonging, and to empower them to speak of who they are in relation to the world of creation and the cosmos. It tends to be relational and inclusive, placing the individual within the context of a larger collective experience, and it provides reference points by which to navigate through life and its challenges, and archetypal characters one can easily identify with.

In *A Long Way Gone: Memoirs of a Boy Soldier*, Ishmael Beah (2007) at times hearkens back to the prewar years in Sierra Leone when his family and village were still intact and partook in long evenings of storytelling under the starlit and moonlit sky. Not only has he drawn sustenance from the foundational communal memories and stories of his early childhood prior to the tragedy that befell his family and his people, but he has also engaged in a healing journey through written and oral presentations of his life story, which provide readers and listeners alike the opportunity to *witness* a personal account of a highly traumatic life experience and gain a deeper appreciation of the complex socio-political and systemic issues that can dramatically impact the lives of innocent children. The value of *witnessing the other,* in other words, authentic listening to the lived experience of another human being, cannot be overstated. Such listening encourages mutual sharing and appreciation of core human and emotional experiences common to all individuals regardless of race, culture, and any other outward differences, and it promotes empathy, a quality which, in turn, promotes connection and inclusivity (White & Epstein, 1990).

With the advent of text (and film), oral traditions where the storyteller personally engages with his or her audience have waned over time and been all but replaced by libraries, bookstores, television, and movie theaters, rendering the relationship with story an increasingly solitary experience. Stories have, to a great extent, become a source of entertainment and, at times, a replacement for or escape from the absence of relationship. I once met an individual who relied on watching movies to better understand what healthy family relationships looked like because of the absence of authentic connection and relationship in her life. In my social work practice with older adults struggling with complex mental health issues and accompanying social isolation, I often found clients addicted to soap operas or with radios and televisions on all day to break the silence of their existence, as many had few links to meaningful relationship. A young single mother propped up her 9-month-old baby in his baby-chair to distract him with a cartoon during one of my home visits. We also see increasing levels of social and emotional isolation and disconnect in today's world with the prevalence of social media. *This story* requires more conscious attention.

A common thread throughout different narrative forms that have emerged over time is related to the symbols and metaphors embedded in the experiences and stories that govern our lives—not only stories we construct about ourselves and the world we live in but also those which others have constructed about us that influence our perception of *self* and *other* and, thus, strongly impact our own life, how we make sense of it, and what resources we are able to access to move forward. Whereas prominent metaphors in traditional stories tended to focus on interconnectedness and collective responsibility, stories today do not carry this value of inclusivity. We see many diverse and divisive narratives in the larger community and the media that center on independence and individualism, which, in turn, encourage the stigmatization, marginalization, and/

or pathologizing of those who fail to meet certain criteria due to economic hardship, mental health issues, cultural or religious background, and many other factors.

In the helping professions, there has been an evolution in the art of using story to engage with these growing individual and social issues. When underlying metaphors negatively shape and cast limitations on the lives of individuals, groups, and communities, the capacity for individual and social change can be supported by identifying more life-giving and transformative metaphors that help people to reframe or restory their lives. This chapter explores the integration of storytelling, poetry, expressive writing, and other creative narrative forms with social work practice and research to stimulate personal and social change.

TRADITIONAL STORYTELLING: THE TRANSFORMATIONAL POWER OF STORY

Lewis Mehl-Madrona (2007), in his book, *Narrative Medicine: The Use of History and Story in the Healing Process*, tells us that individual imbalance and disease is regarded by Indigenous peoples to be an outcome of multiple systemic issues related to lack of harmony and collaboration within the context of the larger community and the natural diversity of all living things. Traditional stories metaphorically reflect this wisdom and hold the power, especially when embedded in a group or community experience, to restore harmony and balance within the individual and in the relational field. As a medical doctor with Indigenous roots—certified in family practice, geriatrics, and psychiatry—Mehl-Madrona has integrated Indigenous storytelling with medical practice, rather than focusing primarily on medical or psychiatric diagnoses (pathology or deficit metaphors) which problematize the individual. His intent is to engage the patient in a story that inspires the ability to transcend the limitations often inherent in medical narratives, thus setting the stage for alternate stories of healing and recovery. (For an interesting discussion of traditional story and ceremony, refer to Chapter 8: Talking with Mental Illness, in Mehl-Madrona, 2007, pp. 199–219.) This same principle can be integrated into social work practice settings where presenting problems of clients are often primarily addressed as individual problems rather than community or social justice issues requiring systemic changes, such as those related to mental health, addictions, poverty, homelessness, or racism.

The essence of traditional storytelling engages multiple aspects of the self within a greater universal consciousness. It draws from concrete life experiences in tandem with the subtle but deep wisdom and spectrum of emotions held in our bodies, minds, and souls. When this is deeply felt yet hard to articulate, it can be accessed or expressed through symbolic representation and metaphor, for example, in the form of poetry or mythical tales. Additionally, we may draw strength from hearing or reading the storied expressions of others whose experience resonates with our own. These poignant expressions may touch that core place within and open the floodgate for emotional release or simply enable us to recognize in a metaphoric parable the opportunity for a transformational outcome—a new perspective on what is possible. This process bypasses the intellectual or rational mind, which may be trapped in unyielding mental constructs, such as deficit perspectives that preclude new learning and opportunities for growth and change. The language of the expressive arts is not based in rational thinking.

Storytellers as Agents of Personal and Social Transformation

Laura Simms, a world-renowned storyteller from whom I had the opportunity to learn more about the art of storytelling at an annual Winnipeg International Storytelling Festival organized by the Arthur V. Mauro Centre for Peace and Justice (https://umanitoba.ca/colleges/st_pauls/mauro_centre/events/1083.html) and an expressive arts workshop organized by the Winnipeg Holistic Expressive Arts Therapy Institute (http://wheatinstitute.com/), has been involved in numerous international storytelling initiatives to aid people in crisis. Some examples are a project with Roma women in Romania, youth programs related to peace building and conflict resolution, and youth struggling with postconflict trauma effects and displacement (Simms, 2003, 2009b, 2011b). She draws from the transformational power of traditional stories (Simms, 2002, 2011a) and develops creative storytelling programs that engage and seek to transform the very difficult stories of the populations she works with. Through storytelling, it becomes possible for individuals to "imagine alternative endings to life stories" (Simms, 2009a, p. 6).

ENGAGING THE LISTENER

Simms reminds us that "[we] are all in need of trusting the inner resources that we have as human beings," of finding the self within the heart (2009a, p. 8). Her premise is that "[within] each individual [lie] . . . the inherent seeds of goodness, compassion, resilience and wisdom that are activated through storytelling" (p. 5). Healing stories thus evoke the innate wisdom and imagination of the listener, which serve as protection from the stresses of contemporary life. Drawing from stories from around the world, Simms creates an atmosphere that brings the listener into the narrative. Listening becomes a body and mind experience as the story comes to life within and engages the imagination.

IDENTIFICATION WITH CHARACTER AND PLOT

Simms explains that the listener "vicariously experiences" the dynamics and plot of the story, identifies with its characters, confronts obstacles and danger, and overcomes challenges. Intense emotions reflected in the story can be safely "confronted without shame" as they are embedded in the narrative but not internalized by the listener. Thus, stories can bring the listener to "the root causes of problems," assist in dealing with many kinds of issues and dilemmas, and "guide [individuals] through subtle stages of emotional development" (Simms, 2009a, p. 7).

OTHER STORYTELLING SKILLS

Simms (2014) identifies the value of face-to-face contact between the storyteller and the listener and attentive preparation of the physical and psychic space before the telling of a story. Whenever possible, there are benefits from *telling* rather than *reading* a story to others because this allows greater spontaneity in delivery as well as eye contact between storyteller and listener. Moreover, it becomes possible to adapt the story to the listener through spontaneous and intuitive improvisation. We may wish to be open to story revisions in order to be more sensitive to the unique situation or needs of the listener. For example, in my telling of one of Simms's stories, *The Giant Who Had No Heart* (adapted from a traditional fairytale and rewritten by Laura Simms, in Simms, 2009a, pp. 19–22), to one of my counselling clients, I adapted it by creating metaphors that shed light on a possible prequel or background to the story—*how the giant lost his heart*. In this way we could begin to explore ways in which, when emotionally vulnerable, the heart may shut down in order for us to feel more resilient and what we might do to *wake it up* again.

Mary Louise Chown (2011), an artist and storyteller in Winnipeg, Canada, describes her intuitive approach to working with terminally ill patients in hospital, hospice, and palliative care settings, and provides selected folktales and patients' stories to demonstrate the power of storytelling in these medically oriented settings. She enters into a patient's personal space very gently, with few, if any, preconceived ideas of how her visits will unfold—often with her dulcimer or autoharp. This requires sensitivity to the receptivity of the individual to having a visit and tuning in to the individual's mood and emotional needs in that moment. Chown (2011) describes her visits with two hospice residents as follows:

> Rose and Agnes taught me how to be with someone who is dying. While it might be true that I helped distract them somewhat from their pain, they were guiding me, teaching me how to listen, how to be present for them, putting aside my own ego and any expectations for a particular outcome.

Once this had happened, they were able to show me what they wanted me to do for them. And what they wanted me to do for them was merely to be present, to listen to them, to be curious about them, and then come up with a story, a song, or a poem that was inspired by our conversations. (p. 64)

In this way, patients had the opportunity to not only listen to a story but to reminisce and review their lives, share important memories, tell their own stories, and feel valued and honored at the end of their lives.

Thus, the telling of a story can become a participatory and dynamic process of cocreation that serves to empower the listener. Simms (2014) describes one such occasion, when sharing a story with a group of young children whose comments were integrated into the story:

For me to include everyone signaled to the children the unspoken fact that the most important aspect of the journey was our participation together. For a storyteller, being present to the actuality of the room expands the joy and the focus tremendously. An inner knowing of confidence arises. It is as if they are saying with their continued focus, "I am able to not only learn and participate, but influence the things that happen in my life." There is a combination of discipline and spontaneity that colors the storyteller moving it from the territory of text into a living art. (See http://www.laurasimms.com/2014/08/31/fieldnote-1-telling-young-children/#sthash.qWPOBOaH.dpuf)

Simms (2014) also emphasizes that working with groups of youth or adults who have experienced conflict and trauma requires a skilful storyteller who is able to create a safe group atmosphere that supports respectful and active listening. The storyteller sets and sustains the tone of the group experience, intuitively using story and inviting the voices of participants—all the while holding the vibration of stories told at the level of *sacred* and *mythical*. In this way, participants are not retraumatized in the process and are able to feel heard and validated while also developing empathy for others. This experience can contribute to catharsis, involving an emotional release or a change in perspective. Storytelling is widely used by professionals and nonprofessionals alike for personal and collective growth and healing with young and old experiencing a wide range of life transitions and traumas (see Resources section at the end of this chapter).

EMERGENCE OF POETRY THERAPY AND INTEGRATION INTO SOCIAL WORK PRACTICE

Poetry and metaphor have to some extent been valued in the practice of social work since its beginnings in the settlement movement with Jane Addams

(Getzel, 1983), and Mary Richmond (1930) and the Charity Organization Society. However, it was not until the mid-20th century, when *poetry therapy* became more established in psychotherapeutic disciplines, that it was more consciously adopted within the field of family social work (Mazza, 1996). It is important to clarify at this point that the term *poetry therapy* does not refer exclusively to poetry but includes various forms of story and writing—the essence of which is the use of metaphor.

A significant portion of the theoretical foundation for the use of poetry, story, and writing in therapy is drawn from psychoanalytic theory, with reference to Freud and Jung, as well as Adlerian, Gestalt, and psychodramatic theories. The resonance between poetry therapy and psychotherapy was attributed to the significant role of symbol and metaphor in each modality. However, while Freud had been concerned with the pathology that may lie beneath the symbols and metaphors used by his patients, Jung—highly regarded in the expressive arts community today—saw these as having emerged from an innate creativity within each individual, a dramatically different foundational premise (Mazza, 2003).

It was in 1963 that Eli Greifer, an American who played a key role in the development of poetry therapy, published a pamphlet called *Principles of Poetry Therapy* and laid the foundation for further development of this work (see https://poetrytherapy.org/index.php/about-napt/history-of-napt/). Formal recognition of poetry therapy was further achieved with the establishment of the Association of Poetry Therapy (APT) in 1969, which in 1981 became incorporated as the National Association of Poetry Therapy (NAPT, http://www.poetrytherapy.org). By this time, many of the professionals using poetry and story included psychotherapists, social workers, and counselors. Though it has received increased attention in family practice with the emergence of narrative approaches and constructivist theory, which holds that through experience, reflection, and meaning-making, people construct their own interpretation and understanding of the world, the application of story and poetry is increasingly seen in all forms of social work practice, including that directed at social change, as well as social work education and research.

Nicholas Mazza is a contemporary social work scholar, poet, and registered poetry therapist who has written extensively about the application of poetry therapy in social work practice and research from 1979 to the present. He describes poetry therapy as follows:

Poetry can be defined with respect to literary genre or the qualities or aspects of language that create an emotional response. The emphasis is on evocative language. Poetry therapy involves the use of the language arts in therapeutic capacities. In addition to the clinical use of pre-existing poems in various modalities, the purview of poetry therapy includes bibliotherapy, narrative psychology, metaphor, storytelling, and journal writing. (Mazza, 1993, cited in Mazza, 2003, Introduction, p. xvii)

Mazza's Multidimensional Poetry Therapy Practice Model

Mazza (2009) promotes the creative use of language, symbol, and story to enhance recognition of the unique histories, contexts, and strengths of individuals, groups, couples, and families, and to facilitate expression, communication, conflict resolution, and meaning-making in a therapeutic setting. He also identifies the value of other "poetic elements" such as "reframing, behavioral enactment, sculpting, music, genograms, scripts, and family drawings" in eliciting creative expression (p. 4).

Mazza (2003, 2009) provides a multidimensional poetry therapy practice model with three distinctive approaches. "Receptive/prescriptive" approaches involve the use of existing poetry that is in resonance with the mood or circumstances of the client and can serve to evoke and validate feelings, promote self-expression, and advance personal and group process, whereas "expressive/prescriptive" approaches involve facilitating the client's own expressive writing in the form of poetry, letters, journaling, or a story (Mazza, 2009, pp. 5–6). Both provide a safe context and structure for the expression of vulnerable feelings. Mazza (2009) further notes that "[p]oetry and other forms of written communication allow the individual to project aspects of self, provide a measure of control, and serve as an emotional safety valve" (p. 6). He provides a few examples of how to stimulate the writing process, such as the use of open-ended sentences or provocative words. When working with couples, families, or groups, the social worker can invite the construction of a collaborative poem where each member adds a line. This potentially allows for the externalization of problems, collaborative problem solving, enhancement of interpersonal relationships, and family or group cohesion. "Symbolic-ceremonial" approaches involve the use of "metaphors, rituals, symbols, storytelling, and performance . . . as a means to deal with life transitions" such as "divorce, geographical relocation, [retirement], death, and loss" (p. 6). Mazza emphasizes the importance of using these methods within the boundaries of one's professional roles and abilities and to be consistent with a professional purpose or plan.

Poetry and Story Approaches and Application in Strengths-Based Social Work Practice

Furman, Downey, Jackson, and Bender (2002) speak to the value of poetry therapy as a *strengths-based* social work approach. Strengths-based approaches are a critical component of social work practice and involve the premise that all individuals have resources and strengths with which to better manage or move beyond the life issues they experience. This shifts attention to client strengths rather than deficits and encourages the development of personal stories that support transformation and growth. Drawing from Cowger and Snively (2002, p. 106), who posit that "[d]eficit, disease and dysfunction metaphors have become deeply rooted in the helping professions, shaping contemporary social work practice through the emphasis on diagnosis and treatment of abnormal and pathological conditions within individuals," Furman et al. (2002) promote the use of strengths-based metaphors in social work practice, with poetry therapy as one way for clients to reauthor their lives by developing alternate metaphors.

To illustrate the strength of this approach, Furman et al. (2002) describe a group poetry process with former patients of a state psychiatric hospital system. This process involved three phases: (1) information on the basics of writing poetry; (2) the reading of existing poetry on themes mutually selected by social worker and clients—themes which fit their circumstances; and (3) reflecting on the poetry read, discussing the readings, writing their own personal poems, and then sharing with the group. The authors note that metaphoric language can help clients more safely discuss issues that are often too painful to address directly. Clients recognized through this process that their marginalized socialization was not primarily linked to mental illness, but rather to the effects of years of institutionalization and loneliness. As a result, clients were able to develop, and identify with, new self-descriptive metaphors; begin to engage in less self-blame; and, increasingly, see themselves as capable of making positive changes in their lives.

Furman et al. (2002) also describe a collaborative poetry writing process that dealt with the issue of fear in a group of war veterans. This elicited discussion about ways of coping with different fears, which fostered group cohesiveness, interdependence, and empathy; the creation of new metaphors; and the exploration of new behaviors in keeping with these metaphors.

The emergence of *found poetry* is worthy of mention, though its use in social work practice is not yet prominent in the literature. Found poetry involves the rearrangement of pre-existing fragments of text found in another primary source, such as words and phrases from a poem, story, media source, or spoken word. The creation of found poetry can be cathartic when experiencing a crisis or life transition. By identifying key words and phrases that resonate with their experience, individuals can produce a poignant expression of their lived experience or even create transformative metaphors that help them to move forward. Found poetry can also be very powerful when done in conjunction with images, for example, in the creation of a collage. It is not only a powerful tool for self-expression, but it can also be a collective expression to promote awareness of social issues. In social work practice, the collaborative poem has been regarded as one form of found poetry (e.g., Furman et al., 2002; Schnekenburger, 2006). In "A Thought Exercise: Thinking Through the Found Poetry of Canadian Abortion Providers," Shaw and Haney (2017) discuss the value and potential role of found poetry in social work practice and research.

The capacity for a skilful poetry intervention to promote honesty, acceptance, empathy, connectedness, and belonging in a group context is also demonstrated by Skudrzyk et al. (2009), with a group of adolescents, in relation to the issue of bullying—specifically, the spreading of rumors through gossip. Not having initially identified the topic for discussion, a counselor read a poem about gossip to the group, entitled *Nobody's Friend* (Anonymous, n.d.). Leaving out lines identifying the term *gossip* itself, the counselor provided a glaring description of gossip with phrases such as "I maim without killing. I break hearts and ruin lives" (Skudrzyk et al., 2009, p. 254). Once group members were able to identify *gossip* and they found that the experience of being the target of gossip, as well as the source of gossip about others, was one they all shared, the facilitator guided them through a process of reflection, discussion, and active listening regarding the feelings engendered as a result of gossip, such as isolation, fear of rejection, anxiety, and depression. This fostered greater mutual understanding and acceptance as well as group cohesion.

In my counseling practice, I am increasingly integrating story and metaphor, which helps to cut through complex client scenarios often trapped in confining thought patterns. In exploring the phenomenon of *emotional shutting down* in particular clients, either due to multiple stressors, crisis, or trauma, I was inspired to write a short story, *The Kingdom That Lost Its Heart*, which metaphorically contextualizes the experience of shutting down and protecting a vulnerable heart at great cost to personal and collective well-being. It also provides a means of transforming that outcome individually and collectively— and waking up the heart. This creative process not only helps me to see, and articulate through a story, the hidden potential within clients to transform their lives despite the apparent hopelessness of their circumstances, but it also provides clients with the important message that their outward presentation is hiding and protecting a vulnerable, though powerful, aspect of their identity that needs to be acknowledged, validated, and reclaimed. This story (see Box 6.1) is also one that lends itself to green social work and the significance of *place*, as it speaks to the interconnectedness of humans with their environment and ecology, the damage done in the absence of the heart, and how to once again awaken the heart individually and collectively to restore humanity and our natural habitat.

Box 6.1

The Kingdom That Lost Its Heart

Inspired by "The Giant Who Had No Heart,"
in *Becoming the World* © 2009 L. Simms
A new story by Elizabeth Krahn

Once upon a time, in a faraway land, was a kingdom of great radiance and beauty. Everyone who passed through the kingdom asked themselves: "What gives this kingdom such beauty?" Some said it was its great wealth, for all of its buildings were made of gold. Others said it was its beautiful mountains, lakes, and forests abounding with wildlife, and the abundance of its crops and orchards. Still others said that they always felt welcomed no matter whom they encountered, for a great spirit of hospitality also abounded in this kingdom. Every day was not only productive in its completion of tasks, responsibilities, and creative ventures, but always closed with feasting and celebration, with story, song, and dance.

Now there lived in this kingdom a young prince who was greatly loved by all. From the time of his birth a special light radiated from him and he was a child of great heart. He basked in the beauty of the kingdom that he would one day rule and serve. He loved every part of it. The only thing that cast a shadow upon his day was when he took part in the hunt to supply wild game for the nightly feast. He found that this was made less painful—it was easier to strike a deer or a rabbit with his arrow—if he removed his heart first and then restored it upon his return to the castle. It became his daily practice to place his heart into a special wooden case that he carefully hid in his bed chamber.

The prince's actions were witnessed by an evil and jealous sorcerer who had been observing the kingdom and searching for a way to rob it of its wealth and beauty. He decided to steal the heart of the prince! So one day, when the prince returned from the hunt, his heart was not where he had left it. He sought high and low for his heart, but it was nowhere to be found. The sorcerer, very pleased with his own ingenuity, appeared to the prince in a dream as a wise seer and provided him with false instructions to find his stolen heart. Leaving the kingdom at once, the prince began a long and desolate journey to find his heart.

But this was not the end of the sorcerer's evil trickery. A master of disguises, he adopted the appearance of the young prince—and no one realized that the prince had actually left. However, since the sorcerer was not that interested in the prince's heart, he wore it only rarely. Thus, it soon became possible to also steal the hearts of the king and queen, who began to yearn for their radiant young prince, who was no longer the shining light that he had once been.

And so the sorcerer came to rule the kingdom. He continued to wear the prince's heart only for certain occasions when it served to provide him with the charisma and charm he needed to tolerate, and in turn be tolerated by, those he ruled, who, after all, kept things going. However, under his rule, the kingdom lost its radiance as the sorcerer confiscated all of the gold from people's homes to fulfil his own desires; the mountains, forests, and lakes lost their beauty and wildlife; crops and orchards lost their abundance; and the spirit of hospitality, with its feasting, stories, and celebration, all but disappeared as more and more hearts were lost. Travelers no longer visited the kingdom, and many who had lived there for generations left in search of their hearts.

In the meantime, the young prince became more and more desolate and utterly lost without his heart. No matter where he went, he found only waste and emptiness. Finally, he could no longer call up the will or the energy to carry on. Ready to give up his search, he stopped at a dreary looking place where the sun never shone. "Why bother going any further when nothing I have encountered so far has brought me any happiness or even solace?" he thought.

He had found a complete wasteland. What appeared to have once been a prosperous kingdom was now laid bare. As he made his way through the winding streets, he found not a soul, nor did he spot any living creature or anything green as even the heart of the land itself had stopped beating. After some time, he came upon an old castle and entered—empty, like everything else he had seen. Making his way through the castle, he came upon the royal bed chamber and, exhausted, fell into a deep sleep. Upon awakening, and gazing solemnly around the room, a beam of sunlight suddenly broke through the heavily clouded sky. As it shone through the window, its ray fell upon a lonely wooden case he had not yet noticed. He opened it with trembling hands and found within it his own heart that he had been seeking for what seemed an eternity. It was still beating, though faintly. With great care and reverence, he placed it inside his chest and began to feel, with every beat, more and more alive and restored—though this was seasoned by the emotional weight and wisdom of his experience.

With his newfound wisdom, he knew exactly what he must do. He made himself a drum and began to beat on this drum slowly and rhythmically for days, weeks, and possibly months, without pause. With every beat of his heart and every beat of the drum, the heart of the land began to awaken. At first, the perpetually gray sky erupted into a gigantic thunder and rainstorm that lasted until all of the dried-up creek, river, and lake beds were replenished. As the prince continued to beat his drum, the land began to sprout new growth until, soon, it was flourishing with every variety of tree, grain, and produce you can think of. This was quickly followed by an abundance and diversity of animals.

But he kept on beating his drum and, as he did so, its intensity only increased and the beating of his own heart strengthened even more.

The beating was so powerful that it could be heard far and wide and those who had left the kingdom either with broken hearts or in search of stolen hearts recognized the beat. As they returned one by one, each constructed his or her own drum and formed in a circle with the prince—all beating in unison. Soon there was great singing and dancing and feasting, and many healing stories were told about the kingdom that lost its heart and how it had been restored—one by one and altogether. Each person had his or her own unique story to share, and each listened with great admiration and respect as stories were told. The prince vowed never to remove his heart again—to approach each and every act of living with his heart, mind, and body working in harmony, as did everyone in the circle. Thus, the power of the drum, the restored hearts of the people, and the healing stories told vanquished whatever was left of the sorcerer's legacy of destruction and despair. The circle grew bigger and bigger, and it has never stopped growing since that day.

Expressive Writing for Personal Healing and Social Change in Social Work Practice

In addition to poetry, expressive writing can take many forms, including journaling, diaries, or memoirs. James Pennebaker has been a prominent advocate of expressive writing as a tool for healing, whether in a counseling setting or as a self-help practice, and has written extensively about the cathartic benefits of writing in relation to emotional, mental, and physical health, including recovery from trauma (e.g., Pennebaker, 1989, 2000, 2010; Pennebaker & Chung, 2011; Pennebaker & Smyth, 2016). DeSalvo (2000) also speaks to the ability of the creative writing process to release emotions that have posed a barrier to mental health and to support increased understanding, personal growth, and the ability to adopt new perspectives.

In his practical guide to expressive writing for therapists and counselors, Pennebaker (2010) provides key elements of the expressive writing process. For example, clients may be asked to write for a minimum of 15 minutes on at least three occasions to see if writing is a fit for them. They are asked to write about what is troubling them versus what the counselor may feel is troubling them, and they are encouraged to write continuously without concerning themselves with editing. Pennebaker advises that the actual written material is best not shared with the therapist or the group because any pressure to do so may increase client stress and be counterproductive. Rather, he suggests that, if the client is ready to share, he or she should be encouraged to do so orally because this provides the opportunity to revise the narrative in order to remain within safe emotional parameters. For the counselor who may wish to use writing as a therapeutic tool with clients who have experienced trauma, it is critical to be adequately educated in the use of this method, as its unskilful use may be detrimental to the well-being of the client (Pennebaker, 2010).

Tilly and Caye (2005) describe the use of writing and poetry with a small group of low-income women parenting sexually abused children—an educational group process led by a child therapist and a parenting social worker who invited a local writer to provide writing classes. Based on the work of Pennebaker (1990) and DeSalvo (1999), women were encouraged to write about trauma and to connect with their feelings as they wrote. Tilly and Caye (2005) offer in their appendix a list of receptive/prescriptive writings that resonated with the women's state of mind and need for acceptance and understanding, and a list of writing prompts, such as "When we speak of friends, as we do tonight, what stories come to your mind about friends? Good friendships are based on trust. Have you lost or found a friend through distrust or trust? Tell us about them" (p. 141). Social workers observed that adding writing to the group process enabled women to more deeply access their feelings, reduce anxious feelings, and have greater clarity of thought. This in some cases led to more constructive problem-solving and parenting skills.

The capacity of the writing process to promote catharsis is also demonstrated in the work of Schnekenburger (2006), a clinical social worker who led a weekly writing group with chronically mentally ill adults in a residential mental health setting for 7 months. Schnekenburger describes the residents as having had "impenetrable shields" at the start of this group process (p. 151). When asked to state their names and a self-descriptive adjective, one woman said, "The End," explaining that medications rendered her incapable of doing things anymore and that her life was over (p. 153). Despite tremendous initial resistance to personal disclosure, the group was eventually able to create collaborative poems when Schnekenburger began to use music, photographs, flowers, rocks, seashells, and colors to stimulate their imagination and senses, which, in turn, evoked deeper feelings and expression. Although one resident spoke little English, was deemed illiterate by other staff and thus an unlikely candidate for the writing group, and sat in silence in the residence much of the time, she was attracted to the energy of the writers' group and began to make spoken contributions to collaborative poems, which Schnekenburger translated. When group members were invited to *paint a picture* of the group with words, this woman enthusiastically contributed the first line: "Waking the heart up" (p. 168). The collaborative writing process promoted growing confidence, self-expression, and meaningful relationships between group members. Furthermore, despite a pervasive belief within the mental health system that these facility residents were the lowest functioning, and thus unable to participate in community programs, the writers' group eagerly submitted poetry to, and attended, a community mental health forum where it received honorable mention. This public recognition did much to alter their confidence and sense of self as individuals and a group.

Cohen and Mullender (1999) describe a poetry group in a service center for homeless and low-income adults that focused not only on personal self-expression within the group but also on organizing readings for the public in order to counter negative stereotypes about homelessness and, thus, promote social change.

STORY AND WRITING AS A TOOL FOR CRITICAL REFLECTION IN SOCIAL WORK PRACTICE AND EDUCATION

Expressive writing is a means by which social workers can process practice experiences and engage in reflection and critical analysis to support personal and professional development. A self-reflexive process as students and practitioners reinforces self-awareness, for example, of unconscious biases and assumptions we may have in relation to the clients we serve. Moreover, the use of poetry and other forms of narrative expression by our clients may uncover hidden stories in oral or written form that may otherwise not have been expressed. Expressive narrative tools have the capacity to sensitize us to the experiences and meaning-making of those we serve, heighten awareness of ethical dilemmas in practice settings, and increase understanding and empathy (e.g., Furman, 2005; Mazza, 1998).

In her role as social work practice instructor, Gold (2012) assigned the reading of memoirs or narratives, written by service recipients who had personally struggled with physical and mental health problems, as a complement to the professional discourse found in social work journals and textbooks. Additionally, in a series of hospital-based seminars for social work practicum students, personal narratives, short stories, and poetry written by both clients and practitioners were used to encourage reflection and dialogue. The seminar was structured so that students read the text aloud and explored a range of meanings and implications for practice.

Another undergraduate social work program offered a human behavior course in which 63 students were paired with older adults in an intergenerational oral history project designed to contextualize human behavior in the social environment (HBSE) theories and concepts (Ames & Diepstra, 2006). As Martin (1995) suggests: "[T]he value of oral history goes beyond gathering facts. It allows individuals and families to ascribe meanings to those events," thus providing social workers with a better grasp of the personal needs and social issues often faced by oppressed individuals and/or groups (p. 8). She adds that oral history is particularly useful in the integration of humanistic values and cites Bennett (1983), who notes that the language of oral history, which includes the meanings individuals ascribe to their experiences, can cross social barriers. Martin likens the social worker to a "midwife," who, in the process of engaging clients in an oral history process, may act as a "bridge between the problems social workers and their clients seek to confront and the clients' own solutions" (p. 9). She also suggests that oral histories conducted with individuals whose functioning is nonproblematic can be beneficial because they provide valuable knowledge for practice with those who do require assistance and supports.

The use of creative writing by social workers to process difficult experiences is demonstrated in a self-published book by David Baxter (2011) called *Emerging*. Based on his experience as an on-call mental health social worker dealing with critical incidents in a hospital emergency ward, Baxter shares poetry written in his retirement—poetry that reflects his process of healing from the crises he has witnessed—and offers critical reflection and poetic analysis of professional and ethical issues one faces in the field. In "One More Time" (pp. 28–29), Baxter describes "Doug," a man with addictions issues who frequently presents in the emergency ward, as "being on the frequent flyer program." Doug is likened to "a giant fir tree" facing "an impending fall" because "[h]is usual meal of booze and drugs [is] beginning to work against his weakened heart." The life and death of a tree is a strong metaphor in this poem. Doug's thick file is described as having "cost the lives of several trees." Baxter makes it clear in the poem that Doug is not a cooperative patient. Rather than graciously accepting the doctor's care, he is "[g]oin fur a smoke . . . [sic]," which brings to mind a tree at risk of burning down. When Doug's physical strength finally falters and the doctor is able to attend to his medical needs without Doug's resistance, his heart stops and medical technology is speedily put into high gear to restore life. Baxter's assessment is that "the prevailing sentiment" of other staff present is to silently query if medical intervention at this point may be "invasive." Would it be more humane to "[l]et the poor guy go[?]" After 6 hours Doug is released from hospital and "never seen again." Baxter appears to allude to a stark contrast between the mandated medical and the mandated social care of people: "Docs, bless their souls, are there to preserve life." On the other hand, social and mental health supports and services, also critical for preservation and *quality* of life, are highly underresourced in our society, resulting in the lack of adequate humane and practical supports and the marginalization of those requiring these services.

Narrative Therapy: The Art of Reauthoring One's Story
Narrative therapy, under the leadership of Michael White and David Epston (1990), is rooted in social constructionism. It focuses on the desconstruction of oppressive stories and construction of liberating and legitimizing ones that have the power to change and transform one's lived reality (Brown & Augusta-Scott, 2007). Narrative metaphor lies at the center of this process and highlights the

premise that all people live storied lives and strive to derive meaning and sense out of their lived experience (White & Epston, 1990). At the foundation of this premise is the notion that the analogies or metaphors we use determine our examination of the world and the realities we construct. Influenced by Foucault's critique of politically legitimized institutions and dominant societal discourses that often judge, categorize, and pathologize individuals on the basis of "expert knowledge" (Foucault, 1980; Nichols & Schwartz, 2007, p. 267), White and Epston (1990) recognized that dominant constructs, discourses, and illness metaphors have the potential to restrict the possibility of positive outcomes for individuals who are problematized.

Narrative therapy thus focuses on *externalizing* the problem so that the individual no longer self-identifies as the problem, seeking positive storylines in the individual's life history that are not in keeping with the *problem-saturated* story, and strengthening these positive storylines to create a new narrative—to reauthor the story. As this new narrative is *thickened*, individuals outside the therapeutic relationship may be recruited to bear witness to the conversation between client and therapist and, thus, validate the individual and strengthen the alternate story (Abels & Abels, 2001; White & Epston, 1990). "As people begin to inhabit and live out the alternative stories, the results are beyond solving problems. Within the new stories, people live out new self-images, new possibilities for relationships and new futures" (Freedman & Combs, 1996, p. 16).

Narrative approaches have been used widely with individuals, families, groups, and communities experiencing a wide range of issues from personal to political. In her role as facilitator of an AIDS support group, Dean (1998) demonstrates how narrative approaches, as established by White and Epston (1990), can be used in a group work context to "create meaning, organize the past, explain the present and consider alternatives for the future" (Dean, 1998, p. 23). Narrative therapy principles and strategies are integrated with group work process to cocreate new stories and meanings within the group context.

Narrative therapy can find a compatible fit with other expressive art forms. For example, Caldwell (2005) advances the integration of narrative therapy principles and strategies with activities such as journaling, videography, and the making of memory books, self boxes, life maps, and time capsules to facilitate the life review process. Working with both the older adult and family members, the counselor engages the family in a collaborative process of creative meaning-making which assists in the deconstruction of problem stories and the coconstruction of stories of resilience. The coproduction of these material representations anchors a life story with tangible objects, images, text, and voice, and it can provide a valuable source of comfort and memory to an older adult, who may be cognitively impaired, and to the family as a whole. This can also be a wonderful way of strengthening intergenerational family bonds.

Gilbert and Beidler (2001) describe narrative therapy approaches in groups for chemically dependent mothers who are residents at an addictions treatment center. Identification with a problem-saturated life of addiction had obscured a deeper sense of self and personal agency to create life change. Arriving at the point where a woman could tell her story and feel heard, validated, and acknowledged was an empowering experience, and each *telling* invoked resonance within other group members, who then reflected their thoughts back to the teller. Daily group experiences provided the opportunity to anchor new self-perceptions and stories, and to rebuild a new identity as a woman without a dependency. Women's stories were also elicited with the aid of puppets that served to represent a woman's life, externalize the addiction, and create numerous story versions about the relationship between the woman and the addiction. Group members participated in these stories, as appropriate, to expand on possible meanings and outcomes.

Narrative approaches also have the capacity to support healing and transformation in the context of larger collective issues, as in Canada's Truth and Reconciliation initiative to witness the Indigenous voices of Canadian residential school survivors (e.g., Younging, Dewar, & DeGagne, 2009); the work of the National Survivors' Association in Rwanda with Tutsi survivors of genocide to strengthen their resistance to the effects of trauma, reclaim their lives and future, and rebuild community (Denborough, Freedman, & White, 2008); and the use of transformative metaphors to elicit stories of resilience with African children orphaned by the invasion of AIDS (Ncube, 2006).

DIGITAL STORYTELLING

With the rise of computer technology, we have also seen the emergence of digital storytelling (DST), which involves the integration of text with sound, video, and still images to create short but poignant visual representations of personal narratives (Couldry, 2008). Joe Lambert (2013), cofounder of the Center for Digital Storytelling (CDS) in Berkeley, California, speaks of the history and vision behind digital storytelling and provides a detailed approach and methodology for the production of dynamic visual narratives. Since 1998, CDS's mission has been to "promote the value of story as a means for compassionate community action," and it has offered "storytelling for professional development, as a reflective practice, as a pedagogical strategy, or as a vehicle for education, community mobilization, or advocacy" on an international scale (Center for Digital Storytelling, http://storycenter.org/). DST is a powerful tool for social change because it provides a means for ordinary individuals to share otherwise marginalized stories in the public domain (such as social media or other community contexts), where they become accessible to a wider audience, thus balancing the playing field in a social climate where such stories would ordinarily not find either a venue or an audience. For examples of case studies with marginalized populations in various parts of the world, where DST is used as a means of educating an international audience, see https://www.storycenter.org/ss-case-studies.

Lenette, Cox, and Brough (2015) promote DST as a useful tool in social work practice. In their research with women from refugee backgrounds, DST provided an opportunity for women to produce powerful and evocative counternarratives to the dominant discourse on the refugee experience. The authors conclude that DST can become a tool for social advocacy to influence policy and practice at a broader political level and also explore ethical considerations.

DST has become a powerful tool in some social work practice contexts because of this capacity to support social work's strong social justice focus. The National Resource Center for Permanency and Family Connections at Hunter College's School of Social Work in New York City, in conjunction with other stakeholders, uses DST as a therapeutic, educational, and advocacy tool to promote improvement in the delivery of child welfare services. This has included the use of digital stories to educate legislators, judges, judicial district staff, and other stakeholders about issues and challenges experienced during legal representation in child protection cases (see the National Resource Center for Permanency and Family Connections [NRCPFC] website at http://www.nrcpfc.org/digital_stories/; also see http://www.nrcpfc.org/digital_stories/about_us.htm and http://www.hunter.cuny.edu/socwork/nrcfcpp/pass/digital-stories/index.htm).

NARRATIVE, STORY, POETRY AS SOCIAL WORK RESEARCH METHOD

Arts-based narrative expression in the form of story and poetry is finding more of a place in qualitative research methodology. According to Leavy (2009, p. 255), "the arts have the capability to evoke emotions, promote reflection, and transform the way that people think in a more powerful way than traditional qualitative research alone." In relying on metaphor, symbolism, and imagination, says Leavy, arts-based research provides representations of marginalized stories that carry authenticity and are compelling and consciousness raising. This elicits understanding and empathy not only for the individual as an isolated entity but for the individual within a social and political context, which may reveal ethical issues, social injustices, and the necessity for individual intervention *and* social change.

There is growing recognition of the relevance of creative narrative method in social work research (Phillips, MacGiollari, & Callaghan, 2012; Riessman & Quinney, 2005). According to Riessman and Quinney (2005), narrative research explores *how* and *why* individuals story their lived experience and the role of meaning-making in this process, not merely narrative content. Within the context of social work, it often involves analysis of self-narratives of individuals who may be in care or otherwise marginalized. There is also increasing evidence of the researcher bringing his or her self, and creative reflection, into the research. This offers authenticity that is more likely to engage and persuade social work students, faculty, and practicing social workers; professionals from other disciplines; or policymakers about the issues being explored.

Tay-Lim and Lim (2013) highlight the value of eliciting children's voices in social research and regarding children as "expert informants about their own lives" (p. 11). In a social work pilot project exploring a creative approach to hearing the stories of young children, D'Cruz and Stagnitti (2010) asked a small group of 6- to 8-year-old children from stable middle-class families to share, through text and drawings, "what it meant for them when parents love and care for their children, and when they do not" (p. 216). They conclude that their study contributes a valuable approach to seeking the perspectives of children about decisions relating to their welfare and can improve social work practice with children.

In exploring experiences of poor working-class mothers and the effectiveness of existing local programs, Foster (2012) uses poetry as a social research method. Some poems produced by women who were part of the research process are discussed and offer insights that provide a counternarrative which challenges dominant ideologies about oppressed people.

In poetic inquiry methods, found poetry is described as a means of working with data in which words from qualitative research interviews are selected and arranged into poems (Butler-Kisber, 2010). Butler-Kisber (2010) identifies Laurel Richardson, a well-known qualitative researcher, as a pioneer in the use of poetry in research who views poetic representation of research data as a way of making research accessible to a wider audience. A researcher-poet can draw from interview transcripts and involve study participants in creating poetry to represent important themes in study findings. Sjollema, Hordyk, Walsh, Hanley, and Ives (2012) use found poetry to examine and more powerfully represent the voices of immigrant women experiencing housing issues and homelessness in Montreal, Canada. The authors identified significant themes that emerged from interviews with women and then selected poignant words and phrases in keeping with these themes, rearranging them into a poetic form without altering the actual words, and attempting to remain true to the interviewee's unique affect and expression.

Using an autoethnographic methodology where the researcher is also being researched in relation to a larger social phenomenon, Gallardo, Furman, and Kulkarni (2009) explore, through self-reflection, the experience of depression by using poetry and narrative. For my MSW thesis, I used autoethnography to explore, from the vantage point of an *insider* (member of the community under investigation) and an *outsider* (social worker and researcher), the life span and intergenerational experiences, stories, and meaning-making of Mennonite women— who during World War II had fled political oppression in Soviet Russia—and adult children of this generation of women born postmigration in Canada (Krahn, 2013). Integrating the voices of each generation to produce two representational collective stories provided insights into the emotional and/or mental health needs of aging refugees and their adult children, who vicariously experienced effects of their parents' traumatic history. In addition to political oppression and war itself, trauma was also related to loss of homeland and subsequent lifelong separation from family and closely knit community members who had either perished or had been subjected to internal displacement to northern regions of the Soviet Union. In the case of adult children, who had often lived in the shadow of their parents' more dominant story of survival, reading their own collective story helped them to depersonalize or externalize life issues that were clearly related to vicarious trauma mutually experienced by their generational cohort. In the case of mother–child dyads where reading each other's collective story was possible, this contributed to deeper intergenerational understanding and/or catharsis.

Based on her experience as a social worker in an emergency and trauma department of a Canadian acute care hospital, Phillips (2007) uses creative writing to provide a subjective account of patient pain and its treatment. Distressed by the medicalization of pain and death, and the power relations in hospital settings that confine social work practice within medical parameters, she presents an alternate discourse on the cultural experience of pain to counter that of the medical chart. She argues that "[a]rts-based methods allow us another way 'into our work,' into conversations of power and the dialogic relations of social work practice." She adds, "It is with such detailed imagination that social workers can consider how to place themselves in relation to acts of power" (p. 200). Phillips believes this is a critical discussion for social workers who wish to pursue social justice in social-clinical care.

There has been an increase in arts-based research methods with Indigenous peoples that incorporate a more collaborative research process, including joint ownership and traditional Indigenous ways of knowing and communicating through story, which more poignantly reflect their needs and values (e.g., Clark et al., 2009; Hart, 2010; Kendall, Marshall, & Barlow, 2013; Transken, 2005). Kendall et al. (2013) reflect on the Western preference for the written word versus other forms of communication, and they quote Ittelson (2007):

The constant obeisance that academics pay at the altar of language may represent an occupational blindness. Written language, in all of its many forms . . . rests firmly on the foundation of the visual arts, and the visual arts, historically and contemporaneously, play an equally large and important role in communicating, recording and analyzing information. (p. 281)

Visual art, storytelling, and other traditional Indigenous practices were strong components of their research process, which explored gaps in health care services to Indigenous peoples in Australia.

Likewise, Clark et al. (2009) used a collaborative approach that involved a participatory action research partnership of Elders, an urban Aboriginal community health and social services agency, Aboriginal university faculty, non-Aboriginal faculty, and research participants to develop culturally safe best practices in social work and human service field education in Aboriginal community health settings in British Columbia, Canada. During this process, issues of power, trust, and relationship related to colonization and its consequences were addressed. This involved mutual storytelling, bridging, and colearning, and acknowledged the value of talking circles, storytelling, and music as traditional ways that lend themselves to research.

CONCLUDING THOUGHTS

There has been an evolution in the art of using story to engage with growing individual and social issues. Storytelling in its many forms—poetry, expressive writing, and other creative narrative expression—can be successfully integrated into strengths-based social work practice with individuals, groups, and/or communities to promote individual growth and social change, and an essential component of this work is the identification of more life-giving and transformative metaphors that help clients to reframe and restory their lives. Social workers' reflexivity in relation to clients' personal stories and meaning-making about their lived experiences is also gaining prominence in social work education and research. Not only do narrative approaches have the capacity to support emotional release, catharsis, and empowerment in recipients of service, but they also have the capacity to deepen the sense of connection between client and professional. In instances where these otherwise marginalized voices are also brought to a wider audience, professional, political, and public awareness and grasp of critical individual and social issues can potentially be heightened in order to strengthen counternarratives that contextualize and respect rather than individualize, pathologize, and stigmatize the needs of individuals and, hopefully, promote more supportive, just, and transformative social institutions and services.

QUESTIONS FOR REFLECTION AND SUGGESTED ACTIVITIES

1. Reflect on the purpose, value, and use of metaphor in all the narrative forms described in this chapter (e.g., strengths-based, transformational, restorying, and reauthoring metaphors versus deficit or illness metaphors) and how you might apply this in your chosen area of practice.

2. Select an actual or fictitious client scenario and seek a metaphor that lies within the problem narrative. How can the client be persuaded to transform that metaphor into something more hopeful and transformative? Find a short story or poem—or write one—that resonates with the emotional impact of the client's story and includes a transformative element.

3. Select a particular aspect of your life that is troubling you and devote a minimum of 15 minutes on at least three separate occasions during a 1- or 2-week span of time to engage in expressive writing. Without planning what you wish to write, and as soon as your pen touches the paper or your fingers hit the keys, continue writing nonstop and refrain from thinking, evaluation, editing, or revision. Reflect on your experience and any insights gained.

RESOURCES

Digital Storytelling

For information about the origins, value, and purpose of digital storytelling; training and workshops; and/or digital stories see the following websites:

CANADA

Community Works, Winnipeg and Toronto: http://www.community-works.ca/digital-stories

North York Community House: https://www.nych.ca/digital-stories

Toronto Centre for Community Learning and Development—Digital Storytelling Toronto: http://www.tccld.org/programs/digital-storytelling/

Youth by Youth: Digital Storytelling Project: http://ucalgarycares.com/category/reading-week-2014/digital-stories/

UNITED STATES

Center for Digital Storytelling, Berkeley: http://storycenter.org/

Small Moments, Big Stories: Forensic Nurses Make Digital Stories—made in collaboration with The Center for Digital Storytelling and International Association of Forensic Nurses (www.iafn.org) © 2010 Seedworks Films (www.seedworksfilms.org).

An excellent short documentary illustrating a reflective group process to support the production of individual digital stories about one's experience in this very challenging field. Important themes relevant and applicable to social workers: https://www.storycenter.org/nurstory/

Silence Speaks: https://www.storycenter.org/ss-case-studies https://www.storycenter.org/case-studies/christensen

Empower: Digital Storytelling and Youth: http://www.empoweryouth.info/our-projects/our-stories/

Expressive Writing

Center for Journal Therapy: www.journaltherapy.com

James Pennebaker, Writing and Health: Some Practical Advice.

Also includes some references for writing, journaling, or diaries: https://liberalarts.utexas.edu/psychology/faculty/pennebak#writing-health

Pennebaker, J. W. The Expressive Writing Method: https://www.youtube.com/watch?v=XsHIV9PxAV4

Narrative Therapy

The following websites provide information on narrative therapy with individuals, families, and communities; educational programs and workshops; journals, articles, and resources; projects; and online stories or therapeutic conversations demonstrating narrative therapy in action:

Dulwich Centre (Australia): http://www.dulwichcentre.com.au/

Narrative Approaches (David Epston, New Zealand): http://www.narrativeapproaches.com

Narrative Therapy Centre of Toronto: http://www.narrativetherapycentre.com/index.html

Poetry

Journal of Poetry Therapy: The Interdisciplinary Journal of Practice, Theory, Research, and Education: http://www.tandf.co.uk/journals/titles/08893675.asp and http://www.tandfonline.com/action/journalInformation?show=aimsScope&journalCode=tjpt20

National Association for Poetry Therapy (Washington, DC)—Promoting Growth and Healing Through Language, Symbol, and Story: http://poetrytherapy.org/ and http://poetrytherapy.org/index.php/journal-of-poetry-therapy/

Youth UpRising: Poetry & Prison Project:
Spoken word by Dre of Hi-Decibels: called "Through the Rain."
http://www.youtube.com/watch?v=eD1B49WK4bQ&feature=relmfu

Storytelling

See the following websites for storytelling workshops, information, and/or resources, including stories, storytellers, journals or newsletters, and journal articles on the benefits of storytelling.

CANADA

Arts Health Network Canada (AHNC): http://artshealthnetwork.ca/

International Storytelling Festival, an annual event organized by the University of Manitoba's Arthur V. Mauro Centre for Peace and Justice: https://umanitoba.ca/colleges/st_pauls/mauro_centre/events/1083.html

Manitoba Storytellers' Guild: http://manitobastorytelling.org/

Storytellers of Canada/Conteurs Du Canada: http://www.storytellers-conteurs.ca/

UNITED STATES

The Healing Story Alliance: http://healingstory.org/

Laura Simms: http://www.laurasimms.com/

National Storytelling Network: http://www.storynet.org/
http://www.storynet-advocacy.org/news/edu.shtml

REFERENCES

Abels, P., & Abels, S. (2001). *Understanding narrative therapy: A guidebook for the social worker.* New York, NY: Springer.

Ames, N., & Diepstra, S. A. (2006). Using intergenerational oral history service-learning projects to teach human behavior concepts: A qualitative analysis. *Educational Gerontology, 32,* 121–135.

Anonymous (n.d.). "Nobody's friend." No source provided; for a similar online version of this poem, google the words: *Nobody's Friend* and *Gossip.*

Baxter, D. (2011). One more time. In D. Baxter (Ed.), *Emerging* (pp. 28–29). Salmon Arm, BC: PetalPress.

Beah, I. (2007). *A long way gone: Memories of a boy soldier.* Vancouver/Toronto: Douglas & McIntyre.

Bennett, J. (1983). Human values in oral history. *The Oral History Review, 2,* 1–15.

Brown, C., & Augusta-Scott, T. (2007). *Narrative therapy: Making meaning, making lives.* Thousand Oaks, CA: Sage.

Butler-Kisber, L. (2010). *Qualitative inquiry: Thematic, narrative and arts-informed perspectives.* London, UK: Sage.

Caldwell, R. L. (2005). At the confluence of memory and meaning—life review with older adults and families: Using narrative therapy and the expressive arts to remember and re-author stories of resilience. *The Family Journal: Counseling and Therapy for Couples and Families, 13*(2), 172–175.

Chown, M. L. (2011). *Now I know the world is round: Stories at the end of life.* Winnipeg, MB: ArtBookBindery.

Clark, N., Drolet, J., Arnouse, M., Tamburo, P. R., Mathews, N., Derrick, J., Michaud, V., & Armstrong, J. (2009). "Melq'ilwiye" Coming together in an intersectional research team—Using narratives and cultural safety to transform aboriginal social work and human service field education. *Pimatisiwin: A Journal of Aboriginal and Indigenous Community Health, 7*(2), 291–315.

Cohen, M. B., & Mullender, A. (1999). The personal in the political: Exploring the group work continuum from individual to social change goals. *Social Work With Groups, 22*(1), 13–31.

Couldry, N. (2008). Mediatization or mediation? Alternative understandings of the emergent space of digital storytelling. *New Media Society, 10,* 373–391. http://journals.sagepub.com/doi/pdf/10.1177/1461444808089414

Cowger, C. D., & Snively, C. A. (2002). Assessing client strengths: Individual, family and community empowerment. In D. Saleebey (Ed.), *The strengths perspective in social work practice* (3rd ed.). Boston, MA: Allyn and Bacon.

D'Cruz, H., & Stagnitti, K. (2010). When parents love and don't love their children: Some children's stories. *Child and Family Social Work, 15,* 216–225. doi:10.1111/j.1365-2206.2009.00662.x

Dean, R. G. (1998). A narrative approach to groups. *Clinical Social Work Journal, 26*(1), 23–37.

Denborough, D., Freedman, J., & White, C. (2008). *Strengthening resistance: The use of narrative practices in working with genocide survivors.* A workshop facilitated for Ibuka: The National Survivors' Association in Rwanda. Adelaide, Australia: Dulwich Centre Foundation.

DeSalvo, L. (1999). *Writing as a way of healing.* Boston, MA: Beacon Press.

DeSalvo, L. (2000). *Writing as a way of healing: How telling our stories transforms our lives.* Boston, MA: Beacon Press.

Foster, V. (2012). What if? The use of poetry to promote social justice. *Social Work Education, 31*(6), 742–755.

Foucault, M. (1980). *Power/knowledge: Selected interviews and other writings 1972–1977.* Edited by Colin Gordon. New York, NY: Pantheon Books.

Freedman, J., & Combs, G. (1996). *Narrative therapy: The social construction of preferred realities.* New York, NY: Norton.

Furman, R. (2005). Using poetry and written exercises to teach empathy. *Journal of Poetry Therapy, 18*(2), 103–110.

Furman, R., Downey, E. P., Jackson, R. L., & Bender, K. (2002). Poetry therapy as a tool for strengths-based practice. *Advances in Social Work, 3,* 146–157.

Gallardo, H. L., Furman, R., & Kulkarni, S. (2009). Explorations of depression: Poetry and narrative in autoethnographic qualitative research. *Qualitative Social Work, 8,* 287. doi:10.1177/1473325009337837

Getzel, G. S. (1983). Poetry writing groups and the elderly: A reconsideration of art and social group work. *Social Work With Groups, 6*(1), 65–76.

Gilbert, M. C., & Beidler, A. E. (2001). Using the narrative approach in groups for chemically dependent mothers. *Social Work With Groups, 24*(3/4), 101–115.

Gold, K. (2012). Poetic pedagogy: A reflection on narrative in social work practice and education. *Social Work Education: The International Journal, 31*(6), 756–763. Special Issue: Arts in Social Work Education.

Greifer, E. (1963). *Principles of poetry therapy.* A pamphlet. New York, NY: published by the author.

Hart, M. A. (2010). Indigenous worldviews, knowledge, and research: The development of an Indigenous research paradigm. *Journal of Indigenous Voices in Social Work, 1*(1), 1–16.

Ittelson, W. H. (2007). The perception of nonmaterial objects and events. *Leonardo, 40*(3), 279–283.

Kendall, E., Marshall, C. A., & Barlow, L. (2013). Stories rather than surveys: A journey of discovery and emancipation. *International Journal of Qualitative Methods (IJQM), 12*, 258–271.

Krahn, E. (2013). Transcending the "Black Raven": An autoethnographic and intergenerational exploration of Stalinist oppression. *Qualitative Sociology Review, 9*(3), 36–73.

Lambert, J. (2013). *Digital storytelling: Capturing lives, creating community* (4th ed.). New York, NY: Routledge.

Leavy, P. (2009). *Method meets art: Arts-based research practice.* New York, NY: Guilford Press.

Lenette, C., Cox, L., & Brough, M. (2015). Digital storytelling as a social work tool: Learning from ethnographic research with women from refugee backgrounds. *The British Journal of Social Work, 45*(3), 988–1005. Retrieved from http://dx.doi.org/10.1093/bjsw/bct184

Martin, R. R. (1995). *Oral history in social work: Research, assessment, and intervention.* Thousand Oaks, CA: Sage.

Mazza, N. (1993). Poetry therapy: Towards a research agenda for the 1990s. *The Arts in Psychotherapy, 20*, 51–59.

Mazza, N. (1996). Poetry therapy: A framework and synthesis of techniques for family social work. *Journal of Family Social Work, 1*(3), 3–18.

Mazza, N. (1998). The place of poetry in gerontological social work education. *Journal of Aging and Identity, 3*(1), 25–34.

Mazza, N. (2003). *Poetry therapy: Theory and practice.* New York, NY: Brunner-Routledge.

Mazza, N. (2009).The arts and family social work: A call for advancing practice, research, and education. *Journal of Family Social Work, 12*, 3–8. doi:10.1080/10522150802383084

Mehl-Madrona, Lewis. (2007). *Narrative medicine: The use of history and story in the healing process.* Rochester, VT: Bear & Company.

Ncube, N. (2006). The Tree of Life Project: Using narrative ideas in work with vulnerable children in Southern Africa. *The International Journal of Narrative Therapy and Community Work, 1*, 3–16.

Nichols, M. P., & Schwartz, R. C. (2007). *The essentials of family therapy* (3rd ed.). Boston, MA: Pearson Education.

Pennebaker, J. W. (1989). Confession, inhibition, and disease. *Advances in Experimental Social Psychology, 22*, 211–240.

Pennebaker, J. W. (1990). *Opening up: The healing power of confiding in others.* New York, NY: Morrow.

Pennebaker, J. W. (2000). The effects of traumatic disclosure on physical and mental health: The values of writing and talking about upsetting events. In J. M. Violanti, D. Paton, & C. Dunning (Eds.), *Post-traumatic stress intervention: Challenges, issues, and perspectives* (pp. 97–114). Springfield, IL: Charles C. Thomas.

Pennebaker, J. W. (2010). Expressive writing in a clinical setting. *The Independent Practitioner, 30*, 23–25.

Pennebaker, J. W., & Chung, C. K. (2011). Expressive writing: Connections to mental and physical health. In H. S. Friedman (Ed.), *Oxford handbook of health psychology* (pp. 417–437). New York, NY: Oxford University Press.

Pennebaker, J. W., & Smyth, J. M. (2016). *Opening up by writing it down: How expressive writing improves health and eases emotional pain.* New York, NY: Guilford Press.

Phillips, C. (2007). Pain[ful] subjects: Regulated bodies in medicine and social work. *Qualitative Social Work, 6*(2), 197–212.

Phillips, J., MacGiollari, D., & Callaghan, S. (2012). Encouraging research in social work: Narrative as the thread integrating education and research in social work. *Social Work Education, 31*, 785–793.

Richmond, M. E. (1930). A plea for poetry. In M. E. Richmond, *The long view: Papers and addresses* (pp. 147–150). New York, NY: Russell Sage Foundation. Retrieved from https://archive.org/details/longviewpapersad00joan

Riessman, C. K., & Quinney, L. (2005). Narrative in social work: A critical review. *Qualitative Social Work, 4*(4), 391–412. doi:10.1177/1473325005058643

Schnekenburger, E. (2006). Waking the heart up: A writing group's story. *Social Work With Groups, 28*(3), 149–171.

Shaw, J., & Haney, C. (2017). A thought exercise: Thinking through the found poetry of Canadian abortion providers. *Journal of Poetry Therapy: The Interdisciplinary Journal of Practice, Theory, Research and Education, 30*(3).

Simms, L. (2002). *The robe of love: Secret instructions from the heart.* New York, NY: Codhill Press.

Simms, L. (2003). The Mother Project: Report for *the Open Society Institute.* Retrieved from http://www.laurasimms.com/wp-content/uploads/2014/02/308edit.pdf

Simms, L. (2009a). *Becoming the world.* A Storytelling Training Program workbook. New York, NY: Laura Simms Productions. See http://www.laurasimms.com/written-word/books/becoming-the-world-2/

Simms, L. (2009b). The Life Force Project: The stories we tell. Retrieved from http://www.laurasimms.com/wp-content/uploads/2012/02/THE-LIFE-FORCE-PROJECT.pdf

Simms, L. (2011a). *Our secret territory: The essence of storytelling.* Boulder, CO: Sentient.

Simms, L. (2011b). Storytelling activity: Peace building and the narrative. Retrieved from http://www.laurasimms.com/making-peace-telling-our-story/ with further description at http://www.laurasimms.com/wp-content/uploads/2012/02/Making-Peace-Telling-Our-Story.pdf

Simms, L. (2014). Storyteller in the field: Fieldnote #1 Telling young children. Retrieved from http://www.laurasimms.com/2014/08/31/fieldnote-1-telling-young-children/

Sjollema, S. D., Hordyk, S., Walsh, C. A., Hanley, J., & Ives, N. (2012). Found poetry—Finding home: A qualitative study of homeless immigrant women. *Journal of Poetry Therapy: The Interdisciplinary Journal of Practice, Theory, Research and Education, 25*(4), 205–217. http://dx.doi.org/10.1080/08893675.2012.736180

Skudrzyk, B., Zera, D. A., McMahon, G., Schmidt, R., Boyne, J., & Spannaus, R. L. (2009). Learning to relate: Interweaving creative approaches in group counseling with adolescents. *Journal of Creativity in Mental Health, 4*(3), 249–261. http://dx.doi.org/10.1080/15401380903192762

Tay-Lim, J., & Lim, S. (2013). Privileging younger children's voices in research: Use of drawings and co-construction process. *International Journal of Qualitative Methods, 12*, 65–83.

Tilly, N., & Caye, J. (2005). Using writing and poetry to achieve focus and depth in a group of women parenting sexually abused children. *Social Work With Groups, 27*(2), 129–142. http://dx.doi.org/10.1300/J009v27n02_09

Transken, S. (2005). Meaning making and methodological explorations: Bringing knowledge from British Columbia's First Nations women poets into social work courses. *Cultural Studies & Critical Methodologies, 5*(1), 3–29.

White, M., & Epston, B. (1990). *A narrative means to therapeutic ends.* New York, NY: Norton.

Younging, G., Dewar, J., & DeGagné, M. (Eds.). (2009). *Response, responsibility, and renewal: Canada's Truth and Reconciliation journey.* Ottawa, Ontario: Aboriginal Healing Foundation. Retrieved from http://www.ahf.ca/downloads/from-truth-to-reconciliation-transforming-the-legacy-of-residential-schools.pdf

7

Singing, Drumming, and Song Stories

Seeking Mino-Pimatisiwin *Through Music*

MARGARET TAMARA DICKS AND DEANA HALONEN

BACKGROUND

This chapter explores the use of music, singing, and drumming for helping and healing. These methods are not new, but they are relatively new to social work practice. Music as a method for healing has been around since time immemorial, within all cultures across the globe. The concept of singer versus nonsinger is a Western phenomenon evolving from Western elitist practices (Dore, Gillett, & Pascal, 2010) that created what Wilken (2005) refers to as the "music-audience dichotomy" (p. 2). Sadly, this dichotomy persists in Western culture, preventing many people from experiencing the benefits of musical participation. Many cultures do not have this belief, and music continues to be integrated into people's day-to-day lives. In Indigenous communities, drumming and singing continue to be important elements of culture, offering connections to the universe and life itself. Music has the ability to evoke deep feeling and affect people's moods, actions, and dreams.

Although music therapy is a young profession built on Western ideals, it is a profession concerned with the healing aspects of music and how music can be used to facilitate healing and wellness. As a profession in Canada, the development of music therapy began in the 1950s with three main players, Fran Herman, Norma Sharpe, and Thérése Pageau. At that time, Herman worked at the Home for Incurable Children in Toronto, Canada. As a music therapist, she has been a tireless advocate of the use of music for those with special needs and became internationally known for her work with children who have muscular dystrophy, cerebral palsy, and other severely physically and, thus, emotionally disabling conditions (Buchanan, 2009). Through her commitment and drive to support these neglected and underresourced children, and to highlight both the needs and the creativity of disabled children in the larger community, Herman developed the first music therapy group project in Canada, known as the Wheelchair Players, a project involving the production of privately and publicly performed musical performances that empowered children to see themselves as more than just their physical disabilities (Buchanan, 2009).

Both Fran Herman and Thérèse Pageau worked toward the development of provincial music therapy associations throughout Canada, Herman in Ontario and Pageau in Quebec (Dibble, 2011). Through her work in organizing music therapy conferences, Norma Sharpe, who was based in Ontario, was instrumental in the development of the Canadian Association of Music Therapy (Dibble, 2011), which was incorporated in 1977 (Kirkland, 2007). Other important figures in the development of music therapy in Canada were Carolyn Kenny and Nancy McMaster, who in 1976 developed the first music therapy training program to be offered in Canada, at Capilano College, North Vancouver (Dibble, 2011).

In the United States, the profession developed in the hospitals utilizing the skills of hospital musicians. Over time, these musicians required more specific training to do their work, and colleges and hospitals began to develop their own training courses and programs (Dibble, 2011). In 1944, the first bachelor of music therapy program was offered at Michigan State College and, in 1948, the first music therapy graduate degree was developed in collaboration with psychiatrist Dr. Ira Altshuler and E. Thayer Gaston (Dibble, 2011). Gaston was considered an important figure in developing the profession further. The National Association of Music Therapy was formed in 1950 and amalgamated with the American Music Therapy Association in 1998 (http://www.musictherapy.org).

The Canadian Association of Music Therapy defines music therapy as follows:

> the skillful use of music and musical elements by an accredited music therapist to promote, maintain, and restore mental, physical, emotional, and spiritual health. Music has nonverbal, creative, structural, and emotional qualities. These are used in the therapeutic relationship to facilitate contact, interaction, self-awareness, learning, self-expression, communication, and personal development. (http://www.musictherapy.ca)

The purpose of this chapter is not to focus on the profession of music therapy per se but rather on the healing role of music and how music relates to social work practice, in particular, drumming, singing, and songwriting. Although music is not the primary element in a social worker's tool box or medicine bundle, social workers, too, are concerned with developing therapeutic relationships, promoting self-awareness, learning, self-expression, communication, and personal development. Musical interventions can only enhance social work practice. Within this chapter we have also included excerpts from an interview with Dr. Carolyn Kenny, an Indigenous scholar and music therapist who has generously provided her wisdom on the role of music as it relates to Indigenous culture and healing.

Developing cultural understanding and creating cultural safety are important ethical imperatives within the profession of social work as highlighted here by the Canadian Association of Social Workers (2005):

> 1.2.1 Social workers strive to understand culture and its function in human behaviour and society, recognizing the strengths that exist in all cultures.
>
> 1.2.2 Social workers acknowledge the diversity within and among individuals, communities, and cultures.
>
> 1.2.3 Social workers acknowledge and respect the impact that their own heritage, values, beliefs, and preferences can have on their practice and on clients whose backgrounds and values may be different from their own.
>
> 1.2.4 Social workers seek a working knowledge and understanding of clients' racial and cultural affiliations, identities, values, beliefs and customs. (CASW/ACTS, 2005, p. 4)

These principles are addressed throughout the chapter but more specifically during the interview with Indigenous scholar Dr. Carolyn Kenny.

Although there is a high level of diversity within Indigenous Nations, the term *Indigenous* will be used in this chapter for the sake of consistency, and specific Indigenous peoples will be identified when sharing cultural practices and history unique to certain groups.

MUSIC AS HEALING

Music is a powerful healing force (Samuels & Rockwood Lane, 1998), which produces vibrations that have the capacity to change every cell in the body. Sound is what our ears pick up from those vibrations moving through air— vibrations of varying rhythms and frequencies. There is a motion with a rhythm and a frequency moving in space, and our bodies pick up the sound with our ears. Other parts of our bodies pick up the vibrations in every molecule, in every cell, throughout the entire body, just like sound brings the vibrations of our own voice into our chest (Edwards, 2016). Music transcends time, using the body as a vehicle for healing. It brings us to places of feeling, is physically accessible, and deeply embodied. The music is inside us, vibrating and changing the patterns of molecules in our cells (Samuels & Rockwood Lane, 1998).

Just as Indigenous traditional dances, particularly men's dances, imitate the natural movements of birds and animals, it stands to reason that music has very likely originated from those who have tried to imitate the sounds of nature. Samuels and Rockwood Lane (1998) describe the natural sounds of the earth, the sound of the gentle wind, the stream, and the ocean as forms of healing music. There is healing in the call of the birds, the sound of the waves, and the sound of the waterfall. When we go to the ocean and listen to the sound of the natural world, when we sit on the edge of a brook next to a waterfall, it is the music of the earth's body that we hear. These sounds of the air, water, fire, and earth moving are the earth's songs. It is that healing energy that we hear in the vibrations going deep into every molecule within every cell in our body, energy that vibrates, shifts into patterns, and changes us. Mother Earth is singing her music to you, and listening to the changes of the earth's body as she moves is healing. Listen to change as she moves in storms, in thunder, in the strong wind blowing; these are all musical songs of the earth.

Places that still have the sounds of the earth are places on our planet that are greatly healing. Sadly, these musical songs of the earth have faded in our contemporary cultures. They are dimmed by technology, computers, iPads, iPods, cell phones, social media, television, even radio. We walk past Mother Earth's music every day, not hearing it and not realizing that this is healing music. A simple way of integrating music into our social work practice is to turn up the volume on nature's healing music and natural sounds, connecting the people we are helping in our social work practice as they listen to them on recordings or, even better, to go out into nature and listen, allowing the earth's magical songs to heal us. It is important to go to these sounds with the intention of balancing yourself and becoming one with the sound. Allow the sounds to go into your body, feeling the harmony of the sounds.

Drumming and Singing

DRUMMING

Although not new within many cultures, one community music intervention that continues to grow in popularity within the helping field is group drumming (Dickerson, Robichaud, Teruya, Nagaran, & Hser, 2012; Fancourt et al., 2016; Stevens, 2005; Stone, 2005). For example, Flores, van Niekerk, and le Roux (2016) provided weekly 45-minute African drumming sessions over a 4-month period, to a group of depressed and anxious children from ages 7 to 12 who were residing at a South African residential facility for youth. The program progressed from facilitator-led structured activities to what the authors called "interactive participant structure" (p. 258). The intent and outcome of the program were to promote the children's emotional and psychological health by providing opportunities for self-expression, relationship building, cooperation, and personal agency. Maschi, MacMillan, and Viola (2012) discuss recreational group drumming in promoting self-care and enhancing well-being for social workers. The recreational drumming program, which was developed by one of the authors, is called the "I-We Rhythm" program and is administered in a 2-hour workshop format. The program highlights the usefulness of musical interventions as it relates to social work practice, along with the teaching of basic rhythm skills while introducing members to various percussion instruments, including the drum. Once these areas are covered, members participate in a group drumming experience (p. 3).

In Winnipeg, Canada, one group drumming program, called *Buffalo Gals Drum Group*, has been offered through the North End Women's Centre for the past 16 years. Amid multiple resources and programs to meet the needs of women living in the North End of Winnipeg, Buffalo Gals is an inclusive women's drum group where members play hand drums and sing Indigenous songs from various Nations. Participants in the Buffalo Gals drum group have shared that the experience of drumming and singing connects them with Indigenous cultures and languages, inspires and empowers them to use their previously silenced voices, and promotes belonging and connections to others in the group, to the healing sounds of the drum, Mother Earth, and all our relations.

Figure 7.1 shows a Buffalo Gals group who regularly sing and play their drums together to experience wholeness and healing. The weekly drumming sessions also allow participants time out of their busy lives to focus on their own well-being, enjoy the mesmerizing and healing aspects of the drum, and to immerse themselves and their child(ren) in language and culture of Indigenous peoples. Similar to what the Maori people in New Zealand find, "to experience Maori music is to experience Maori culture . . . Music is so imminently tied to who the Maori are that beautifully, it serves to both sustain culture and to propel them into their [brighter] future" (Clements, 2015, p. 46).

Bruce Perry (2015), a world renowned pediatric neuroscientist, reminds us that prior to European contact, Indigenous peoples had effective healing tools in dealing with the fallout of trauma. He highlights that "Aboriginal healing practices are repetitive, rhythmic, relevant, respectful, and rewarding, they are experiences known to be effective in altering neural systems involved in the stress response in both animal models and humans" (xi). From an Indigenous perspective, Kenny (2006) adds, "Repetition is a fundamental concept in traditional, Indigenous societies because the cycles of the Earth, the phases of the sun and moon, the developmental stages of peoples' lives, the processes of healing all depend on repetition for keeping the world in balance" (p. 167).

Figure 7.1 Drumming and singing. Photo courtesy of Deana Halonen. Used with permission of all subjects.

As highlighted in both these perspectives, repetition is important in promoting healing, which explains why the repetitive sound of the drum is therapeutically beneficial. When you drum in time with others and are able to connect through sound, you are either energized by the experience or, depending on the tempo, relaxed by the experience (Ho, Chinen, Streja, Kreitzer, & Sierpina, 2011; Owen, 2012). There is a natural pull from one drummer to the next, which is known as entrainment. Dimaio (2010) describes entrainment as a "pull exerting from one vibrating object to another vibrating object" (p. 106). Rhythm is a part of our everyday life, from the sound of our hearts beating, to the rhythm of our breathing, to our sleep-wake cycles (Stevens, 2005) and, for women, their monthly moon (menstrual) cycles. We are all made up of and surrounded by rhythms. When we tune in to our bodily rhythms, we find ourselves living in the present moment and, when we are able to live in the moment, our stress levels decrease, our blood pressure goes down, and our muscle tension subsides and with this comes a sharpened ability to focus our mind and think more clearly.

From the literature on drumming as a therapeutic musical intervention, we see a variety of drumming techniques that social workers can use in their work, including call and response, heartbeat rhythms, sculpting, rumble (Hannigan & McBride, 2011), and soundscape (Venkit, Godse, & Godse, 2012).

Call and response is like a conversation between a soloist and the rest of the group. A facilitator or group member plays a rhythm and the rest of the group responds by mirroring back the rhythm (Hannigan & McBride, 2011). *Heartbeat rhythms* reflect the heartbeat of the person playing; drummers are asked to match their heart rate, which "increases concentration and relaxation" (Hannigan & McBride, 2011, p. 3). Drumming in unison to a slow steady beat can also have a calming effect on the group. One example of *sculpting* might include a facilitator directing a group member, or a section of the drum group, to play louder or softer, faster or slower while the rest of the group keeps the original rhythm in the background. *Rumble* is described as "drummers collectively drumming into musical chaos" (Hannigan & McBride, 2011, p. 4) to mark a transition or get members' attention.

Venkit, Godse, and Godse (2012) describe *soundscape* as "a landscape described in sound" (p. 134). Members of a group are asked to create their own soundscape with the remaining members guessing at what sounds are being created. For more information on techniques for drum circle facilitation, see the Resources section at the end of this chapter.

SINGING

Although not all group drumming programs mention singing in their programs, singing and drumming are typically not separated within Indigenous practices. Singing is an intimate act of expression, and the sounds created through singing are unique to every person (Summers, 2014). The voice can be understood as a barometer for what is occurring for the person emotionally, physically, psychologically, and spiritually. If the voice is suppressed, then the person loses his or her inherent need to express and the benefits associated with self-expression. In her video, *Singwalk: An experience of environmental vocal exploration* (https://www.youtube.com/watch?v=N3NiqcTKwok) Oddy states, "in our society, the idea of singing openly in a public space is . . . probably always considered to be a transgression. Many of us, we repress the desire to voice into the world due to a fear of social reprimand." In my [Tamara's] master's thesis, *Exploring Drumming/Song and Its Relationship to Healing in the Lives of Indigenous Women Living in the City of Winnipeg*, one participant shared the following:

> It was something that was given to me from my friend. . . . when she encouraged me to sing. She told me that I had a beautiful voice. She said, "You have a nice voice, you have a strong voice. Use it. Don't let people take that away from you." So it really encouraged me and helps me to have that confidence. (Dicks, 2014, p. 83)

Samuels and Rockwood Lane (1998) describe how Peter Halprin, a doctor and musician, experiences the voice as powerful and capable of evoking deep emotion. One can hum, chant, or sing to create music and rhythm.

Sometimes people need to be encouraged to use their voices and, once they have the courage to sing, they can experience the health benefits associated with this act of expression. Through encouragement and integrating voice work into their practice, the social work practitioner can play a role in promoting self-acceptance and confidence within the people they are supporting.

Storytelling and Music

Just as drumming and singing can affect positive change, so too can storytelling. It is a powerful technique that offers inspiration and hope that all of us can make positive changes in our lives. Storytelling is an important aspect of Indigenous worldviews, a powerful medium of life instruction and a means of conveying values, feelings, actions, and dreams. Stories also serve as essential links to the past and provide a means of surviving into the future. Storytelling is the oldest art, is universal to all people, and the basis of all other arts, including music (Lanigan, 1998).

Everyone has a story, and honoring stories can provide an important healing dimension to our lives, especially in cases where people have been deeply impacted by social, political, and economic marginalization (Baskin, 2016). Storytelling through music can focus on social problems, as well as social justice, and serve as a way to build bridges between communities. As Musicians Without Borders say: "[W]ar divides . . . music connects." In their work, they "use music to bridge divides, connect communities and heal the wounds of war" in countries around the globe (see https://www.musicianswithoutborders. org/#ourwork).

In Canada, contemporary Indigenous music serves as a healing mechanism, building bridges and moving Indigenous peoples and members of the non-Indigenous dominant society alike beyond the truth of Canada's colonial history to reconciliation (Truth and Reconciliation Commission, 2015). Through telling stories about the long-hidden Indigenous history, spirituality, and values, contemporary music can educate about misunderstandings, mistrust, and negative stereotypes that are still perpetuated today. Barney and Mackinlay (2010) concur with this in their work with Indigenous Australian musicians who have been impacted by the Australian child welfare system. Discussing the history of Indigenous popular music and thematic concerns of Aboriginal musicians, Gibson (1998) asserts that "themes of self-determination, land rights, resistance to cultural loss, rewriting Australian national history, dispossession, and calls for social justice remain common features of the traditions of Aboriginal popular music" (as cited by Barney & Mackinlay, 2010, p. 8).

A women's four-member group known as the Ulali Project highlights aspects of their cultural worldview in the hand drum song *Mahk Jchi* (the Heartbeat Drum Song), reminding us to stand tall, sing, dance, and never forget who we are and where we come from. Two of the originators of this group are Pura fé and Jennifer Kreisberg, both descendants of the Tuscarora Nation in the United States. The YouTube video of their song can be found at https://www.youtube.com/watch?v=bOn4vIybDU8.

From this song we see the important role the arts play in promoting Indigenous identity and, therefore, health. This song highlights the value of relationships, connection, and promoting the idea that you must understand where you come from to maintain a healthy Indigenous identity. Through *Mahk Jchi* and other music of Ulali Project, we see that cultural continuity through music is as important today as it was in the past, and drumming and singing continue to play a vital role in Indigenous cultural revitalization, the health of Indigenous peoples (Archibald, 2012; Broad, Boyer, & Chataway, 2006; Chandler & Lalonde, 1998; Goudreau, Weber-Pillwax, Cote-Meek, Madill, & Wilson, 2008), and the social movements that pull people together in reclaiming this traditional form of healing.

One musical endeavor that promotes positive images of Indigenous peoples of North America, as well as social justice, is the work of *A Tribe Called Red*, a Canadian Juno Award–winning music group that blends instrumental, hip-hop, reggae, and dancehall with elements of Indigenous music, particularly vocal chanting and traditional drumming. A Tribe Called Red promotes inclusivity, empathy, and acceptance among all races and genders in the name of social justice. Strong supporters of the *Idle No More Movement*, these positive role models provide a modern gateway into urban and contemporary Indigenous cultures and experiences, celebrating all of its layers and complexity through music, song, and dance. For an example of A Tribe Called Red's music combined with Inuit throat singing and traditional Hoop Dancing, see their video at Tribal Spirit Music https://www.youtube.com/watch?v=3S4tCA_12Io.

"Music has been described as 'the universal language' and that goes for hip-hop, as well" (Trainin Blank, 2016, p. 2). While combining social work, rap music, and hip-hop may seem an odd combination, Trainin Blank introduces the reader to a few programs offered in the United States as well as Canada, such as Hip-Hop Heals and Hip-Hop Therapy, which have provided a bridge between clients and those who work with young people. One social worker, Nakeyshaey M. Tillie Allen, commented that "[m]any young people are products of failed relationships . . . are hurt. . . . If they can find someone to relate to, they'll do it. They don't want to be alone . . . [and] gravitate toward gangs, music, popular culture" (Trainin Blank, 2016, p. 2). Another, Lauren Collins, describes her program as follows: "Hip-Hop Heals is a group therapy program for at-risk youth and young adults, whose passion for rap encourages an acceptance of therapy . . . and provides a comfortable forum for honest self-examination while helping participants find their way along the path to personal growth" and healing (p. 1).

Collins began her work, states Trainin Blank (2016), with court-mandated African American and Hispanic males, 18 to 25 years of age, residing at Palladia-Starhill, an alternative to incarceration, in Bronx, New York. When Collins first started, she found that:

> not all of her clients were into hip-hop, some really didn't like it. . . . When they saw her . . . they started laughing, wondering what she'd know about hip-hop. They didn't want to talk to her. She started playing a Tupac song, "calming and equalizing them . . . [which] started a discussion . . . [and] opened [them] up" [quoting Collins]. . . . She helped them understand that the songs topically had relevance to what brought them to jail and found the hip-hop program "made a huge impact." It helped unite the group and foster camaraderie. (p. 1)

In Canada, social worker Stephen Leafloor, better known as Buddha, founded Blue Print for Life, offering creative consulting, project management, and training in the fields of social work and education (Trainin Blank, 2016). Buddha is well known as one of the oldest B-boys, and he and his team "[do] social work through hip-hop programs through[out] the Canadian Arctic and First Nations communities. . . . This work has been described," Leafloor says, "as the most important social outreach in the Arctic in 20 years. . . . We also work with youth from a 24-hour lockup and inner-city youth, including Sudanese refugee kids in Calgary, Alberta, and other locations" (Trainin Blank, 2016, p. 2).

In projects studied by the Aboriginal Healing Foundation, the healing benefits of music, songwriting, and poetry were discussed by healers, program facilitators, and program participants alike. Carla Johnston, who incorporated songwriting into a literacy program for women incarcerated at Pine Grove Correctional Centre in Prince Albert, Canada, reported "singing and song-writing really does boost self-esteem and pride, as well as getting back to feeling comfortable with art and music" (Archibald, 2012, p. 48). At the correctional center, Johnston facilitated a project where a group of women created a song collaboratively. They wrote it themselves, with each woman writing a sentence or a phrase; then together they created a melody and, finally, recorded the song.

In another project funded by the Aboriginal Healing Foundation of Canada, Mike McInnes used songwriting in his social work practice on Eskasoni First

Nation, in a group called *Tunes and Talk* where participants, mainly residential school survivors, wrote songs, did some voice work, and jammed. Archibald (2012) offers the words of Mike McInnis, a healer from Nova Scotia, who states, "[w]hen you have secrets stuck inside of you, it's sometimes easier to put it into arts and music than to talk" (p. 49). There is pride "because a good song is something that makes you proud . . . builds a person up . . . makes life bigger than what you're feeling" (p. 49). In addition, "[I]t raises consciousness and starts making you write or create about personal issues or changes that you want to see in society—social justice" (p. 50). Ernie Blais, a Métis fiddler and square dancer in Winnipeg, Manitoba, also spoke about music as a universal language and the many benefits of holding weekly gatherings with music and dancing, such as camaraderie, joy, and stress release (Archibald, 2012, p. 50). Traditional healer Janice Longboat spoke about the changes she saw in a group of women who came together to sing, which was often the beginning of these women finding their voices (Archibald, 2012, p. 29). For Haudenosaunee women, singing is a part of their gardening tradition as "[w]e sing to our seeds before planting—without a voice, you couldn't offer this spiritual part" (Archibald, 2012, p. 29).

Songwriting and creating your own song can be rewarding and very therapeutic, as well as a positive way to vent emotions. Somehow, putting feelings into a song is easier than talking about those same feelings. "Writing songs can range from short and simple efforts, using popular music for the base, to extremely elaborate spill-your-guts original masterpieces" (Lorenzato, 2005, p. 79). Writing songs can be done individually with children, youth, or adults simply by beginning with a popular melody and a format for adding one's own words. More elaborately, it can be done through developing the lyrics, or encouraging both the choice and/or the creation of one's own melody and lyrics. Songwriting can also be accomplished with groups of people choosing or creating their own lyrics and/or melodies, as described by Carla Johnston, a woman who has worked with incarcerated women (Archibald, 2012).

In preparing to write this chapter, our relative *Dewe-igan* (the drum), Margaret Tamara (also referred to as Tamara) and Deana spent time with Carolyn Kenny discussing the use of music, singing, and drumming in the practice of helping people. The next section uses excerpts from that discussion to elaborate on a philosophical orientation to music, singing, and drumming, as well as some practical examples of their use in helping and healing.

STORY SHARING AND CONVERSING WITH *DEWE-IGAN*, DR. CAROLYN KENNY, TAMARA DICKS, AND DEANA HALONEN

Sharing stories is a long-practiced tradition among Indigenous peoples and is used in everyday life to teach, to heal, to promote the ethic of noninterference, and, ultimately, to build connections and enhance relationships.

Because relationships are central to Indigenous ways of knowing and doing (Wilson, 2008), we will discuss the power of drumming and song from this relational point of view beginning with some explanation of the word *dewe-igan*. *Dewe-igan* is a nonspecific term for drum in the *Anishinabemowin* language and is the term we will use in this story-sharing segment. The *Anishinaabe* (Ojibway) people have more than one name for the drum, depending on the type of drum and purpose for which it is played (Fontaine, 2013). Other terms include "*gimishoomisinaan,* meaning Grandfather, or *manidoo odewe'iganan,* meaning God's drum" (Vennum, 2009, p. 282). Like all of our relatives—the *two-leggeds,* those that swim (fish, water creatures), those that crawl, those that fly (birds, creatures with wings), those that stand (the trees)—the drum is animate, complete with physical, emotional, psychological, and spiritual aspects, and as *Dewe-igan* is animate and central to our discussion, we have invited him/her to take part in the following conversation. See Figure 7.2 for a picture of *Dewe-igan*.

In the spirit of building relationship, we would like to now draw the readers' attention to the conversation between our relative *Dewe-igan*, Dr. Carolyn Kenny, and Tamara and Deana, the writers of this chapter. Dr. Carolyn Kenny, originally from the United States, is a respected Indigenous scholar/author, music therapist, and educator who now lives in Vancouver, Canada. In this next section, we use excerpts taken from a conversation with Dr. Kenny that

Figure 7.2 *Dewe-igan* (the drum). Photo courtesy of Deana Halonen.

elaborates on a philosophical orientation to music, singing, and drumming, as well as some practical examples of their use in helping and healing. The drum (*dewe-igan*) also participates.

DEWE-IGAN: *Tansi, Boohzoo* [hello], my friend, and can you tell us where on Turtle Island your ancestors reside? Where do you come from? What is your story?

CAROLYN: Well, I'm 70 years old. I have two children and five grandchildren. My ancestry includes Choctaw from Mississippi, on my mom's side, and my dad is Ukrainian, first-generation Ukrainian American. I was adopted by the Haida Nation 20 years ago and so I have a family there in Massett, Haida Gwaii, Canada, and my Haida name is Nang Jada Sa-ets. I was adopted into that Nation. It's very, very important to me and I am close to my relatives there.

I was trained as a musician from an early age. I actually had polio when I was a child and part of the rehab was dance. I could never be a really great dancer because I had certain limitations with my legs, but I danced for many years from age 3 until age 21 and, through dancing, I discovered music. I also studied classical and popular voice, and classical piano. Later in life, when we had the spontaneous children's music workshops with the Musqueam people, I took on percussion instruments. They were used in our music practice with the kids and the adults that we worked with. Then in university I studied the flute and continued my voice lessons as well as piano and guitar.

DEWE-IGAN: *Eya'* [yes], music has been your loyal companion for many years.

DEANA: From what you shared, music has been a healing force in your life from a young age. Are there any other stories you would care to share on music's healing qualities?

CAROLYN: At age 50, I took up the cello as it was a very healing instrument for me at that time in my life. My mother had just passed away and the cello gave me so much. It was so healing for me personally to be able to play the cello. I discovered the cello while working in Norway teaching music therapy. A friend held a dinner for seven of us. When she opened the door to her house, her 15-year-old daughter was standing there. She didn't say anything to me. She just came to me, took my hand, and walked me into her room, where she started playing the cello for me. I'm getting teary-eyed even remembering that. It was 20 years ago. It was so powerful and healing, her playing, the tears started coming. When I returned home to Turtle Island, I knew that I had to start making the cello my own. I did that for quite a few years, although I'm not doing that anymore because I have arthritis in my hands. But it was so healing for me to play it for those 5 years to recover from the loss of my mother. You know the grief . . .

DEWE-IGAN: Hmm, the music resonated with your grieving heart.

TAMARA: That is a powerful story. It reminds me of how powerful music is for those dealing with grief and loss. My second practicum in music therapy was in palliative care and is where I met Susan, a beautiful person who was dying of cancer when we met. During our time together, Susan often requested the song *I Have a Dream* by the Swedish band ABBA. It was the theme song of Susan's cancer support group. The lyrics gave the women a sense of hope and strength in facing their illnesses.

A week before Susan died, she gave me this letter (which I include here). After all these years, I still hold on to her letter because it continues to remind me of the powerful role music plays in creating connections and supporting people through grief and loss.

I am writing this letter in case I do not see you again as I am doing very poorly. I have not been able to eat for over a week and I can no longer stand up. Before I go I want to thank you for all the good times we have had in the hospital with our music and art therapy. I feel I am blessed to have gotten to know such a beautiful person as yourself. Good luck in your pursuit of spiritual fulfillment. I believe you are on the road to true happiness, which so few people attain. Love, your friend in heaven and on earth, Susan.

DEWE-IGAN: Eya' [yes].

CAROLYN: Then of course in our native ceremonies I attended, there were always instruments. I participated in the Salish Guardian Spirit Dance Ceremonials, which were part of, but not my entire MA. I was studying ethnomusicology at the time and that was my major paper. In the 1970s, there was a moratorium on any researchers coming into native communities. But because I was native, and because I made friends with the Musqueam people through our children's spontaneous music workshops, I was able to know about and participate in the winter ceremonials. The Salish Guardian Spirit Dance ceremonials are a form of community shamanism. So if you're attending those ceremonies, there is drumming and you are part of the transformation process for the person being cured. What every one of us does we do on behalf of the other, which is what the Elders say. So that means whether it's for good or bad, you're not doing things just for yourself, it's for everybody. So you can see that happening there. Same with the Mescalero Apache; I was part of the initiation ceremonies for young women. It's a similar thing, women are dancing and the men are playing the drums and you are part of the transformation, not only of the young girls but of yourself, for everybody in the community. So I've been very fortunate to have many wonderful experiences with music in different contexts.

DEWE-IGAN: Eya' [yes], you have been fortunate.

DEANA: From an Indigenous perspective music is part of a broader context; it was integrated more fluidly into all parts of life. Would you agree with this?

CAROLYN: Absolutely, in our native societies there was not this sense of silos, like everything being separated. We believe everything to be connected. I don't think the idea of connection is fully understood by most people. It is a very deep idea, a very spiritual idea that comes with consequences and responsibilities. This is missing in a lot of the dialogue we are having about life on earth; it has become a catchphrase people use, "Oh yeah, that's what native people believe." It doesn't go beyond the surface, which is really too bad. If we do things from this place of deep understanding, then it brings with it a sense of radical mutuality because we are invested with every part of our beings, in the well-being of our people, all our relations, and our earth mother. We are invested so we have to take care of not only ourselves, it's a collectivity.

DEWE-IGAN: Eya' [yes] he, he [chuckling]. I like your words, "radical mutuality."

TAMARA: This theme reminds me of my own work with Indigenous women drummers and singers who also spoke about the value of connected-ness and responsibility. My friend Joan talks about these concepts as they pertain to her experience as a drummer sitting at the big drum with other women:

When you're singing and drumming and focusing solely on what you're creating with each other, you're not just connecting with yourself, or with the other women. You're connecting with the energy around you—the animal world from the skin of the drum, the plant world with the ring and the smudge, spirit when you sing those songs and sound a drum that's been blessed. (Joan, 2014, as cited by Dicks, 2014, p. 78)

JOAN: Talks about connecting with others beyond the human form and that it is important to be cognizant of these connections and responsibilities for those relationships, as well as for balance in those relationships.

CAROLYN: I would add, music, too, is in everything. As my friend, Fran Goldberg, shared: *You are the music.* So there is an intimacy. The person is the music. I also believe that music comes from your ecology because it is all around you, constantly a part of you, so the question is: *Are you listening, are you listening to the music?*

DEANA: Ann Clements (2015) would agree with you and Fran as she shares, "All Maori *waiata* [songs] stem from emotions that the gods displayed during creation" (p. 132). So from this perspective music is foundational to Maori society, culture, and expression. It is all around them and part of them. Can you say more about music being land-based?

CAROLYN: Absolutely, it continues to be land-based. I get a great comfort and energy and knowledge from, say, the river. The river is a great example of adaptability, of energy, and of shifting patterns. There is a great quote from James Youngblood Henderson. In one of his articles, he says "Anybody who believes that things will remain the same are confused." And I love that quote. The river reminds us that things are always changing, Mother Earth is always changing. So for me, joining that energy on Mother Earth is important. It's something that a lot of music therapists don't talk about, but it's very integrated into my work. And that really leads us to this whole notion of the ecology of being. In all of that for me there's a kind of radical mutuality with Mother Earth and I write about this in my book, *Music and Life in the Field of Play* (2006)—that we are an ecology. We are just like a field of daisies. We get conditions whether we grow or not. We get conditions from the earth, from the people around us, from our environment. Some people call it ecological therapy, but they talk and write about it in a very abstract way, like Klaus Riegel or Urie Bronfenbrenner talk about systems. For me, the ecology is about the earth and joining it in a kind of radical mutuality in everything we do. We are energy systems because we are part of nature. There's a self-generating of new life and that is a resource for us in terms of healing, in terms of just listening to the next steps that you need to take on the way to healing. If we had done that we wouldn't be in the mess we are in today with the environment.

DEWE-IGAN: *Eya'* [yes], a deep listening, there lies the music.

TAMARA: Yes, that reminds me of the question you posed to Walker Stogan on the meaning behind the music of the Salish Guardian Spirit Dance Ceremonials. He told you to go into the Long House and listen. In your book you write about it and add, "As music therapists, we use this same 'listening principle' in our work. Music is a resource pool. It contains many things—images, patterns, mood suggestions, textures, feelings, and processes. If selected, created and used with respect and wisdom, the clients will hear what they need to hear in the music, and use the ritual as a supportive context" (Kenny, 2006, p. 171).

DEWE-IGAN: *Eya'* [yes], *he he* [chuckling], I'm always telling my young friends to quit fooling around and start listening to their hearts, *he he*, lot of wisdom in there, you know.

DEANA: Yes, we agree. We think this is true for all of us. Social workers need to develop this listening principle within their relationships and in the music choices they make. So far we have talked about foundational values such as the importance of connection, relationships, responsibility, deep listening, and music as land-based or as an ecology of being. How do you think these cultural imperatives and concepts might relate to the novice social worker or helper in using music in the work they do?

CAROLYN: Most importantly, the first thing to do in terms of educating people in other professions, who are not music therapists and who are not Indigenous, is to try and encourage them to develop a consciousness about the things that I've just been talking about. That has to come first because that's the source of Respect. I think there's a lot of training that goes on with just giving people lists of things to do, and most often the training in music therapy programs does not go to a deeper level of consciousness. We have something precious with our native traditions. I would be reluctant to give them a recipe, even though it's probably what they're used to. It is about consciousness-raising and I feel it's the ethical way to go, that has to come first. The other very important thing in terms of giving them ideas like how to use a drum that matches what we've been talking about, is that they need to have a guide. I would say that it's important to work with an Elder, a Knowledge Keeper, or a Medicine person—to have a person with experience with how to use the drum and how to use songs. I don't know what happens there [in Manitoba, Canada], but in the Haida tradition [on the Pacific West Coast] and most of the traditions I have worked with, songs are owned by the people and they have to be gifted to someone who is not in their tribe, or not native, and given in a formal way as a gift before those songs can be used by others. There is so much New Age appropriation of Indigenous cultural practices, you know, with people pretending to be shamans who fly in for one day, make everyone into a shaman while making a lot of money doing it. So I guess I'm a little bit oversensitive about that kind of thing. It's the kind of consumerism and commercialism that has its source to a great degree in the United States, so even if you are all doing that, or not doing that, that is what people have come to expect.

TAMARA: Yes, we agree there are clear dangers in the appropriation of Indigenous cultural practices. And yes, you can't respect something you don't understand. This is foundational in the training of both social workers and music therapists. Social workers must develop their deeper levels of consciousness through whatever creative processes they choose, be it music, visual arts, dance, storytelling.

CAROLYN: I would say this is especially important for social work students be-cause they have so many pieces of paper to keep, protocols to follow, and forms to fill out. There are plenty of accountability systems and people to deal with above any clinical work to be done. Sometimes it makes it very difficult, when you have all that going on, to be still enough to really sink into that other place where consciousness lives. So this is an opportunity to invite them to participate in that deeper place. Through coming to an understanding of Indigenous ways.

Another thing to remember that might help is that every single person living on this earth has Indigenous roots; it's a question of accessing that, and acknowledging that. So some of this is about their own self-awareness, exploring their own roots. That's one way of helping them understand that music belongs to all of us. All cultures had forms of music to develop their consciousness and very often those were drums, but not always. For example, the Chumash people, they don't use drums. They use rattles made of shells. They didn't use drums until recently, the last 20 years or so, but their original culture used things from the sea, and things that came from the water and the beach, to make instruments.

DEANA: Yes, that is true, reminds me that the big drum was only recently introduced to the Mi'kmaq from the East Coast of Canada in the late 1980s (Tulk, 2007). It makes sense that you use what the land offers you. Your ecology influences your musical expression. What advice do you have for non–music therapists that are a bit nervous about using music in their social work practice?

CAROLYN: I feel music belongs to everybody. It's not like music therapists have ownership of music, not by a long shot. I think people just need to be authentic, be aware of the music that means something to them, be very sensitive about the music that is important to others, and feel free to use that music for establishing relationship, for entering beauty, and enjoying the senses through music. I think if that is done it is such an elegant way to approach music, without having all the formal training. It opens up new pathways. Music is an extraordinary spiritual thing. Just by doing those simple things they can do a lot of good with bringing music into their work.

DEWE-IGAN: *Eya'* [yes], our world can do with more beauty . . . more music.

TAMARA: I am glad you pointed that out, *Dewe-igan*, as Carolyn talks about the concept of beauty in her written work as well. She talks about the "moral responsibility the Navajo have towards beautifying the earth" (Kenny, 2006, p. 179). In discussing the work of the music therapist, Kenny (2006) shares that you are not "doing something" to your patients and clients. You are "being with" them as an equal participant in "beautifying the world" (p. 180). We too can do the same. We can take up this moral responsibility and beautify our world. She does not refer to beauty the way our consumer-driven pop culture manufactures and defines it; it is not a superficial physical form of beauty but she rather calls us forth to look more deeply into the beauty that lies within the human person, including within oneself. According to Kenny (2006), the human being is an aesthetic and at the same time the music therapist strives to create "the best conditions [for their clients] to have an aesthetic experience that will enable *epiphanies*, moments of deep transformation" (p. 170). Social workers would do well not to forget about the aesthetic in their work as they become immersed in policy and procedures, where beauty can easily be forgotten or ignored.

DEWE-IGAN: *Eya'* [yes], like I said, our world needs more beauty, not less. Gotta make sure those young social workers don't get lost in all that paperwork, thinking that's the only way to help [*sic*]. Less paperwork, more beauty, *he he* [chuckling]. Maybe teachers don't want to hear that, but I think it is worth repeating, *heh heh*.

TAMARA: *Miigwech* [thank you], *Dewe-igan*, for your thoughts. Carolyn, can you say something about the importance of music and cultural continuity or cultural revitalization within Indigenous cultures?

CAROLYN: Well, we have seen it happen a lot, especially with the youth when we can get our boys, especially the young boys, dancing in the powwows and getting them on the drum. I'm sure you've seen some of this, too. It actually can turn around those kids. There's such a big problem with gangs in Winnipeg and I had some friends, retired now, who were working with adolescents, who brought those kids into the circle through guidance from experienced dancers and drummers. Finding their culture gave them a sense of belonging they previously found in gangs. This was something very concrete; it was the music, the dance, and the guidance from the Knowledge Keepers and Elders that all worked together to turn those kids around. The sad thing is that so much of our native culture is lost, so once you cut the babies off from the Elders, if one generation loses the language, the cultural knowledge is buried. It's written in books, but it's not the same as learning it from your *Nokomis* (grandmothers) or *Mishomis* (grandfathers). So people are trying to recover things now, and I think that is an incredibly noble thing to do, to capture things before everything is lost.

DEANA: This next question ties into cultural continuity and identity. You often hear people talking about the idea of blood memory (Dicks, 2014, Torrie, 2004) and the emotional experience they have upon hearing the beat of the grandfather drum for the first time. People become very emotional and have shared that the sound of the drum seems to help them feel reconnected to their Indigenous roots? Have you heard of this?

CAROLYN: Absolutely. In fact, that's happened to me. I mean, it's happened to me a couple times, where, in ceremony, for no apparent cognitive reason, the music, the drum in particular, brought me back to what I would call the heartbeat of my own cultural heritage, from the Haida, or it didn't nec-essarily have to be from the Haida Gwaii or the Choctaw. It was just the connection. If one can become aware of that heartbeat, that's where life starts; it comes from Mother Earth. If you ever see the Taiko drummers who live on an island just off the coast of Japan, they are monks, both men and women, who spend their whole life just connecting with the heartbeat of the earth. That's where Taiko drumming comes from and that was one of the times that I was floored. The drumming was so strong and I felt connected. I found a place where I belonged.

DEWE-IGAN: My friend *bawdywaywidun banaise* [Edward Benton-Banai] talks a lot about my role in creating connection, and belonging, and how important this is for our people.

TAMARA: Yes, that's right, *Dewe-igan*, *miigwech* (thank you) for reminding me. He talks about this in his book, The *Mishomis* book: *The Voice of the Ojibway* (Benton-Banai, 1979). He also shared his understandings in a video series produced by Torrie (2004), in Episode 1: The Drum:

> The drum reminds us of who we are as Anishinaabe. Even if you did not grow up learning about the culture and you were totally disconnected through adoption or what have you, when you first hear the drum the blood memory of who you are comes back, the drum reminds you of this. (Torrie, 2004, cited in Dicks, 2014, p. 73)

> Our late friend Layne Redmond (2009) talked about this in relation to women from other parts of the world. Layne noticed that women from different parts of the world also hungered for the teachings they acquired from the frame drum—teachings that reflected their own cultural practices that they had forgotten or lost. Through learning the songs and dances associated with the frame drum, many women reconnected with their cultural roots. Although Layne Redmond died of breast cancer in 2013, you can find more about her work on YouTube: https://www.youtube.com/watch?v=8oOnwYrsWE0.

> So, yes, connection can occur on so many different levels, connecting to one's identity, to culture, and to community (Dicks, 2014; Goudreau, et al., 2006; McCabe, 2007; Pedri, 2011).

CONCLUDING REMARKS

For Indigenous peoples around the globe, music is the universal language. Drumming and singing are part of age-old traditions of integrating creative arts into celebrations, ceremonies, and healing rituals. The growing acceptance of the healing power of music, drumming, and singing among therapists, mental health professionals, and social workers situates traditional Indigenous approaches to health and well-being on the leading edge of therapeutic healing.

As Carolyn Kenny (2016) warns, if we want to use music, drumming, and singing in traditional ways within our social work practice, it is essential that we "develop a consciousness about these things and a deep respect" for those Indigenous knowledges, traditions, and ways of helping and healing. Kenny reminds us that there is a lot of training and a deeper level of consciousness required before we begin to use lists of things to do in incorporating music, singing, and songwriting into our practice of social work. With drumming, it is essential that we have not only received instruction on how to use a drum but also that we have someone to guide us in our work. It is essential to work with an Elder, a Knowledge Keeper, or a Medicine person and to have a person with experience of how to use the drum or how to use songs.

QUESTIONS FOR REFLECTION

1. Has music played a healing role in your life? If so, how could you use what you learned in your work as a social worker?
2. What does the drum signify to you in your background? If it has some significance, what does it signify and when is it played?
3. What role does music play in the process of decolonization?
4. How can music lead to or contribute to individual and collective change and transformation?

RESOURCES

American Music Therapy Association: http://www.musictherapy.org/

Canadian Association for Music Therapy/Association de musicotherapie du Canada: http://www.musictherapy.ca/en/

Musicians Without Borders: https://www.musicianswithoutborders.org/ #ourwork: Using music to bridge divides, connect communities, and heal the wounds of war in projects around the world.

Social Work Through Hip Hop (BluePrint for Life): Promoting physical and mental health in youth: http:// www.blueprintforlife.ca/ and http:// www. blueprintforlife.ca/ about/

Indigenous Drumming and Throat Singing: https://www.bing.com/videos/sear ch?q=indigenous+drumming+and+throat+singing&qpvt=Indigenous+Drum ming+and+Throat+Singing&FORM=VDRE

DRUMMING
World Music Drumming: http://www.worldmusicdrumming.com. World Music Drumming workshops and information from various parts of the world. See website for workshops and resources available and/or offered throughout the year, as well as publications: http://www.worldmusicdrumming.com/wmd-resources/

Pow Wow Trail—The Drum: https://www.youtube.com/watch?v= 5auRmbhkwes. First episode of a television documentary series produced by Jeremy Torrie (2004). Winnipeg, MB: I. C. E. Productions/Arbor Records Ltd. Winnipeg MB.

UpBeat Drum Circles: Drum Circle Training, with Christine Stevens, MSW, MT-BC, MA—Valencia, California: http://www.ubdrumcircles.com. Christine offers healing retreats and drum circle facilitation workshops. She has a number of resources on her website, including several videos highlighting techniques that people can use for self-healing or within their work as helpers.

When the Drummers Were Women, with Layne Redmond (musical historian and drummer): https://www.youtube.com/watch?v=8oOnwYrsWE0. A valuable resource for all women interested in drumming. You can find a synopsis of the work Layne Redmond was involved in this video.

THROAT SINGING

Inuit Throat Singing—National Geographic: http://video.nationalgeographic. com/video/exploreorg/inuit-throat-singing-eorg

Throat Singing—A unique vocalization from three cultures: http://www. folkways.si.edu/throat-singing-unique-vocalization-three-cultures/world/ music/article/smithsonian. The three featured videos include N. Sengedori of Mongolia demonstrating Khoomei throat-singing; Mark van Tongeren, an ethnomusicologist specializing in Khoomei; and Nukarik (Inuit) sisters Karen and Kathy Kettler demonstrating traditional Inuit throat singing practiced by women in their community.

REFERENCES

Archibald, L. (2012). *Dancing, singing, painting, and speaking the healing story: Healing through creative arts.* Ottawa, ON: Aboriginal Healing Foundation. Retrieved from http://www.ahf.ca/downloads/healing-through-creative-arts.pdf

Barney, K., & Mackinlay, E. (2010). "Singing trauma trails": Songs of the stolen generations in Indigenous Australia. *Music and Politics, 4*(2). doi:http://dx.doi.org/10.3998/ mp.9460447.0004.202.

Baskin, C. (2016). *Strong helpers' teachings: The value of Indigenous knowledges in the helping professions.* Toronto, ON: Canadian Scholars' Press.

Benton-Banai, E. (1979). *The Mishomis book: The voice of the Ojibway.* St. Paul, MN: Indian Country Press.

Broad, G., Boyer, S., & Chataway, C. (2006). We are still the Aniishinaabe Nation: Embracing culture and identity in Batchewana First Nation. *Canadian Journal of Communication, 31*(1), 35–58.

Buchanan, J. (2009, March). Fran Herman, music therapist in Canada for over 50 years. *Voices: A World Forum for Music Therapy, 9*(1). https://voices.no/index.php/voices/ article/view/367/290.

Canadian Association of Social Workers (CASW/ACTS). (2005). *Guidelines for ethical practice*. Retrieved from http://www.casw-acts.ca/sites/default/files/attachements/ CASW_Guidelines_for%20Ethical_Practice_e.pdf

Chandler, M. J., & Lalonde, C. (1998). Cultural continuity as a hedge against suicide in Canada's First Nations. *Transcultural Psychiatry, 35*(2), 191–219. http://journals. sagepub.com/doi/pdf/10.1177/136346159803500202

Clements, A. C. (2015). Maori Waiata [Music]: Re-writing and re-righting the Indigenous experience. *IK: Other Ways of Knowing, 1*(2), 132–149.

Dibble, C. (2011). *An inquiry into the collective identity of music therapists in Canada*. (Master's thesis). Wilfrid Laurier University, Faculty of Music: Music Therapy Program, Waterloo, Ontario. https://web.wlu.ca/soundeffects/researchlibrary/ ChristineLeeAnneDibble.pdf

Dickerson, D., Robichaud, F., Teruya, C., Nagaran, K., & Hser, Y. (2012). Utilizing drumming for American Indians/Alaska Natives with substance use disorders: A focus group study. *The American Journal of Drug and Alcohol Abuse, 38*(5), 505–510.

Dicks, M. (2014). *Exploring drumming/song and its relationship to healing in the lives of Indigenous women living in the City of Winnipeg*. (Unpublished master's thesis). University of Winnipeg, Winnipeg, MB.

Dimaio, L. (2010). Music therapy entrainment: A humanistic music therapist's perspective of using music therapy entrainment with hospice clients experiencing pain. *Music Therapy Perspectives, 28*(2), 106–115.

Dore, C., Gillett, S., & Pascal, J. (2010). Community singing and social work: A new partnership. *UNESCO Observatory*, Faculty of Architecture, Building and Planning, The University of Melbourne refereed e-journal, *2*(1). http://education.unimelb.edu. au/__data/assets/pdf_file/0008/1105928/dore-paper.pdf

Edwards, C. (Director and Producer). (2016). *I got rhythm: The science of song*. CBC. The Nature of Things with David Suzuki. Retrieved from http://www.cbc.ca/ natureofthings/episodes/i-got-rhythm-the-science-of-song

Fancourt, D., Perkins, R., Ascenso, S., Carvalho, L., Steptoe, A., & Williamon, A. (2016). Effects of group drumming interventions on anxiety, depression, social resilience, and inflammatory immune response among mental health service users. [Report] *PLoS ONE, 11*(3). doi:10.1371/journal.pone.0151136.

Flores, K., van Niekerk, C., & le Roux, L. (2016). Drumming as a medium to promote emotional and social functioning of children in middle childhood in residential care. *Music Education Research, 18*(3), 254–268. http://dx.doi.org/10.1080/ 14613808.2015.1077798

Fontaine, J. (2013). *Gi-mi-ni-go-wi-ni-nan o-gi-ma-wi-win zhigo O-gi-ma-win* [The gifts of traditional leadership and governance] (Doctoral dissertation). Trent University, Peterborough, ON.

Gibson, C. (1998). We sing our home, we dance our land: Indigenous self-determination and contemporary geopolitics in Australian popular music. *Environment and Planning D: Society and Space*, 163–184.

Goudreau, G., Weber-Pillwax, C., Cote-Meek, S., Madill, H., & Wilson, S. (2008). Hand drumming: Health-promoting experiences of Aboriginal women from a northern Ontario urban community. *Journal of Aboriginal Health, 4*(1), 72–83.

Hannigan, P. D., & McBride, D. L. (2011). Drumming with intimate partner violence clients: Getting into the beat; Therapists' views on the use of drumming in family violence treatment groups. *Canadian Art Therapy Association Journal, 24*(1), 2–9.

Ho, P., Chinen, K., Streja, L., Kreitzer, M., & Sierpina, V. (2011). Teaching group drumming to mental health professionals. *Explore, 7*(3), 200–202.

Kenny, C. (2006). *Music and life in the field of play: An anthology.* Gilsam, NH: Barcelona.

Kenny, C. (2016). Personal interview between writers and Carolyn Kenny.

Kirkland, K. (2007). Music therapy in Canada. *Voices Resources.* Retrieved from http://testvoices.uib.no/community/?q=country-of-the-month/2007-music-therapy-canada

Lanigan, C. (1998). Aboriginal pedagogy: Storytelling. In L. A. Stiffarm (Ed.), *As we see . . . Aboriginal pedagogy* (pp. 103–120). Saskatoon, SK: University Extension Press.

Lorenzato, K. (2005). *Filling a need while making some noise: A music therapist's guide to pediatrics.* London, UK: Jessica Kingsley.

Maschi, T., MacMillan, T., & Viola D. (2012). Group drumming and well-being: A promising self-care strategy for social workers. *Arts & Health: An International Journal for Research, Policy and Practice, 5*(2), 142–151. http://dx.doi.org/10.1080/17533015.2012.748081.

McCabe, G. (2007). The healing path: A culture and community derived Indigenous therapy model. *Psychotherapy: Theory, Research, Practice, Training, 44*(2), 148–160.

Oddy, N. (2011). A fieldwork of vocal discovery: Self-exploration through community singing. In F. Baker & S. Uhlig (Eds.), *Voicework in music therapy: Research and perspective* (pp. 83–99). London: Jessica Kingsley.

Owen, P. (2012). *Rhythm as an intervention for health and mental health difficulties: A comprehensive literature review.* Doctoral dissertation available from ProQuest Dissertations and Theses Database. (UMI No.3540346).

Pedri, C. (2011). *Gna-Giidadowin: Exploring our way of life through Anishinaabe song and drum* (Unpublished master's thesis). Royal Roads University, Victoria, BC.

Perry, B. (2015). Foreword. In C. Malchiodi (Ed.). *Creative interventions with traumatized children,* (pp. xi-xii). New York: Guilford Press.

Redmond, L. (2009). When the drummers were women. *Drum! Play better faster.* Retrieved from http://drummagazine.com/when-the-drummers-were-women/

Samuels, M., & Rockwood Lane, M. (1998). Healing yourself with sound: Music as healing. In M. Samuels & M. Rockwood Lane (Eds.), *Creative healing: How to heal yourself by tapping your hidden creativity* (pp. 216–240). New York, NY: Harper Collins.

Stevens, C. (2005). The healing drum kit for personal wellness and creative expression. [drum, guidebook, rhythm cards and CDs]. Boulder, CO: Sounds True.

Stone, N. (2005). Hand-drumming to build community: The story of the Whittier Drum Project. *New Directions for Youth Development, 106,* 73–83.

Summers, S. (2014). *Portraits of vocal psychotherapists: Singing as a healing influence for change and transformation* (Doctoral dissertation). Retrieved from Antioch University Repository & Archive at http://aura.antioch.edu/etds/134.

Torrie, J. (Producer and Editor) (2004). *Pow Wow Trail Episode 1: The drum.* Television documentary series. Winnipeg, MB: I. C. E. Productions/Arbor Records. Winnipeg MB. Retrieved from https://www.youtube.com/watch?v=5auRmbhkwes

Trainin Blank, B. (2016). Hip-hop social work. *The New Social Worker: The social work careers magazine*. Retrieved from http://www.socialworker.com/feature-articles/practice/Hip-Hop_Social_Work/

Truth and Reconciliation Commission. (2015). *Truth and Reconciliation Commission of Canada: Calls to action*. Retrieved from http://publications.gc.ca/collections/collection_2015/trc/IR4-8-2015-eng.pdf

Tulk, J. E. (2007). Cultural revitalization and Mi'kmaq music-making: Three Newfoundland drum corps. *Newfoundland and Labrador Studies, 22*(1), 259–286.

Venkit, V., Godse, A. A., & Godse, A. S. (2012). Exploring the potentials of group drumming as a group therapy for young female commercial sex workers in Mumbai, India. *Arts & Health: An International Journal for Research, Policy and Practice, 5*(2), 132–141. http://dx.doi.org/10.1080/17533015.2012.698629

Vennum, T. (2009). *The Ojibwa dance drum: Its history and construction*. St. Paul, MN: Minnesota Historical Society Press.

Wilken, B. (2005). *Three northwest First Nation perspectives on the practice of drumming and singing: Expanding the dialogue on purpose and function* (Unpublished master's thesis). University of Saskatchewan, Saskatoon, SK.

Wilson, S. (2008). *Research is ceremony: Indigenous research methods*. Winnipeg, MB: Fernwood.

8

Theater, Drama, and Performance

DEANA HALONEN

This chapter draws on creative methods from role playing to applications of script-making, acting, and performing used in social work with children, youth, and other populations in schools, mental health agencies, and in community organizations where social work practice and research sometimes combine for powerful results. As with most of the expressive arts, drama has been used not just for entertainment but also as therapeutic intervention for individuals, groups, and communities. The purpose of this chapter is not to train in the therapeutic methods of drama therapy, but rather to explore the use of drama, theater, and performance in social work practice, education, and inquiry for growth, development, and transformation.

PSYCHODRAMA, DRAMA THERAPY, AND ROLE PLAY

Drama techniques and drama therapy have both been used in psychological programs since the first half of the 20th century, such as in Gestalt group therapy (Perls, Hefferline, & Goodman, 1951) and in Moreno's (1946, 1953, 1959, 1969, 1975) and Wilkins's (1999) psychodrama, and they are still being implemented in various different contexts. In his earliest work, Moreno (1953) described five "instruments as essential to the psychodramatic method." These are as follows:

1. The *stage*, either the formal stage or structure, being three-tiered with a balcony or circular, multileveled with the actors raised slightly above the audience;
2. The *protagonist*, that is the person who is the subject of the psychodrama and its principal actor;

3. The *director*, who uses a set of professional skills to facilitate the intervention and to ensure the safety of the protagonist and the group;
4. The *auxiliary ego or auxiliaries*, who are the people who assist in the action by taking on roles; and
5. The *audience*, who are the people witnessing the drama. (p. 81)

With the aid of the director and the collaboration of group members, "protagonists explore scenes from their lives in which they play themselves and, when it is useful to the action, other people or things. These scenes may be imaginary, addressing what could have happened, what should have happened or things yet to be" (Wilkins, 1999, p. 22). The possibilities for the scenes are "limited only by the experience and imagination of the group" (p. 23).

The director's function is that of a co-producer, "putting a set of professional skills at the service of the protagonist in such a way as to facilitate the action" (Wilkins, 1999, p. 23). Kellerman (1992) also discusses the professional roles of the psychodramatist. These are as follows:

1. *Analyst* with the task of empathizing and understanding;
2. *Producer* with the function of theater director and the responsibility "to create a stimulating work of dramatic art" (p. 48);
3. *Therapist or agent of change* toward growth and healing; and
4. *Group leader* with the task of managing the group process.

Moreno (1953) described the auxiliary ego as "a therapeutic agent who provides the assistance the protagonist needs in exploring or resolving a situation, issue or relationship" (p. 233). He conceived of psychodrama as "an opportunity to get into action instead of just talking, to take the role of important people in our lives to understand them better, to confront them imaginatively in the safety of the therapeutic theater, and most of all to become more creative and spontaneous" (Moreno, 2014, p. 50). Moreno believed that "every person in a psychodrama group has the potential to be a therapeutic agent to the others and, because of this, protagonists are usually invited by directors to pick the person(s) in the group who seems the 'best fit' for the necessary role (which may be another person, an aspect of the protagonist, or even an object)" (Wilkins, 1999, p. 25). Spontaneity and intuition generally best guide this choice.

In social work, role play, or simulations of real-life case scenarios, are used both in social work education and social work practice in a wide variety of ways. In social work education, role play has been an accepted practice for helping undergraduate and graduate students acquire both counseling and group work skills (Carillo & Thyer, 1994; Cohen & Ruff, 1995; Regan, 1994; Shebib, 2014). Although skill development can be accomplished in a variety of ways, the experiential learning technique of role playing provides low-anxiety situations for the application of practice skills, the acquisition of initial and advanced interviewing and communication skills, and increased self-awareness of one's skill levels (Dennison, 2011). Additionally, reverse role playing also helps in developing an understanding of the other person's perspective, increasing both empathy and empathic skills (Shebib, 2014). When social workers in training place themselves in various roles, they "begin to understand client experiences thereby intensifying their frame of reference" (Harrawood, Parmanand, & Wilde, 2011, p. 199), enhancing empathic abilities and understanding of clients' situations, defenses, feelings, and responses.

In social work practice, role plays can be incorporated in a wide variety of ways when working with individuals, families, or groups. Commonly used with families, role playing can be used to examine the many aspects of families, such as communication styles, patterns and barriers, family dynamics, inter- and intrafamily relationships, and more, to increase awareness of how individual family members are experiencing the various aspects of the family. Additionally, role playing provides opportunities to explore possibilities for transformation, growth, and development within the family system. Although this requires extensive knowledge and training in family therapy and skills in facilitating role plays, using expressive arts exercises with individuals and families can assist individuals and/or families to begin exploring various aspects of self and self within family in an emotionally safe, nonthreatening environment, allowing time to process the emotions and reflect on actions, feelings, and thoughts.

Some common role-play exercises used in social work practice with families can involve family members role playing themselves in a typical daily activity, then collaboratively identifying individual thoughts, feelings, and cognitions they experienced at specific places in the role play. For example, when Johnny said . . . ; when Dad yelled . . . ; when Mom left the room . . . ; when Suzy started to cry . . . . Another variation involves individual members role playing another family member in a typical daily activity or situation that has been identified as a concern. It is common to switch roles between generations and/or genders; for example, Johnny role plays Dad or Mom, while Dad or Mom role plays Johnny or Suzy.

A common role-play or improvisation exercise used with individuals is the *Empty Chair* (Perls, Hefferline, & Goodman, 1951), where clients are invited to role play a situation that has been identified as a problem or concern, both as themselves and as someone or something else, by moving between the two chairs and the two different roles. A Gestalt therapy technique, this exercise requires clients to imagine someone—either representing themselves or part(s) of themselves, a behavior pattern, a family member, a friend, and so on—is seated beside them in the empty chair. Then they alternate between role playing themselves when occupying the chair they have been sitting in—speaking, gesturing, and otherwise communicating—and role playing the other self, part(s) of self, behavior pattern, person, when occupying the second (empty) chair. Generally, through experiencing this expressive technique, people are able to develop a greater understanding of feelings, thoughts, actions, and communication as a result of this exercise, and this helps people to move from talking about something toward the fullness of the experience, including sensations, affect, emotions, cognitions, and movement.

In *The Expressive Arts Activity Book*, Darley and Heath (2008) offer a visualization drama exercise in which individuals create a circle of people using images glued onto paper with dialogue balloons in which to create a record of the visualized interaction. Leading questions might include the following: Are these family members? If so, who are they? For example, are these friends, strangers, or coworkers? Where are they? What is happening? Individuals then create an improvisation in their mind imagining what each person is thinking or saying and then use the dialogue balloons to record their words. Limiting the images available, the facilitator can direct the scenario more specifically. Different questions can also be used to direct the scenario, for example: What would they say to one another if they met at . . . (various locations); at home; on the phone; using text messaging? Like the Empty Chair, this experiential visualization allows for the opportunity to increase awareness of feelings, thoughts, actions, and communication, as well as explore possibilities for transformation, growth, and development in an emotionally safe, nonthreatening environment.

According to the North American Drama Therapy Association (NADTA), drama therapy is the "intentional use of drama and/or theater processes to achieve therapeutic goals" (2017, home page at http://www.nadta.org/what-is-drama-therapy.html) and involves integrating role play, stories, improvisation, and other techniques with theories and methods of therapy. It is an "active, experiential approach that facilitates the client's ability to tell his/her story, solve problems, set goals, express feelings appropriately, achieve catharsis, extend the depth and breadth of inner experience, improve interpersonal skills and relationships, and strengthen the ability to perform personal life roles while increasing flexibility between roles" (NADTA, 2017).

Chasen (2011) rooted his innovative model of drama therapy in neuroscience and designed it specifically to develop social, emotional, and expressive language skills in children with autism spectrum disorders. Using scenarios based in his own practice, Chasen (2011) describes in detail a 30-session drama therapy program which uses creative and playful tools such as guided play, sociometry, puppetry, role play, video modeling, and improvisation.

Many of these creative and playful tools, including storytelling, have been adapted for and used in social work practice to assist and support people through the process of developing awareness, identifying strengths and areas of resilience, and exploring alternatives and options for growth, development, and transformation. Guided play, puppetry, Image Theater, and drama have been used extensively with children and adolescents, for example, in supporting their growth, development, and transformation.

Storytelling and Performance

Storytelling and performance have long been at the root of drama, theater, psychodrama, and drama therapy. Performance, both public and private, is also a key element in the formation, sustenance, and building of social movements. A social movement is a network of people engaged in sustained, contentious, collective action (Tarrow, 1998). Through a communicative process (Fraser, 1997), a collective action frame or a new way of looking at the world develops. An example of this is the development of the civil rights movement in the United States. Even with being locked out of halls of power and civil society, this movement was able to nurture "resistance based in churches, civic organizations, and their own press and allied cultural workers (musicians, artists, theater makers, etc.)" . . . build "coalitions across region, race, and class" . . . and sustain their "struggle against American apartheid over the course of decades" (Bogad, 2005, p. 48).

Scheherazade of Baabda, a theater project in the Baabda prison of Lebanon, devised by drama therapist Zeina Daccache, encourages inmates "to find their voice, culminating in performances that see the audience placed claustrophobically in the centre, with the actors circling them" (Shetty, 2014, p. 1963). Also having worked in men's prisons with drug dealers, rapists, and murderers, Deccache's mission is to "ensure the humane treatment of all prisoners" (p. 1963). In Beirut's Baabda prison, the women "readily admit to their crimes, most of which seem to be innocuous social niceties or understandable reactions to violence: riding a bicycle; smiling at her father's male friend; begging not to be raped. All this, too often, when they were barely out of puberty" (Shetty, 2014, p. 1963). The Daccache project reveals that many "feel free for the first time because it's the first time they can talk about anything they want. In their discussions, bitterness has been replaced with acceptance . . . even about painful experiences such as domestic violence and rape" (p. 1963). With the desire to enlighten, as well as entertain, the pieces the women have created are "charming, amusing, and surprisingly, in praise of love" (Shetty, 2014, p. 1963). *Scheherazade's Diary*, a documentary about the project, was shown at New York's Human Rights Watch Film Festival, in New York City, June 12–22, 2014 (http://ff.hrw.org/film/scheherazades-diary).

During the 1900s, particularly the latter portion, a new conception of life emerged that is both radically different from the previous mechanistic view of the world, holistic, and ecological (Capra, 2002, 2007). Scientists have discovered that the world is a "network of inseparable patterns of relationships"; the planet as a whole "is a living, self-regulating system"; and evolution is "a co-operative dance in which creativity and the constant emergence of novelty are the driving forces" (Capra, 2007, p. 14). In science, the network perspective began in the 1920s in the field of ecology, and subsequently scientists began to use network models at all levels of living systems, viewing organisms as networks of cells and cells as networks of molecules, just as ecosystems are understood as networks of individual organisms. Life in the social realm consists of living networks of communications, involving language, culture, and the experience of community (Capra, 2007).

In social work, the ecosystems and ecological perspectives have been universally accepted as a framework for thinking about and understanding networks in their complexity. The ecological perspective makes clear the need to view people and environments as a unitary system within a particular cultural and historic context. Both person and environment can be fully understood only in terms of their relationship, in which each continually influences the other (Germain, 1979; Germain & Gitterman, 1996, 2008; Pardeck, 1988; Saleebey, 1992). The application of the ecological perspective can best be understood as a shift away from the individual as the core focus of intervention, to looking at persons, families, cultures, communities, and policies, and identifying and intervening upon strengths and weaknesses in the transactional processes between these various systems.

In social activism, Grace Boggs (1997) urged a move away from the 1960s style of activism based on protest, to an emphasis on positive action. She asserted that change begins with each of us, quoting Gandhi: "Be the change you want to see in the world." While recognizing that personal transformation alone will not change social conditions, Boggs emphasized doing what is in our control as a necessary prerequisite to larger efforts. "One of the most important qualities of revolutionary leadership is the ability to transform yourself, to evolve and change as reality changes, and as you learn from your own experiences and the experiences of others" (Boggs, 1997, p. 140).

Storytelling as a traditional form of education passes on values, practices, experience, and knowledges that affirm the collective identity of the group. Popular education also affirms collective identity and stresses "dialogue, group learning, and valuing the participants' experience as the foundation for further learning and knowledge." Even as artists facilitate community-based art, trained educators facilitate popular education, because they are "able to question critically different perceptions of reality and custom, and contribute to the formulation of new knowledge that addresses the problems of poor communities and the actions those communities want to undertake" (Razack, 1993, p. 57).

Storytelling in Education: Freire's Pedagogy of the Oppressed

Popular education, which originated with Paulo Freire, a Brazilian pedagogue, also affirms collective identity but is based on rethinking received wisdom in a dialectic with lived experience. Freire's (1996) principle of dialogue holds that a democratic and dialogical interaction between educator and learner allows participants to interrogate, reflect on, and reimagine experiences, concerns, and perspectives collectively to transform personal and social reality. Rather than positioning learners as empty vessels wherein educators *deposit* educational matter through the ritualistic educational pedagogy of information dissemination and memorization known as the "banking method" of education (Freire, 1996, p. 53), Freire, in his work among peasants, generated a process whereby learners stand back from that which is familiar to them to perceive it in a more critical light (Scott, 1996). This process is "a means by which one can reflect critically on one's actions with a view to transforming it" (Mayo, 1997, p. 365); and it is referred to as praxis, a key concept in Freire's thinking and pedagogical work (Allman & Wallis, 1990).

Freire's pedagogical concept of praxis refers to the process of creating, negotiating, or applying knowledge through experience and informed action in the context of sociocultural values (Freire, 1996) with the intention to change these values. Dialogue, praxis, and conscientization actively engage with the lived realities and cultural power embedded in one's social reality—positioning the lived experience as knowledge in this context (Freire, 2006). This foundation of communal engagement and dialogue, that embeds the critical learning imperative of Freire's pedagogy, offers a "language of possibility" (Freire, 1985, xii–xiii) and tools for development and transformation.

Freire's (1996) pedagogy aims to shift learners from an object status (something acted upon) to a subject status (acting upon their knowledge). This enhances agency and ability to act upon, transform, and create new possibilities for their world(s). Brazilian theater practitioner Augusto Boal similarly aims to empower people, through theater, to become aware of oppressive contexts so that they can change it collectively, providing a method to Freire's pedagogy of the oppressed (1996) and pedagogy of hope (2006).

Storytelling in Theater: Community-Based Theater

Community-based art is a field in which "artists, collaborating with people whose lives directly inform the subject matter, express collective meaning"

(Cohen-Cruz, 2005, p. 1). It spans performances, including theater, committed to social change along with those whose purpose is the conservation of local cultures, sometimes incorporating both at once. Community-based art practices range from grassroots oral storytelling to formal techniques created by professional artists, while its theories build not only on ideas about art but also on concepts from education, therapy, sociology, anthropology, the emerging field of dialogue studies, and community organizing. According to Boal (2002), the role of art is "not only to show how the world is, but also why it is thus, and how it can be transformed" (p. 36).

In community-based theater, public protests, skits, storytelling gatherings, ritual, dance, music making, and theater are some of the ways that people make and enact group meaning. Community-based performance scholar-practitioner Richard Green described the field as "of the people, by the people and for the people" (1993, p. 23), relying on artists guiding the creation of original work or material adapted to, and with, people with a primary relationship to the content (Cohen-Cruz, 2005). However, over time, community-based performance has become less about homogenous communities and more about different participants exploring common concerns together, both building and reflecting community.

Flash mobs, for example, have been used to draw attention to a wide variety of social issues, to organize a show of dissent, or to create a shared moment of random kindness and beauty. A form of Community Theater, a flash mob is an unrehearsed, spontaneous, contagious, and dispersed mass action (Mitchell & Boyd, 2016). Participatory performance art, flash mobs have been used around the world as a revolutionary tactic for political protest and for raising awareness to local, national, and global issues. Examples range from performing some kind of playful activity in a public location to organizing spontaneous mass actions:

1. *Grandmothers to Grandmothers Campaign's* flash mobs on World Aids Day (December 1) 2016, with hundreds of grandmothers and grand-others in cities across Canada participating to call the world's attention to the scale of the global AIDS epidemic and the massive role African grandmothers are playing in response to this issue. See the video at http://www.grandmotherscampaign.org/flashmobs.

2. *Idle No More* movement's flash mobs throughout the winter of 2012–2013 across the United States and Canada in a collective demand for governments worldwide to "honor Indigenous sovereignty and to protect the land and water" (http://www.idlenomore.ca/vision). Using traditional music and round dance to bridge generations and cultures, creating space for building peace, unity, and community, the

flash mobs were orchestrated to send the message "we are here, our culture is strong, and we will not be silent in the face of destruction" (Kuttner, 2012). See the YouTube videos of the Idle No More Flash Mob in the Mall of America, in Minneapolis, Minnesota, United States on December 30, 2012, at https://www.youtube.com/watch?v=zy-Vp_DDgRw and the December 22, 2012, Idle No More Flash Mob in Portage Place, Winnipeg, Manitoba, Canada at https://www.youtube.com/watch?v=fl0zDNyGjWk.

3. *Dancing Inmates* from Cebu Provincial Detention and Rehabilitation Centre (CPDRC), a maximum security prison in the Philippines, performing Michael Jackson's "They Don't Care About Us" (2010). Implemented as daily exercise and as an enjoyable way of keeping the prisoners mentally and physically fit, the choreographed dance regimes grew into monthly performances, a regular part of a rehabilitation program, and the inspiration for the creation of several documentaries, musicals, and drama films drawing attention to the stigma of incarceration and the use of therapeutic music and dance in healing, rehabilitation, and restoring dignity. See the YouTube video at https://www.youtube.com/watch?v=mKtdTJP_GUI.

THEATRE OF THE OPPRESSED

Augusto Boal's (2000) integration of Freire's *Pedagogy of the Oppressed* (1970/1996) into Theatre of the Oppressed is an example of the emergence of new knowledge out of people's experience. A Brazilian theater director, playwright, activist, and revolutionary, Boal's work extends into popular theater pedagogy, activism circles, therapeutic models, and social work, aiming to empower marginalized populations and their allies by rehearsing creative and collaborative problem solving (Ivey, 2015). Boal (2000) moved from agitprop, a form of theater that tells audiences what they should do, to Forum Theater, a story-based approach that uses an arsenal of theater techniques and games that seek to motivate people, engage audiences in discussions about what they want to do, restore true dialogue, and create space for participants to rehearse taking action. It begins with the idea that "everyone has the capacity to act in the theater of their own lives; everyone is at once an actor and a spectator—we are spect-actors" (Boal, 1996, p. 27). Theatre of the Oppressed (see Figure 8.1) encompasses many forms or branches including Image Theater, Forum Theater, Invisible Theater, Street Theater, Newspaper Theater, Rainbow of Desire, and Legislative Theater, all of which involve games, images, sounds, and words (Boal, 1992, 2000, 2002, 2006a, 2006b).

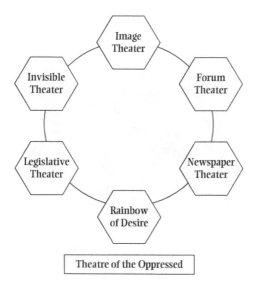

Figure 8.1 Forms of Theatre of the Oppressed. Diagram produced by Deana Halonen. Based on the work of Augusto Boal.

Image Theater

Image Theater is one of the more widely used forms of Theatre of the Oppressed (Saxon, 2016), in which activists, students, or any group are invited to form statues that represent a moment in time of an oppressive situation. The image serves as a springboard for critical group reflection in order to both understand the situation better and to try out possible solutions. Through the process of creating and working with the image, participants decode the situation, dissecting each character's personality, motivation, and range of possible actions, and, finally, explore possible actions that they themselves can take in their lives. In a Creative Arts and Expressions in Social Work Practice course, taught by Tuula Heinonen and Deana Halonen, as an elective course in a bachelor of social work degree program, exercises involving Image Theater are often used to involve students in the exploration of local issues. In Figure 8.2, a group of students express oppression through a group sculpture.

While Image Theater starts with a frozen image, it quickly moves toward interventions by participants, acting in character to collaboratively and spontaneously name their oppression and its source and then explore courses of action. The final stage is to reflect on what happened with participants and, if appropriate, write up the actions that seem most viable. In Figure 8.3, a group of students use group sculpture to depict overcoming oppression.

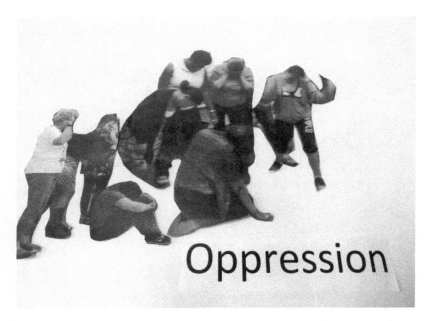

Figure 8.2 Image Theater depicting oppression. Collage produced by Deana Halonen.

Figure 8.3 Image Theater depicting overcoming oppression. Collage produced by Deana Halonen.

Forum Theater

In Forum Theater, several people who share a particular social oppression or *ism* each tell a story that localizes how that ism plays out in their lives. Using the stories as building blocks, the group makes a scene in which they all feel represented and performs it for an audience that also identifies with that problem. The effort is to build on the particulars to create one story that stands for the many. That is why, after performing the scene, a liaison between actors and audience, also known as *the joker*, can discuss the problem with the spectators and ask, "Can anyone imagine anything the protagonist might do to ameliorate the situation?" If anyone has an idea, the scene is replayed, stopping at whatever points spectators want to replace the protagonist and try the idea out. The spectators thus become spect-actors, and the room full of people who share the concerns get to see a number of possible solutions enacted.

Forum Theater is a form of participatory theater that provides an opportunity for creative, community-based dialogue. The theater, often referred to as *Stop Theater* (Diamond, 2007), is created and performed by community members who are living the issues under consideration. The process begins with workshop participants creating a short play, which is then performed once for the audience, or spectators—the ones who watch—but who are also in the process of enacting their change agent abilities and transforming into spect-actors—the ones who watch and take action. The spect-actors experience the play, which provides an opportunity to see the situation and the problems being presented. The story builds to a crisis and stops there, offering no solutions. Then, the play is performed a second time, with spect-actors (audience) able to freeze action at any point where they see an incident of oppression. A spect-actor (audience member) yells "Stop," comes into the playing area, replaces the oppressed character, and tries out his or her idea. The other actors respond in character, enacting the intervention. This process continues until several solutions are explored, the crisis is alleviated, or the problem is solved. For an example of Forum Theater using theater for social change, see the video at https://www.youtube.com/watch?v=NbYx01re-ec for a collection of scenes from the 2009 Forum Theater production, *To the Core*, put on by students at Mount Royal University, Calgary, Alberta in Canada.

Invisible Theater

The main objective in Augusto Boal's work in theater is "to change the people—'spectators,' passive beings in the theatrical phenomenon—into subjects, actors, transformers of the dramatic action" (Boal, 1979, p. 122). Using theater as discourse, the "spectator assumes the protagonic role, changes the dramatic action, tries out solutions, discusses plans for change, in short, training for real action . . . rehearsing for the revolution" (p. 122). Invisible Theater involves presentation of a scene in a public place rather than that of a theater or a space recognized as theater, before people who are not spectators, such as a restaurant, sidewalk, shopping mall or marketplace, train, or a line of people. The people who witness the scene are those who are there by chance and during the spectacle must not have the slightest idea that it is a "spectacle" (Boal, 1979, p. 144).

Thus, the goal is to make the intervention as realistic as possible so that it provokes spontaneous responses. The scene must be loud enough to be heard and noticed by people, but not so loud or conspicuous that it appears staged. Because it is real life for them, bystanders can and will engage with the scene, removing barriers between performers and spectators and creating very accessible conflictual situations in which people can rethink their assumptions and engage with sensitive issues (Mitchell, 2016).

An Invisible Theater performance will be only as strong as the reaction or thought processes it provokes in the audience. Thus, it is important to anticipate and rehearse potential responses from spectators. It is also a good idea to test out the scene with people who did not participate in its creation to see what responses it is likely to provoke.

In its pure form, Invisible Theater never divulges that it is theater, which requires significant preparation and rehearsal, and actors to remain in character even when the action moves in unexpected and challenging directions. People who encounter an Invisible Theater performance should experience it as reality and forever after think that it was real. The many scenarios played out on the ABC News Show *What Would You Do?* used a version of Invisible Theater to generate discussion. The program features actors acting out scenes of conflict, ethical dilemmas, or illegal activity in public settings, while hidden cameras videotape the scene. The focus is on whether or not bystanders intervene, and how. Variations of the scenarios are also included, such as changing the genders, races, or clothing of the actors to see if bystanders do react differently. Even though the host and news correspondent, John Quinones, does appear at the end of each scenario, revealing the theatrical nature of the scene, and interviewing bystanders and witnesses about their reactions, *What Would You Do?* is a good introduction to the power and possibility of Invisible Theater (Mitchell, 2016).

In education, community activism, and social work, practitioners have been using, adapting, applying, or testing out Boal's theories in practice. Drawing from Boal's (1979) detailed step-by-step descriptions of every stage of the work, the major forms taken by Theatre of the Oppressed (Boal, 1979, 2000) and the games and exercises used to lead up to them (Boal, 1992, 2002), and possibly their experience of having participated in one or more of Boal's workshops, there has been an explosion of activity around the world and a broad range of strategies utilized in the application of the various forms of Theatre of the Oppressed.

Applications: Readers Theater, Theater for Living, and Playback Theater

Readers Theater   Readers Theater, also known as chamber or interpretive theater, is a form of theater in which actors do not memorize their lines and instead read plays, poems, stories, or scripts specially designed to draw attention to issues of oppression or any of the *isms* experienced locally or globally. It is an interpretive activity in which readers use their voices to bring characters to life, enabling the audience to visualize the characters and the actions.

Contemporary Readers Theater has been heavily influenced by Augusto Boal, whose forms of Theatre of the Oppressed emphasized creating interactive improvisational performances where the focus is on the audience's reaction to the central theme of performance. Unlike traditional theater, readers direct their lines to the audience rather than looking at the persons with whom they are speaking. Unlike storytelling, Readers Theater has several storytellers who represent the narrator and the various characters identified in the story. The drama is enacted in the minds of the audience, who listen to the story and create mental pictures of what is happening. Readers Theater is "an act of involvement, an opportunity to share, a time to creatively interact with others, and a personal interpretation of what can be or could be" (Karabag, 2015, p. 20).

In education, Readers Theater is used extensively as a reading and learning tool that adds fun and excitement to oral reading activities, and helps stimulate interest in reading and learning. Promoting collaborative teamwork and cooperation, it helps improve oral language and communication skills, confidence, and self-esteem, while developing reading fluency and listening skills. It can promote learning across all subject areas by providing an opportunity for students to interpret stories and communicate meaning. When readers write or develop their own scripts, it can also enhance writing, problem-solving, and critical thinking skills. In their *How-To Kit* on *Readers Theater*, the Northwest Territory Council on Literacy offers five easy steps for what you need to do:

1. Choose a script or have participants choose a book, newspaper articles, or stories from which to develop a script.
2. Adapt the script. Participants identify speaking parts and break the story down into dialogue.
3. Assign parts. Participants should read through the various parts, trying them out to get a feel for them, then choose their own roles.
4. Highlight parts and rehearse. Participants practice reading their lines, to themselves, to each other, at home, and in groups.

5. Perform. The cast reads the play, using tone, inflection, and gestures to make the characters come alive for the audience.

Their extensive tips for finding and choosing a script, writing a script, creating an original script, implementing Readers Theater, and using various different styles, including circle reading, cooperative reading, and group reading, offer lots of ideas on using Readers Theater with people of all ages and reading abilities, including English as a Second Language (ESL) learners.

In social work, Readers Theater is often used to introduce case studies, develop empathy, and deep understanding of social issues or oppression as experienced by real (often live) people locally, regionally, or globally. Just as in education, Readers Theater can involve creating an original script or combining many stories to write a script. The audiences of Readers Theater are often moved significantly toward their own personal growth, collaborative development of solutions, and transformation.

Theater for Living   *Theater for Living* views the world through a systems theory lens, recognizing that the binary poles of the oppressor and the oppressed are both part of the same large organism living in some kind of dysfunction. It approaches the community as a living organism, acknowledging that structure is created by patterns of behavior, and creating plays that help us investigate ways to change the behaviors that create the structures, not just the structures themselves (Diamond, 2007). Theater for Living, having grown directly out of Boal's *Theatre of the Oppressed*, focuses on creating the best art possible that tells the true story of the living community. The "invitation in Theater for Living is to engage in the struggles of the characters, not to break the oppression (getting rid of what we don't want), but to create a healthy community, or safety, or respect (getting what we do want)" (Diamond, 2007, p. 43).

Living systems all have something in common, *autopoiesis*, which is defined as "a process whereby a system produces its own organization and maintains and constitutes itself in a space; e.g. a biological cell, a living organism, and to some extent a corporation and a society as a whole" (Principia Cybernetica Web, as cited by Diamond, 2007, p. 45). Understanding the configuration of relationships, and that structure is the material embodiment of the pattern of relationships, helps us to understand that in order to change the local and global structures that seem to control our lives, we must work to change the patterns that create those structures (Capra, 2002).

Community exists when a group of people share geography, values, experiences, expectations, or beliefs, and those people can be members of many different communities, creating layers of communities within structures. Communities exist within each other, overlapping each other, yet seemingly separate from each other, arising from a complex, highly nonlinear dynamic. It is created by a social network involving multiple feedback loops through which values, beliefs, and rules of conduct are continually communicated, modified, and sustained. It is a living organism surrounded by a boundary of ideas, information, beliefs, and behavior that is distinct to that specific community (Diamond, 2007). When we, as social workers, embrace the systems view, we come to see that living things, individuals, families, communities, organizations, even nations can change and grow in healthy ways, because they want to or because they do so naturally. Change cannot be imposed, and, even in instances where the impulse to change has come from an outside stimulus, actual behavior change occurs from within.

Diamond (2007) reminds us that "art is a process . . . the result of an individual or a group creating. It can be an image of serendipitous juxtaposition . . . subsistence economies, or human life that happens in the street every day" (pp. 72–73). Theater for Living employs social artistry, in an improvisational way, enacting an interactive process that engages the living community at a deeply creative level. Both the process itself and the result of the process can be transformational. Part of the power of Theater for Living is its authentic voice—it is the people from the community who are living the issues under investigation, the experts in their own lives, who create and perform the theater. The actors must remain true to their characters, really listen, observe, and have no exterior agenda. Their main focus is to tell the truth of the character in that moment, and allow their responses to emerge from the situation. If the actor is going to initiate an action, it must be to explore this moment, this idea that has come from the community.

Being authentic in a Theater for Living performance comes from its purpose, which is the creation of true dialogue. It is this authenticity, honesty, and dialogue that creates the environment which enables the community to understand new perspectives on the issue. Through making its own discoveries, the community experiences deep learning and opportunities for growth and transformation.

Diamond's (2007) *Theater for Living* is essential for social workers interested in the power of theater for evoking community healing. Complete with extensive descriptions of the various aspects of this form of interactive community theater, activities, and games useful in empowering participants and community members, examples of productions in communities around the world, and case studies, Diamond's work allows us insight into ideas that are large, daring, and challenging, and the steps to implementation are precise and accessible. Included in the Appendix are numerous games and exercises, based on and adapted from Boal's publications, *Games for Actors and Non-Actors* (1992, 2002), that are often used in applying Theater for Living.

Playback Theater   *Playback Theater* is a community-building improvisational theater in which personal stories are transformed into theater pieces on the spot. Combining artistic expression and social connection based in deep, empathic listening, Playback Theater brings together the roles of *teller, conductor, actors,* and *audience,* and various modes of thought to promote healing and well-being. People alternate between the roles, with the *teller* telling a personal story, while the *conductor* facilitates the telling by interviewing the teller in a friendly and attentive manner. As the story is told, *actors* (often between two and four) listen attentively, trying to put themselves in the teller's shoes, while avoiding judgment. After the story is told, the *actors* improvise a theater peace in which they reflect back the story with empathy. Then roles switch and another member of the *audience* becomes the *teller* sharing a personal story, and so on.

The improvisations can have a powerful effect on all—the *tellers* not only hear their own story, they also witness it, gaining perspective and a sense of being truly heard. *Actors* and *audience* often resonate with the *teller's* story, strengthening bonds of understanding, enhancing relationships, and building community. Playback Theater is thought to require the intersection of three fields of an event: the aesthetic, which helps enhance audience identification; the social, the here-and-now context of the group; and ritual, in which the conductor and actors carry the audience across a threshold and bring them safely (Fox, 2007), uniting aspects beneficial for healing—art, storytelling, and social connection (Haneji, 1998) within a meaningful framework.

Playback Theater can be learned by people without previous acting experience, like social workers, who work to create an atmosphere that promotes inclusiveness, appreciation, and playfulness. It has been used in a wide variety of fields of practice, including mental health (Moran & Alon, 2011); the aged (http://playbackwinnipeg.blogspot.com/); marginalized groups, refugees, and displaced persons (Weinblatt, 2000); and victims of violence and bullying (Salas, 2005). Playback performances in schools, workplace settings, and institutions can often avert issues that need to be addressed. Change happens, or movements toward change, from the reality that the *audience* reveals to itself in an organic way, through the people and their own responses. Dialogue of this sort, which reflects the experience and awareness of community members, is a way for a community to develop, allowing people to become mindful of the collective.

Jonathan Fox, developer of the original *Playback Theater* company in New Paltz, New York, defines an oppressed person as "a person who has no place to tell their story" (Fox, 1986, p. 32). Providing that place, Playback Theater facilitates stories that are fragments of lives, often chaotic, half-understood by the teller, without clear beginnings, endings, or climaxes. It is the task of the conductor, the actors, and the musician to receive that raw material, filter it through their understanding and inspiration, condense certain aspects of it, expand others, and present the teller and audience with a theater piece. This process allows the teller and audience members to see their experience crystallized, made clear, and cohesive. In scenes where a transformation is appropriate, the teller has a chance to be the refiner, to craft the raw material of life. A series of moments from the confusion of ordinary life becomes the subject for intense artistic focus and expression where the moments are comprehended, celebrated, and entrusted to the community's reservoir of self-knowledge (Salas, 1983).

In Winnipeg, Canada, Dana Ranguay, a social worker, social activist, and community capacity builder, founded the *Red Threads of Peace Project* in conjunction with the Gas Station Arts Centre, following training at the Playback Centre in New York. Using Playback Theater techniques and specialized training in creating supportive performance with people with cognitive disabilities, processes for historic trauma, racism, bullying, and social justice, Dana and other members of the troupe conduct and perform Playback Theater in a wide variety of settings. They have facilitated theater based projects in First Nations, youth at risk, newcomer, senior, LGBTTQ, and marginalized communities. For detailed descriptions, videos, and photos of various projects they have been involved in, see their blog entries at http://playbackwinnipeg.blogspot.ca/.

In addition to the tremendous power for growth, development, and transformation in individuals, families, and communities, theater has also been used extensively in social work research and inquiry. The qualitative nature of social research lends itself very well to using creative methods for collecting data and for the dissemination of research findings.

THEATER IN RESEARCH: PERFORMATIVE INQUIRY

Performative inquiry is the exploration of a topic or issue through performance (Fels & McGiven, 2002), which "opens spaces of intertextual play with which social responsibility and individual and communal response may be investigated" (p. 30). It provides a momentary entrance into "other worlds embodied in play and reflection" (p. 32) and "is a research methodology that recognizes and honors the absences, journey-landscapes, and space-moments of learning realized through performance" (p. 30).

Performative inquiry describes the burgeoning use of performance and dramatization as a mode of inquiry that addresses social issues with goals of change and has been taken up by researchers in anthropology, sociology, health sciences, social work, and education. It has been referred to as docu-drama, nonfiction playwriting, theater of re-enactment (Saldana, 2008), reality theater, performed ethnography, performance science, research-based theater, data-based readers theater (Donmoyer & Yennie-Donmoyer, 2008), and popular theater (Conrad, 2004).

Performance is innate to humans and pervasive in our social interactions. "Humans are socialized from childhood, to imitate, to pretend, to role play, to ritualize, and to storytell. It is thus a simple transition to act on our performative impulses by developing artistically rendered work that reflects our dramatic nature" (Saldana, 2008, p. 196). Performance offers a metaphor for all that is done in qualitative inquiry, both in the doing of the research and in the representation. Performative inquiry encompasses all the senses and offers an important lens for thinking about inquiry that is relational, participatory, and geared to action, social change, and transformation.

In their work *Sharing the Talking Stones*, Linds, Goulet, Episkenew, Ritenburg, and Schmidt (2015) use performance inquiry, including both Image and Forum Theater, in their data collection and adapt Forum Theater workshops using theater games, and other activities, to create space for Indigenous youth to critically examine the choices they make that affect their health. Initially, theater games such as blind games, energizers, and community-building activities (Boal, 1979; Diamond, 2007) are used to develop trust, to get to the real work—the issues in stories and scenes—and encourage youth to sustain their engagement through the repetitive practice required to develop the clarity of expression needed to communicate with an audience.

Following games, the next step in their workshop process is Image Theater (Boal, 1979) enabling participants to create static, silent, group images to represent their stories. Through an interactive discussion process, alternative ways to change power relationships are explored, and possible solutions tested in new images, leading to a new round of possible actions. Finally, Forum Theater scenes are developed and enacted to explore the thoughts, feelings, and deeper motivations of the various characters involved; reflect on possible actions; and develop other solutions (Linds et al., 2015).

Other researchers have used theater and performance to disseminate the results of their research. Eve Ensler, for example, uses Readers Theater to share the extensive data collected in interviews with over 200 women from over 60 countries around the world about their views on sex, relationships, and violence against women. *The Vagina Monologues*, an episodic play of several monologues, was written by Ensler, a playwright and activist, offering a piece of art like nothing seen before. *The Vagina Monologues* ran for 5 years in New York and then toured throughout the United States. After each performance, Ensler found women waiting to share their own stories, leading her to see that the performances could be a mechanism for moving people to end violence against women and children and propelling her to found VDay. Through the VDay movement, Ensler allows groups around the world to produce a performance of the *Vagina Monologues* play, or one of its many adaptations, and use the proceeds for local projects and programs that work to end violence: (http://www.vday.org/about.html#.Wr8UtHKovnN).

For a TedX2004 presentation entitled *Happiness in Body and Soul*, in which Ensler shares how a discussion about menopause with her friends led to talking about all sorts of sexual acts on stage, waging a global campaign to end violence toward women, and finding her own happiness, see the video at http://www.ted.com/talks/eve_ensler_on_happiness_in_body_and_soul#t-1000359.

CONCLUDING THOUGHTS

Drama and performance techniques are used in social work practice, education, and research to collaboratively examine issues both locally and globally in working with individuals, families, groups, and communities. Role play, storytelling, and performance encourage finding voice; growth and change as we reimagine experiences; reflection and dialogue to transform personal and social reality; development of solutions; and transformation and the creation of healthy communities, safety, and respect.

Freire's (1996/2006) *Pedagogy of the Oppressed* and *Pedagogy of Hope* in popular education allows educators and learners to interrogate, reflect on, and reimagine experiences, concerns, and perspectives collectively to transform personal and social reality. Boal's (1979/2000) *Theatre of the Oppressed* in community-based theater involves a wide variety of theater forms for exploring common concerns, as well as building and reflecting community. Extending into community activism and social work with the goal of empowering marginalized populations and their allies, Image, Forum, Invisible, Legislative, and Newspaper Theater provide opportunities for creative, community-based dialogue, change, and transformation. Diamond's (2007) *Theatre for Living* and *Playback Theater* both employ social artistry, in an improvisational way, enacting interactive processes to engage living communities at deeply creative levels in evoking community healing.

Performative inquiry or the exploration of issues through performance (Fels & McGiven, 2002) and dramatization (Saldana, 2008), use popular theater techniques to address social issues with the goal of change and transformation. Encompassing all of the senses, performative inquiry offers a lens for thinking about research that is relational, participatory, and geared to action.

QUESTIONS FOR REFLECTION

1. What ways have you experienced role play in your social work education? How would you modify those role-play exercises to

incorporate collaborative explorations of therapeutic interventions, and enhance self-awareness, empathic abilities, and understanding of clients' situations, feelings, and responses?

2. Have you experienced the expressive *Empty Chair* technique in your social work education or in practice? If so, how did it increase your awareness of feelings, thoughts, actions, and communication? How did it explore possibilities for transformation, growth, and development?

3. How can expressive arts help you to be the change you want to see in the world?

4. Which form of Boal's *Theatre of the Oppressed* moves you to use theater technique(s) and game(s) to motivate people, engage them in true dialogue, and create space for them to rehearse taking action toward change, growth, and transformation?

RESOURCES

North American Drama Therapy Association Website—Includes a video short gallery, testimonials, information, and fact sheets regarding drama therapy itself and its application with people of all ages and social needs, FAQ, bibliography, and drama therapy listserv: http://www.nadta.org/what-is-drama-therapy.html

A Forum Theater performance by a troupe from SC State University to engage their audience in problem solving: https://www.youtube.com/watch?v=vcLcXeXJVDU

A TEDx Talk about the process and applications of Playback Theater, published May 20, 2011 by Jo Salas, the cofounder of Playback Theater: https://www.youtube.com/watch?v=R-UtiROCm6E

Red Threads of Peace Playback Theater Project, Gas Station Arts Centre, Winnipeg, Manitoba, Canada:

Introducing Red Threads of Peace [Video]: http://playbackwinnipeg.blogspot.ca/search?updated-max=2015-10-28T22:57:00-07:00&max-results=7&start=7&by-date=false

Meet our Troupe [Video]: http://playbackwinnipeg.blogspot.ca/p/project-member-biographies-elena-anciro.html

REFERENCES

Allman, P., & Wallis, J. (1990). Praxis: Implications for "really" radical education. *Studies in the Education of Adults, 22*(1), 14–30.

Boal, A. (1979). *Theater of the oppressed.* London, UK: Pluto Press.

Boal, A. (1992). *Games for actors and non-actors.* New York, NY: Routledge.

Boal, A. (1996). Politics, education and change. In J. O'Toole and K. Donelan (Eds.), *Drama, culture and empowerment: The IDEA dialogues* (pp. 47–52). Brisbane, Australia: IDEA.

Boal, A. (2000). *Theatre of the oppressed.* London, UK: Pluto Press.

Boal, A. (2002). *Games for actors and non- actors* (2nd ed.). New York, NY: Routledge.

Boal, A. (2006a). *The aesthetics of the oppressed.* New York, NY: Routledge.

Boal, A. (2006b). *The rainbow of desire: The Boal method of theatre and therapy.* New York, NY: Routledge.

Bogad, L. (2005). Tactical carnival: Social movements, demonstrations, and dialogical performance. In J. Cohen-Cruz & M. Schutzman (Eds.), *A Boal companion: Dialogues on theatre and cultural politics* (pp. 46–58). New York, NY: Routledge.

Boggs, G. (1997). Martin and Malcolm: How shall we honor our heroes? *Monthly Review: An Independent Socialist Magazine, 49*(2), 140.

Capra, F. (2002). *The hidden connections.* New York, NY: Doubleday.

Capra, F. (2007). Foreword. In D. Diamond, *Theatre for living: The art and science of community-based dialogue* (pp. 14–18). Victoria, BC: Trafford.

Carillo, D., & Thyer, B. (1994). Advanced standing and two-year program MSW students: An empirical investigation of foundation interviewing skills. *Journal of Social Work Education, 30,* 377–387

Chasen, L. (2011). *Social skills, emotional growth and drama therapy: Inspiring connection on the Autism spectrum.* London, UK: Jessica Kingsley.

Cohen, M., & Ruff, E. (1995). The use of role play in field instruction training. *Journal of Teaching in Social Work, 11,* 85–100.

Cohen-Cruz, J. (2005). *Local acts: Community-based performance in the United States.* New Brunswick, NJ: Rutgers University Press.

Conrad, D. (2004). Popular theatre: Empowering pedagogy for youth. *Youth Theater Journal, 18*(1), 87–106. doi:10.1080/08929092.2004.10012566.

Darley, S., & Heath, W. (2008). *The expressive arts activity book: A resource for professionals.* Philadelphia, PA: Jessica Kingsley.

Dennison, S. (2011). Interdisciplinary role play between social work and theater students. *Journal of Teaching in Social Work, 31*(4), 415–430. doi:10.1080/08841233.2011.597670.

Diamond, D. (2007). *Theatre for living: The art and science of community-based dialogue.* Victoria, BC: Trafford.

Donmoyer, R., & Yennie-Donmoyer, J. (2008). Readers' theater as a data display strategy. In J. G. Coles & A. L. Knowles (Eds.), *Handbook of the arts in qualitative research* (pp. 209–224). Thousand Oaks, CA: Sage.

Fels, L., & McGiven, L. (2002). Intercultural recognitions through performative inquiry. In G. Bauer (Ed.), *Body and language: Intercultural learning through drama* (pp. 19–35). Westport, CT: Ablex.

Fox, J. (1986). *Acts of service: Spontaneity, commitment, tradition in the non-scripted theatre.* New Paltz, NY: Tusitala.

Fox, H. (2007). Playback theatre: Inciting dialogue and building community through personal story. *The Drama Review, 51*(4), 89–105.

Fraser, N. (1997). *Justice interruptus: Reflections on the "postsocialist" condition.* London, UK: Routledge.

Freire, P. (1985). *The politics of education: Culture, power and liberation.* Westport, CT: Bergin and Garvey.

Freire, P. ([1970] 1996). *Pedagogy of the oppressed.* London, UK: Penguin.

Freire, P. (2006). *Pedagogy of hope.* London, UK: Continuum International Publishing Group.

Germain, C. (1979). *Social work practice: People and environments , an ecological perspective.* New York, NY: Columbia University Press.

Germain, C., & Gitterman, A. (1996). *The life model of social work practice: Advances in theory & practice* (2nd ed.). New York, NY: Columbia University Press.

Gitterman, A., & Germain, C. (2008). *The life model of social work practice: Advances in theory & practice* (3rd ed.). New York, NY: Columbia University Press.

Green, R. (1993). Of the people, by the people and for the people: The field of community performance. *High Performance, 16*(4), 23–27.

Haneji, K. (1998). *What playback theatre did provide: Experience through playback theatre at four institutions for mental disorders* [Leadership course essay]. Retrieved from http://www.playbackcenter.org

Harrawood, L., Parmanand, S., & Wilde, B. (2011). Experiencing emotion across a semester-long family role-play and reflecting team: Implications for counselor development. *The Family Journal: Counseling and Therapy for Couples and Families, 19*(2), 198–203. doi:10.1177/1066480710397122.

Ivey, S. (2015). *Forum theatre performance, TEDxColumbiaSC.* TEDx Talk/OTR Films. Retrieved from https://www.youtube.com/watch?v=vcLcXeXJVDU

Karabag, S. (2015). Secondary school students' opinions about readers' theatre. *European Journal of Educational Research, 4*(1), 14–21.

Kellerman, P. (1992). *Focus on psychodrama: Therapeutic aspects of psychodrama.* New York, NY: Routledge Press.

Kuttner, P. (2012). Case study: Idle no more and the round dance flash mob. *Beautiful trouble: A web toolbox for revolution.* Retrieved from http://beautifultrouble.org/case/idle-dance-flash-mob/

Linds, W., Goulet, L., Episkenew, J., Ritenburg, H., & Schmidt, K. (2015). Sharing the talking stones: Theatre of the Oppressed workshops as collaborative arts-research with Aboriginal youth. In D. Conrad & A. Sinner (Eds.), *Creating together: Participatory, community-based and collaborative arts practices and scholarship across Canada* (pp. 3–19). Waterloo, ON: Wilfred Laurier University Press.

Mayo, P. (1997). Tribute to Paulo Freire (1921–1997). *International Journal of Lifelong Education, 16*(5), 365–370.

Mitchell, T. (2016). Invisible theatre. In A. Boyd & D. Mitchell (Eds.), *Beautiful trouble: A toolbox for revolution* (pp. 66–68). Berkeley, CA: OR Books in partnership with Counterpoint Press.

Mitchell, D., & Boyd, A. (2016). Flash mob. In A. Boyd & D. Mitchell (Eds.), *Beautiful trouble: A toolbox for revolution* (pp. 46–47). Berkeley, CA: OR Books in partnership with Counterpoint Press.

Moran, G., & Alon, U. (2011). Playback theatre and recovery in mental health: Preliminary evidence. *The Arts in Psychotherapy, 38*(5), 318–324.

Moreno, J. L. (1946). *Psychodrama* (Vol. I). Beacon, NY: Beacon House.

Moreno, J. L. (1953). *Who shall survive?* Beacon, NY: Beacon House.

Moreno, J. L. (1959). *Foundations of psychotherapy* (2nd ed.). Beacon, NY: Beacon House.

Moreno, J. L. (1969). *Action therapy and principles of practice.* Beacon, NY: Beacon House.

Moreno, J. L. (1975). *Psychodrama* (4th ed.). Beacon, NY: Beacon House.

Moreno, J. D. (2014). *Impromptu man: J. L. Moreno and the origins of psychodrama, encounter culture, and the social network.* New York, NY: Bellevue Literary Press.

North American Drama Therapy Association (NADTA). (2017). Fact sheet on Drama Therapy with Children and Adolescents. Retrieved from http://www.nadta.org/assets/documents/children-adolescent-fact-sheet.pdf).

Pardeck, J. (1988). An ecological approach for social work practice. *The Journal of Sociology & Social Welfare, 15*(2), 133–142.

Perls, F., Hefferline, R., & Goodman, P. (1951). *Gestalt therapy: Excitement and growth in the human personality.* New York, NY: Julian Press.

Razack, S. H. (1993). Story-telling for social change. *Gender and Education, 5*(1), 55–70.

Regan, S. (1994). A mutual aid based group role play: Its use as an educational tool. *Social Work With Groups, 15*(4), 73–87.

Salas, J. (1983). Culture and community: Playback theatre. *The Drama Review, 27*(2), 15–25. doi:10,2307.1145490.

Salas, J. (2005). Using theatre to address bullying. *Educational Leadership, 63*(1), 78–82.

Saldana, J. (2008). Ethnodrama and ethnotheatre. In J. G. Coles & A. L. Knowles (Eds.), *Handbook of the arts in qualitative research* (pp. 195–207). Thousand Oaks, CA: Sage.

Saleebey, D. (1992). Biology's challenge to social work: Embodying the person-in-environment perspective. *Social Work, 37*(2), 112–118.

Saxon, L. (2016). Image theater. In A. Boyd & D. Mitchell (Eds.), *Beautiful trouble: A toolbox for revolution* (pp. 62–63). Berkeley, CA: OR Books in partnership with Counterpoint Press.

Scott, S. (1996). Conscientization as the object of practice. In H. Reno and M Witte (Eds.), *37th Annual AERC proceedings.* Tampa, FL: University of South Florida.

Shebib, B. (2014). *Choices: Interviewing and counselling skills for Canadians* (5th Canadian ed.). Toronto, ON: Pearson Canada.

Shetty, P. (2014). Drama therapy. *The Lancet, 383*(9933), 1963.

Tarrow, S. (1998). *Power in movement: Social movements and contentious politics.* Cambridge, UK: Cambridge University Press.

Weinblatt, M. (2000). *Small steps towards change: A parable from Azerbaijan.* Mandela Centre for Change, The Higher Source. Retrieved from http://www.mandalaforchange.com/resources/articles/small-steps-towards-change-a-parable-from-azerbaijan/

Wilkins, P. (1999). *Psychodrama.* London, UK: Sage.

9

Expressive Arts for Transformation and Change

TUULA HEINONEN, DEANA HALONEN,
AND ELIZABETH KRAHN

A review of the chapters in our book, after we have spent time writing them, focuses us on what we have said collectively and what this offers to readers. This chapter reflects what was outlined in Chapters 1 and 2 regarding the content and orientation of the book, including the elements we view that are central. A summary of chapters describing expressive arts approaches and methods follows.

Chapter 3 discussed the use of visual arts, namely drawing, painting, and collage. For many people these methods are most familiar from primary school and may bring back memories from childhood art classes and classroom activities. For some, they may bring a fear of being judged as unable to draw or paint that harks back to their early years. However, art for expressive, therapeutic, and social change applications does not require artistic or technical skill or experience. Collage-making can offer an alternative method when technique and artistic talent are a concern for participants. There are many possible ways to make use of these media in working with people, whether in social work or other fields of professional practice. It can also be helpful for practitioners to make use of visual arts methods to process and express the feelings that emanate from challenges in their work or epiphanies that result from their practice. Although there seems to be little time for professionals to reflect on their practices and what they learn from their work with individuals and groups, it is important to take some time to do this so that growth, learning, and reflexivity can result.

Individual, group, and community visual art-making has the potential to generate change and lead to transformation. Many examples can be found in academic journals, websites, and videos that attest to the power of visual art to help people express deep feelings, reflect on their ideas, and heal from life difficulties experienced. Professional support from a practitioner who is experienced in use of the arts is very helpful to facilitate these processes, whether with individuals or groups. Community projects that involve visual arts can often be found when people want change in society, for example, to address perceived injustice, oppression, dangers, and other issues adversely affecting a collective. It can feel empowering to join with others in a common cause and demonstrate collective concerns through group murals that are drawn, painted, and/ or collaged by those who come together. Such activities are often accompanied by media attention sought by participants to draw attention to the issues that concern them. Some of the applications of visual arts at individual, group, and community levels were described in Chapter 3.

Chapter 4 on photography and video methods considered the many ways that viewing photographic images, taking photographs, and producing videos can enhance the lives of diverse populations, both individually and collectively, to achieve individual and social change and transformation. Photographs as still images offer records of events, people, societies, and other subjects of interest to photographers. The context related to the images is often significant in making sense of the meaning of the photograph. Photographs can be used to elicit information, to create a historical record, or to depict significant events as they occur. In qualitative research, photographs taken by participants and the stories they tell about them compose the data in photovoice, a method that is meant to attend to voices of those who have not often been heard, for example, those who experience homelessness.

From the conception of an idea for a video project to its production and dissemination, those who participate are affected in various ways. Essentially, videos tell stories, discuss ideas and highlight perspectives related to events, and explore social issues. Those who participate in making videos may find it challenging, empowering, disturbing, and/or comforting, depending on how they relate to the video's content and their engagement with it. From our research for this chapter, we were intrigued by the ways in which photographs had played roles in social work practice over the years and the various settings in which photography, both in practice and in research, had been applied. We found that videos were a newer format that has found an important niche in social work for those who have ideas and experiences they want to address.

Chapter 5 described the possibilities of integrating movement and dance with social work or other human services. Health aspects of physical movement aside, there are numerous benefits that can be achieved by expression through bodily movement, even when it involves only a small range of motion or experiencing enjoyment through creating a dance with others. As Roche's examples showed, expression through movement and dance can suit all people, including those whose lives have been affected by trauma, ill health, and many physical challenges. Further, all age groups can benefit and realize improved well-being. Very little in social work literature is evident on the potential or existing application of movement or dance in practice. Knowing about the field and how the use of movement and dance could be a resource to social work and other professions is important to explore.

Chapter 6 has taken us through the evolution of story in its many forms and shows that the original essence of a good story remains intact. Just as traditional storytelling had the potential to unite and anchor a group of individuals in a collective sense of meaning, identity, and belonging, so too does story in its various expressions do so today. Thus, a storyteller and, since we all tell stories, each one of us, has the capacity to be an agent of personal and social transformation. When a story involves an exchange between two or more individuals (as opposed to with a fictional character in a book), there is potential for authentic listening, connection, and catharsis—of seeing and witnessing the other—and this builds community.

A common thread throughout different narrative forms that have emerged over time—traditional and other forms of storytelling (including digital story), poetry, expressive writing, and narrative therapy—are the metaphors embedded within the story. Of particular value is the art of using transformative metaphors versus the pathology or deficit metaphors that in our modern world are so prevalent in health care and other social systems that impact recipients of social work services. This resonates strongly with strengths-based social work approaches. In addition to describing the art and the skills involved with these narrative forms, the chapter provided a wide spectrum of applications with different populations and social needs, including social workers themselves, who can benefit from using story and expressive writing for their own personal and professional growth. Those who are in the margins can also find themselves to be a powerful agent of social change when they are empowered to share their stories with larger audiences in safe contexts and by consent, such as through public presentations of poetry and digital story or through arts-based research.

Singing, drumming, and song stories for helping and healing were the focus of Chapter 7, which explored the incorporation of music and songs into people's day-to-day lives as important elements of culture, offering connections to the universe and life itself. Music is a universal language and a powerful healing force. It transcends time, enables us to feel, is physically accessible, and deeply embodied. Music is not only inside of us, vibrating and changing the patterns of molecules in our cells, it is in the ecology surrounding us, the natural sounds of the earth, offering connections to others, all our relations, and to life itself.

When we are singing and drumming, we are not just connecting with ourselves or with other people; we are connecting with the energy around us, and all relations beyond the human form. It is important that we are cognizant of these connections, and the responsibilities for those relationships and for balance in those relationships, when incorporating music, singing, and drumming into our social work practice.

Chapter 8 explored theater, drama, and performance, drawing upon creative methods from role playing, script-making, acting, and performing used in social work with children, youth, and marginalized populations, in schools, mental health agencies, and community organizations. In these places social work practice and research often combine for powerful results, particularly for awareness, growth, development, and transformation. Storytelling and performance, long at the root of drama, theater, psychodrama, and drama therapy, are also the key elements in the formation, sustenance, and building of social movements and communal engagement. In social work practice and education, it offers possibilities and hope, as well as various tools for change, development, and transformation.

Popular education, based in Freire's work and Boal's work, extend into popular theater, activism circles, therapeutic models, and social work, aiming to empower marginalized populations through rehearsing creative and collaborative problem solving. Community-based theater provides springboards for critical group reflection, transformation of personal and social realities, and the creation of healthy communities, cultural safety, and respect.

Performative inquiry provides insight into areas that are difficult to access through talk alone and has been taken up by researchers in social work, education, health sciences, sociology, and anthropology. Researchers are incorporating performance and theater games to develop trust, build relationships, create spaces for clarity of expression, and critical examination in various phases of research projects.

CONCEPTS AND PRINCIPLES IN OUR ORIENTATION TO SOCIAL WORK AND EXPRESSIVE ARTS

The topics in this book have opened up what is possible in bringing expressive arts into social work and exploring what others, many of whom are not social workers, have achieved. Although social work practitioners, researchers, and educators have found ways to integrate expressive arts in their work, evidence of interest in this topic in the social work literature is relatively recent.

For practitioners, it may be that this is due to heavy workloads and lack of time, limited mandates, or a lack of knowledge and confidence to innovate. Social workers are often expected to deliver services according to established agency policies and practices for which social services are funded; few resources may be available for new initiatives or work that is added to existing tasks. However, there may be room for building in expressive arts if these can improve outcomes for the benefit of social work clients (e.g., youth, individuals and/or groups experiencing serious physical or mental health challenges or addictions, children in foster care, and more), and when social workers have skills, knowledge, and supervision to support such work. For example, the group Red Threads of Peace: Playback Theatre, founded by Dana Rungay in Winnipeg, Canada, perform and offer workshops with the goal of "building empathy and community connection through the power of Playback" (see http://playbackwinnipeg.blogspot.ca/).

Social work books and journals increasingly publish reports of studies by social work researchers that include expressive arts. Some of these have been discussed in this book and include, for example, photovoice, digital stories, and poetry and performance inquiry integrated into research studies. In research with children, older persons, newcomers, and others for whom verbal communication or language limitations pose challenges, expressive arts have enabled their inclusion in research projects.

Educators in social work have been able to draw on a range of creative methods from drawing, music, story, poetry, collage, role play, and theater, with experiential sessions that enhance awareness, empathic understanding, critical thinking, and creative problem-solving skills, as well as skills for social work practice with individuals, families, and groups who use social work services. However, very little has been written on the effectiveness of expressive arts applications in social work education. Social work pedagogy and teaching practice on this topic could offer interesting and useful material for discussion and dissemination at professional conferences and in journal articles.

There is much room for integrating into social work a range of expressive arts. As interest and knowledge regarding this kind of innovation in practice increases, social work research and education will more often include expressive arts as complements to social work. In addition, more social workers educated in expressive arts specialities will contribute their knowledge to social work. The greater complexity of people's lives today and the issues and problems that occur at different life stages and transitions require social work to innovate and respond effectively. We have described in this book the many powerful and promising ways to practice, research, and teach through drawing on expressive arts approaches and methods. We also recognize that learning, sharing, and innovating are needed when new conditions, situations, and challenges call for change.

The significance of place is taken up in relation to geographical locations such as neighborhoods and communities where people live, work, interact, and play. Long histories of experiencing a place mesh generations, events, and processes together where one person's history to the land as place is bound up with another's. Stories are often ways to account for such histories, and so too are the photographs taken of people over a long period of time. People will have their unique perspectives of place because rarely is one person's experience of it the same as another's, even if they lived as neighbors.

Individuals seek change in their situations, and it is known that the arts have a transformative potential that can help. This book discussed and provided examples about how expressive arts, when used in social work practice, can respond. At the same time, social change and transformation are needed to address urgent issues such as environmental challenges and climate change. Bringing these issues into the social work curriculum will help students, in their social work practice roles, to consider environmental issues and act based on their knowledge.

Indigenous people in many parts of the world stress the need to halt the damage to the environment and the earth itself and to be critical of unbridled economic activity because it destroys the air, land, and water that sustains us and all living things. Environmental justice and green social work scholars and advocates draw our attention to these issues, challenging us to talk with our students and colleagues to intervene on behalf of the environment and the future of all.

Social justice is a goal contained in the social work codes of ethics in many countries where social workers practice. In current Western thought, individuals tend to be regarded as solely responsible for their own lives, and their struggles and challenges may be pathologized (e.g., as a mental health diagnosis) or attract judgement and/or discrimination (e.g., refugees who require social supports upon entry to a country of refuge; Indigenous peoples who experience the tremendous challenges in reclaiming their identity after generations of cultural oppression). Yet it is clear that larger social, economic, and political contexts involving corporations and government systems are very much implicated in creating the lived experiences of such populations— systems that often reap benefits while those with less power and control are required to support their goals. Those who seek social justice aim for fairness and equity in society by raising their voices, finding allies, and working with them to develop action plans. Use of expressive arts, such as large murals or paintings (e.g., *Guernica*, painted by Pablo Picasso in 1937 about the horror of war), films, street theater, and even contemporary dance are powerful methods that can be used to raise awareness about injustice. Likewise, storytelling and other creative narrative approaches can provide counternarratives to narratives that fuel injustice. Such counternarratives not only have the potential to raise social awareness, but they can support empathy and respect for the *other*, personal growth, and social change by challenging stereotypical and/or prejudicial perspectives.

Social action may involve similar strategies but might be implemented in different ways depending on social history, political context, cultural traditions, and other factors. For example, social justice in a mining town in Bolivia may be related to a long struggle for better working conditions, benefits, and salaries of miners whose lives are adversely affected by conditions set by employers. Bolivian miners and their families may have developed culturally specific ways of seeking social justice to seek redress, such as marches and street theater. The Raging Grannies with chapter groups (gaggles) across North America and now internationally have their own signature style and strategies for social action that can teach social work much about community organizing at the front line. Their international website invites *grannies* to enter in the following way: "Please pour yourself a cup of tea and join us inside. We are out in the streets promoting peace, justice, social and economic equality through song and humour" (http://raginggrannies.org/). There are many ways to conduct social action without violence. The expressive arts offer useful and creative examples to draw from.

Cultural safety is a concept discussed mostly in Chapter 7 in relation to Indigenous people that goes beyond cultural awareness and competency by adding consideration of power in relationships between professionals and Indigenous people. Seeking and receiving health and social services often sets up an unequal relationship, especially where services are shaped by what Indigenous people may view as a foreign culture. Finding ways to go beyond awareness of cultural difference and building skills toward cultural competence can help; however, cultural safety is more challenging to resolve.

Finally, in our construction of elements important to social work and expressive arts is an assertion that all people need to have opportunities for creative expression, not simply to enhance leisure but as a compelling need to achieve well-being. Whether people participate with others or alone to experience the arts at different stages in their lives, there are clearly benefits from such activities, for example, through social interaction and support, physical activity, skill development, dealing with trauma or illness, and the joy of finding one's voice. All chapters of the book discuss these topics in relation to the specific expressive arts approaches and methods, with examples that illustrate them.

At the ending of this book, we have found many other topics to explore in further writing, for example, on the benefits and challenges of combining these and other expressive arts approaches and methods together; on learning from participants about the long-term outcomes of participating in expressive arts individual, group, and community activities and initiatives; and in explicating our own experiences and knowledge drawn from our many combined years of work in practice, research, and education. We welcome ideas, insights, and experiences from readers who would like to share what they have done and learned through use of expressive arts in social work and other human professions.

Index

CPSIA information can be obtained
at www.ICGtesting.com
Printed in the USA
BVHW070113091019
560579BV00004B/8/P